Analysis
and
Design

Analysis and Design

A Handbook for Practitioners and
Consultants in Church and Community Work

GEORGE LOVELL

With a Foreword by
LESLIE J. GRIFFITHS

BURNS & OATES

First published 1994
BURNS & OATES
Wellwood, North Farm Road,
Tunbridge Wells, Kent TN2 3DR

ISBN 0 86012 234 4

Typeset by Search Press Limited
Printed and bound in Great Britain by
Biddles Limited, Guildford and King's Lynn

To Reg and Madge Batten
My beloved mentors
Throughout three decades of my ministry

Contents

Foreword

I've known George Lovell for most of my life. It was he who brought me into membership of the church when I was a teenager and it's to him that I've turned at most of the key moments of my life for help with my work. I've had the thrill too of working with him a number of times, mainly in various countries of Africa. I think I've read everything he's written over the years. So, I reckon I've seen George Lovell's work from many different angles of view. It's a privilege to be asked to write this Foreword for this latest book.

I know a man who repairs cars. He can take an engine to pieces, right down to the last nut and bolt. Then, when he's done his repair, he can put the pieces back together again. And the miracle (for my untechnical brain it's no exaggeration to call it that) is that, when the key's turned in the ignition, the engine seems always to start at once.

I drive a car most days of my life. If anything goes wrong or needs checking, I have to resort to the car's handbook just to open the bonnet. And what I see inside the bonnet is simply one of life's mysteries as far as I'm concerned. Wires and plugs; metal and plastic; dipsticks, camshafts and radiators—to think that my everyday work depends upon such things as these!

My everyday work depends upon much more than a car, of course. It depends upon the people I work with, my own aptitudes, the various focal points of action and reaction, the structures within which my work is done, available resources, and people's expectations of me. My work is coloured and shaped by the values I consider important, the degree of fulfilment I find in what I do, and the frustrations that come from being prevented from achieving what I set out to do.

My mechanical friend knows how to take a car engine to pieces, do his repair, and then reassemble the motor. George Lovell knows how to take a piece of work apart, identify and address the elements that aren't functioning very well, and then put the whole thing back together again. But that's only the beginning. What George goes on to do (or, to be more exact, what he does whilst analysing a piece of work) is to enable the person whose work he's looking at to recognize and identify its constituent parts, examine the way those parts inter-relate, strip the whole thing down if necessary, and then put it all back together again. Here he scores heavily over any mechanic I've ever known. For no mechanic has ever persuaded me that I could cope with the intricacies of a motor engine. Yet George Lovell has more than once helped me to look at my work, to analyse its inner dynamic, and to identify the critical path which would help me achieve the objective of a more effective output. Again and again, in more than a quarter of century of patient (yet innovative) work with people as varied as you can imagine—from Methodists on council housing estates to nuns in religious community, amongst those living in communities divided by boundaries as harsh as those in Ulster or as subtle as those in suburbia—George Lovell has helped church workers look critically at what they're doing and find ways of handling what they see. His has been a charismatic ministry and the whole church is deeply in his debt.

With this book, a further important step has been taken. We know that our author can analyse and reflect upon a piece of work, and that he can design and sculpt models for doing it better. Many people have seen him do it. But George Lovell is no Paul Daniels, a magician who reduces his audience to speechless wonder before the mystery of it all. He has shown so many of us how well he works with people, helping them to acquire some of his own analytical and synthesizing skills. The large majority of those who've attended Avec courses can testify to this. But now a third dimension opens up. Here, in this book, George Lovell is offering a service to people who want to help others with their work, people who want to work as he works. This is a book for consultants as well as practitioners. In its pages, the author shares the treasures of his life's work, the fruits of his labours, the depths of his wisdom and long experience. It is a generous offering from a big-hearted man.

I welcome this book because it fills a gap that needed filling for a long time. I'm convinced it will enable us understand George Lovell a little better; it will help all of us who want to know how to look critically at the work we do; and it will help any who want to help others analyse and reflect on their work.

June 1994
Leslie J. Griffiths
President of the Methodist Conference 1994–95

Preface: The Purpose and Structure of this Book

Thinking to good effect about work aimed at promoting the human and spiritual development of people in church and society is one of the most absorbing, worthwhile and rewarding activities. It is absorbing because it is about temporal and ultimate matters of human life and destiny. It is worthwhile and rewarding because the quality of any work we do with people is directly related to the quality of the thinking that we ourselves put into it. Sometimes thinking things through can be straightforward. But, for many reasons, it can be extremely difficult. Our knowledge and understanding of human affairs is always partial no matter how much experience and knowledge we have and how sharp our analytical faculties are. Psychological, sociological and theological explanations of any and every human phenomenon abound and many of them are mutually contradictory. Which should we use? To complicate things further we have to think as clearly as we can about the feelings we bring with us to the task and those generated by our emotional involvement and investment in the work—feelings which suffuse our thinking and play all kinds of tricks upon us and our thoughts. We encounter difficulties in thinking practically, theoretically and theologically about complex human situations and making decisions which have profound consequences for us. Whatever the circumstances, thinking about work with people about whom we deeply care activates many levels of belief and touches the raw nerves of our unfulfilled vocational aspirations.

All this makes it difficult to think at all, and even more difficult to "think straight". Consequently it makes heavy intellectual, spiritual and emotional demands upon us. Quite often people with considerable academic experience and competence say to me that they are surprised to find themselves deeply satisfied but quite tired after thinking about human situations for a couple of hours. They are surprised because they had not found other studies anywhere near as tiring. They were also surprised to realize that they had not previously given themselves to this combination of thinking and feeling. Thinking feelingly but constructively is an expensive but creative activity. And, this thinking has to take place in situations that are alive and very demanding. One of three things can happen: thinking time is squeezed out and people give up trying to think things through and become hyperactive; or they think more and more deeply without following it through with action; or they look for ways of thinking and acting which are more effective and satisfying.

An increasing number of people who are searching for more effective and satisfying ways of thinking about their work are looking for help to the behavioural sciences and adult education. I know this from my own experience. Over the past twenty years I have been privileged to work with thousands of people—men and women, ordained, religious and lay—of eight denominations engaged in a very wide spectrum of church and community work at all levels in Great Britain and in some twenty other countries. I have spent equal amounts of time working in the Anglican, Methodist and Roman Catholic Churches. I never cease to be amazed and excited by the far-reaching effects of helping people to think for themselves more systematically, thoroughly and deeply about their work and their part in it through using the approaches and methods described in this book. What happens is that they see possibilities and potential they had not seen before; they are animated; they are able to do things they did not previously think they could do; they experience greater job satisfaction; developments occur in people and their environment; workers and people gain a greater control over their lives and circumstances; they discover more effective and satisfying ways of thinking about their work with people. *My experience convinces me that a most important need in church and community work today is to get people, separately and together, at all levels in the church and in the community, to think for themselves more creatively and consistently about their work and what they do, or must do, for the common good, for human and spiritual well-being and the development of people and their environment in the light of the insights from the social and behavioural sciences and pastoral theology.*

But the time and energy to think is strictly limited! It simply is not possible to think in a thorough-going way about everything all the time. Doing so would paralyse us. This does not mean, as some infer, that there is little point in trying to think about anything in depth. On the contrary, it points us to the vital importance of selecting carefully just what we should be thinking about at any particular time. Of itself that requires thought. Life is, in fact, sustained by an ever changing pattern of doing things without thinking, doing and thinking at the same time, and thinking before doing. Human and spiritual development occurs when the combination of thought and action is creatively integrated.

Several things help us to do this kind of thinking. First, we need to be convinced that it is of vital importance that we do think for ourselves. This is necessary for our own growth and development as well as for the good of the work and it is part of our response to Jesus' command that we love God with our minds as well as our hearts. While the thinking of others informs our own thinking, it is no substitute for our own thought. Second, we need to believe that we can think for ourselves. Many of us come to this belief only when others believe that we can think for ourselves and help us to do so. Third, we all need, from time to time, people who will help us to think for ourselves. I refer to such people as non-directive workers and consultants. The response to such help is almost always positive. Tools are the fourth thing we need: tools which we ourselves can use to help us to think things through and tools which enable us

16

to help other people to think through things. Fifth, we need to know about ways of working with people in groups, churches, communities and organizations which enable them to think and act for the common good. (Most of the help I have received of this kind comes variously from community development, behavioural sciences, adult education, theology and particularly pastoral theology.) Sixth, we need an atmosphere of thought which reinforces all this and which leads people to make the arrangements to facilitate it.

The purpose of this book is to provide conceptual tools which enable individuals and groups to think more creatively about work for development in churches, communities and organizations.

A core process comprising a series of stages of thinking is at the heart of the various things which over the past thirty years have equipped and helped me to think about my work, have helped me to help others to think about their work and have helped them to do the same. Essentially this process, thoroughly tested and researched, comprises a series of stages of thinking which helps people to move from experience through critical and imaginative thought to creative action. The stages involve studying things as they are, defining what needs to be done and working out how to do things in relation to reference points (purpose, things to avoid, beliefs, resources and needs) and in a context of meditation, reflection and prayer. Reference points are important because the ability to think can be used for good or evil. Consequently, checking out our motivation and purposes is an important part of the processes and procedures described in this book. The process has a strong thrust towards thoughtful action: it directs and eases people towards that even when it is holding them back from precipitate action to get them to think things through. This process is at the heart of that tradition of church and community development work which has its roots in adult education rather than social work. It integrates into the methodology of ministry and mission relevant aspects of the behavioural sciences. Basically, therefore, this book is a contribution to the *means* of doing the work of the kingdom. This is an important correction to the propensity in the Church to talk about visions and ideals and to neglect the means of achieving them in specific social contexts. Visions are important; without them we perish. Visions of what things ought to be like help us to know whether we have arrived, or not, just as photographs of places do. But they do not help us to find our way through the labyrinthine pathways of thought, decision-making and action involved in moving from where we are to where we want to be; directions and the means of travelling are needed to do that.

Thus this book is about the shaping and sculpting of work with people so that every aspect of it, from considering the initial ideas to the evaluation of any action taken, makes its best contribution to human and spiritual development. I use the word sculpting to indicate that it is a practical craft using technical and theological knowledge about ways and means of working with people for development and an art form using intuitive skills and creative imagination. I describe sequences by which clergy, religious and laity can sculpt the work they do with people by thinking through it more systematically and systemically. These sequences help people to articulate, conceptualize, analyse, and evaluate their work experiences and ideas and to design, plan and carry out programmes most likely to achieve their purposes. Once these sequences have become embedded into the habitual working practices of clergy, laity and organizations they will form an infrastructure which gives depth to the work and enhances its quality and value. In turn this makes for better workers and more proficient working organizations and churches. This book illustrates and describes these sequences and methods and discusses the underlying theory and theology. It has the following four parts.

Part One: Examples of Work Analysis and Design demonstrates that clergy, religious and laity think quite naturally about their work and themselves as workers in terms of cases, problems, situations and projects. Each chapter gives a worked example of a systematic approach to one of these ways of thinking about their work. The subject-matter of these examples is of interest: an ecumenical church in faction over children at communion; a sense of failure; a bishop wanting to get the diocese to translate theology into social action; a small group of Jesuits putting into practice their "preferential option" for the poor in Northern Ireland. Having described the examples, essentials of the mode of analysis and design are discussed.

Part Two: Approach and Method considers the basic stages underlying processes described in Part One. It considers these processes, basically non-directive, and how they can be harmonized with the inner rhythms of the workers. It also considers the relationship between workers, their work and their context. The chapter on "designing" is important. Little has been written on this vital aspect of work sculpting. People generally find it more difficult than analysing, about which much is written! Neglect of this leads workers to opt for standard designs for church and community work which may or may not fit. The basic equipment for analysing and designing is considered in Chapter 7 and includes: spoken and written words and the relationship between them; questions; diagrams; hypotheses.

Part Three: A Commentary on The Approach takes the discussion of the approach a stage deeper and examines the theoretical and theological nature of the process which is based on the non-directive approach to church and community development. It discusses the ways in which it is a developmental process aimed at producing changes for the better in people and their environment. It shows that the approach is experiential but not limited to the experience of the workers and that it is both inductive and deductive. It considers the part beliefs play in this work and demonstrates that commitment and conviction are, along with abilities to think and skills to act, key factors in the quality of the work done.

Part Four: Application considers difficulties experienced by those who are persuaded but daunted by the approach, including: feeling intellectually inadequate; the difficulties of finding time and energy; the fear of losing control. The approach is shown to be relevant to all kinds of church and community work: it contributes towards providing a more highly skilled and satisfied church and community development work force; it helps people to have a subjective purchase on work and life; it contributes to the de-privatization of religion; it builds up egalitarian working relationships, co-operation and dialogue in a competitive and pluralistic society; it can be used to develop work consultancy infrastructures which service and support workers, and it provides data about church and community work. This part concludes by showing that these approaches engender a spirituality which, of itself, is a medium of human and spiritual development.

The parts are presented in the order: practice, methods and practice theory, underlying theory and theology, application and current contextual relevance. This order helps those who prefer to proceed from the particular to the general and from practice to theory. But the way in which the book is written means it could be read in reverse by those who prefer to work in the opposite direction.

By its structure the book models the inductive method: it starts with descriptions of representative experiences of the process in action; draws out the generic structure of the process; considers the essential nature of the process and the theory and theology upon which it is based; then returns to its application as it discusses difficulties and describes uses. Inevitably this method, and my desire to produce a handbook for practitioners and consultants, means that, in returning to aspects of the analytical processes, there is some repetition in order that sections should be self-contained.

So, by way of summary, this book is about a particular way of analysing and designing work with people in church and community. It shows what it looks like in practice and as a conceptual schema (Chapters 1–5); it describes how to use it and the approaches and equipment required to do so (6–8); it examines the nature of the activity and its theology (9–10); it considers principal daunting factors (11); and it describes its contemporary uses and relevance (12). This is set out in the following figure, *A Diagrammatic Overview of The Book*.

My hope is that this book will engender more creative action through promoting better understanding, extended discussion and wider use of this approach to analysis and design and that it will stimulate and help others to examine and conceptualize their own approach to studying and planning their work in church and community.

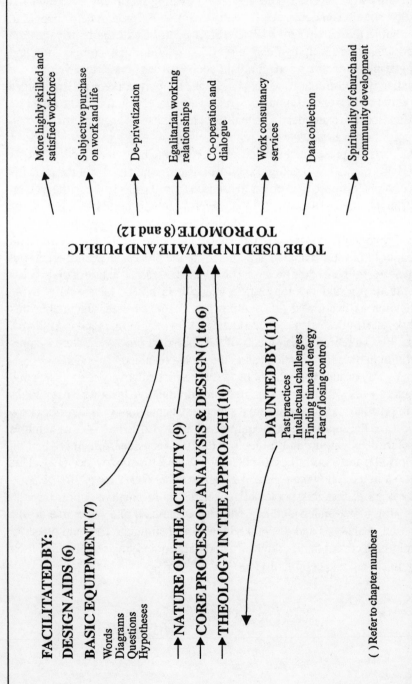

FACILITATED BY:

DESIGN AIDS (6)

BASIC EQUIPMENT (7)

Words
Diagrams
Questions
Hypotheses

NATURE OF THE ACTIVITY (9)

CORE PROCESS OF ANALYSIS & DESIGN (1 to 6)

THEOLOGY IN THE APPROACH (10)

DAUNTED BY (11)

Past practices
Intellectual challenges
Finding time and energy
Fear of losing control

TO BE USED IN PRIVATE AND PUBLIC
TO PROMOTE (8 and 12)

More highly skilled and satisfied workforce

Subjective purchase on work and life

De-privatization

Egalitarian working relationships

Co-operation and dialogue

Work consultancy services

Data collection

Spirituality of church and community development

( ) Refer to chapter numbers

A DIAGRAMMATIC OVERVIEW OF THE BOOK

List of Displays

List of Figures

Acknowledgements

Vast numbers of people have contributed to the development of the approaches described in this book. Some have done so through allowing me the privilege of studying their work with them and entering into their vocational aspirations and struggles. They showed me just what would and would not work for them and their situations. General acknowledgement is too bland a recognition of the ways they allowed and helped me to forge my tools of analysis and design on the realities of church and community work. But naming them is impossible. Others have made incalculable contributions through the work we have done together to provide training and consultancy services through Avec. Colleagues became soul friends as we used all our resources to analyse profoundly and design perceptively. To all of them I am eternally indebted and particularly to the Avec Associates, the part-time staff (Charles New, Howard Mellor and Michael Bayley) and to my colleague for more than twenty years, Catherine Widdicombe. I cannot begin to express my debt to her for her continuous support, her utter dedication to the work and her unfaltering commitment to the Christian beliefs and vision through which she saw the vital importance of the non-directive approach to church and community work.

I am indebted to the Avec Trustees, who encouraged and enabled me to "harvest" the work of Avec during 1991–93, and to The Leverhulme Trust, which enabled me to continue my research and writing through granting me a Leverhulme Emeritus Fellowship in 1993. I am also indebted to the people of the Victoria and Chelsea Methodist Circuit who have given me a spiritual base, graciously affirmed my ministry and generously contributed towards my stipend.

Then there are those who have helped me more directly with the writing of this book. I am deeply indebted to those who graciously gave me permission to publish Chapters 1, 3 and 4 after reading my manuscript. The minister central to the case study and the bishop with whom I studied his work situation must remain anonymous but I am free to name the Portadown Team of Jesuit Priests and the person with whom I worked, Paddy Doyle.

Margaret O'Connor has read and commented on every part of it. Her suggestions have greatly improved the text. Her enthusiasm for the book and her moral support gave me much-needed encouragement. Several other people read various parts in draft and made helpful suggestions: Michael Bayley, Paul Bunyan, David Deeks, Leslie Griffiths, Peter Russell, Ann Sutcliffe, John Stevinson and Catherine Widdicombe.

Valerie Tredinnick, my part-time secretary for many years, has typed and re-typed the whole of the book with great care, cheerfully and patiently and without any hint of complaint or irritation when I produced yet more revisions.

Reg and Madge Batten to whom I dedicate this book are the initial inspiration for the approach which is at the heart of it. They continue to be beloved mentors. Reg has added value to my ministry beyond description through hundreds of hours of the richest consultative conversations I have experienced.

Molly, my wife, has allowed me the freedom and provided the domestic environment within which I could give myself unreservedly to this book. Not only has she given me her full support, she has also helped with the typing and the proof reading. She has lived through the low and high moments with me.

I acknowledge with deep gratitude all this help, support and reinforcing encouragement.

I also acknowledge permission from the Guilford Press to reproduce the figures on p. 188.

George Lovell
September 1994

Part One

Examples of Work Analysis and Design

Orientation

There are several different ways in which we consider church and community work. We think and talk about our general and specific *problems* and about stories of difficult relationships which I will call *cases*. (A case is a sequence of events in which I, the worker, experienced inter-personal difficulties which led to a deterioration in working relationships. Cases are, of course, problems. They are differentiated because they need a different kind of analytical treatment from those problems that do not have a story-line.) Also we think in terms of the *situations* in which we work and the *projects* with which we are concerned. These vary enormously from the care of people in a street to international religious and secular organizations. We talk about each and all of these aspects in relation to how we feel about them and our job; how we see ourselves featuring and functioning and how we would prefer to do so; our beliefs, hopes, purposes, fears and, increasingly, about the wider socio-religious context in which we and our work are set. Recurring subjects emerge from these different modes of engagement with people (e.g. authority, communication, evaluation, leadership) and issues (clericalism, deprivation, injustice, racism, sexism). Subjects and issues form other natural ways in which we think and talk about our work. They facilitate the study of generic themes and the general application of findings. The approach I am describing centres on specific work situations and pursues subjects and issues which prove to be relevant in direct relation to them. Adopting a non-directive approach makes this possible. This approach is a common denominator to the contents of this book and therefore a generic issue which I inevitably bring to all my work. (I discuss this further in Chapter 9.)

It was only after many years of practising and promoting these methods of working on cases, problems, situations and projects that I realized I was using what seemed to be four natural categories. Consequently I had to check whether they were natural or whether they were introduced by my approach and methods. Going back over my experience of listening to people talking in their own way about their work convinces me that they use these categories quite naturally to present their experience and thinking. Undoubtedly the methods we have used have sharpened up the categories, but they did not invent or impose them. They fit like a glove. Whilst it is natural to think in one or other of the given categories (case, problem, etc.) the most appropriate one is not always obvious. Workers sometimes focus on a problem when they need to focus on a situation, or on one case when they need to examine the implications of a series of similar cases. Consideration is given in Chapter 5 to choosing the appropriate method.

This Part illustrates and discusses ways of using these natural categories (problems, cases, situations and projects) in order to tackle our work and the subjects, issues and feelings related to them more effectively and efficiently. It demonstrates the processes of analysis and design in the study of four examples of church and community work. There are two main aspects of each of the examples: the people and their work; the analytical processes and those engaged in them. In this book my concern is with the analytical processes and so I have chosen examples which best illustrate them. The example in Chapter Two was presented and worked on by women and men; the other three examples happened to be presented by men but they were worked on equally by women and men. Consequently the examples represent the analytical work of people of both sexes from several denominations, ordained, religious and lay people. Together they made the processes work. It is necessary to say this because, by their very nature, these processes direct attention away from themselves, and those who are deploying them, towards the human situations to which they are being applied; away from the analysts and designers to the presenters and the subject-matter. This is right: to be analytically effective processes and procedures need to be other-directed and structurally unobtrusive. To achieve our purposes we need to focus our attention on these processes.

CHAPTER ONE

Working on Cases

The first part of this chapter is the analysis of a case that occurred a few years ago in a non-conformist church formed by the uniting of Methodist and U.R.C. congregations. It was written by the minister who was central to the events.

I. A CASE STUDY

1. Family Communion

I am the minister of a church that wants its children to feel they are part of the family. Every Sunday morning they join the adults for a joyful culmination to morning worship. On the monthly Communion Sunday this is a little difficult, as their arrival after adult celebration creates an awkward second climax, and the teachers complain that the morning is too long, that they have to miss Communion themselves, and that the children are given strange ideas about a mysterious rite from which they are excluded. The exception is Easter Sunday, when the children are present for Communion, and come forward with the adults to receive a blessing.

Once, when all this was being fully discussed by a teachers' meeting I attended, the teachers started asking why we did not have Family Communions. My wife, who leads the Junior Department, felt particularly strongly about it, pointing out that our two young daughters were able to partake at a local Anglican church and at conferences, and claiming that children in her class feel rejected when they were invited to the Table at Easter only to be refused the bread and wine. I was asked whether I would be prepared to include the children fully in the next Easter Communion. I said that I would if it were left to me, but that this was a question to be opened up at the next Church Meeting; and in anticipation they planned a Junior Church Council which would lead up to an Easter Family Communion.

At the Church Council I brought the matter to the attention of the elders, who considered it carefully. One of them declared herself adamantly against children's partaking, but she agreed with those who thought members would be in a better position to discuss Family Communion if they had experienced one. Accordingly the Council decided to place the issue on the agenda of the Church Meeting in the form of a recommendation: that a Family Communion be held at Easter, in the light of which the question could be fully explored.

At the Church Meeting, however, the subject touched off an explosion of anger and confusion. Five people (two elders, one of whom had missed the last Church Council, and a teacher who had been absent at the relevant teachers' meeting) opposed the whole idea at length. Children wouldn't understand, would spoil the atmosphere, had to learn to wait; Communion was not to be used as a guinea pig; Church Council had taken unfair advantage by recommending .... Equally impassioned arguments favoured Family Communion, and my wife, with the other teachers of her department, said she would rather keep her class out altogether at Easter than have them dismissed with a blessing. By way of compromise I suggested a family meal of biscuits and squash, but was accused of trivializing the sacrament. I would not allow a vote on the issue, and said that with feelings running so high a Family Communion this Easter would not help any of us. But I did not know how to handle the deadlock. Someone suggested I preach a series about Communion. I agreed, said the discussion would have to be reopened at a later date, and moved on to the next item on the agenda. (A radical proposal affecting the whole future of our church, which was accepted without opposition!)

Since then, there has been a conspiracy of silence about Family Communion. Other discussions (e.g. children's work) have always stopped short of this topic, there has been no comment when the occasional child has taken the elements (including a party of mentally handicapped young people brought by a social worker to that particular Easter service), and I have never felt objective enough to preach my promised series of sermons. Privately one or two people have admitted surprise that all this fret and fever should have been for nothing. Junior Church has ceased the practice of attending Easter Communion for a blessing. And the teachers seem less certain that they have the backing of the members.

This case, like all other cases, tells the story of a causally connected sequence of events. It is the kind of pattern that occurs in every aspect of human life. Workers often talk about critical aspects of their experience in church and community work in this way.

In this particular case the central theme was children and communion. The Junior Church teachers wanted family communions but the consideration of the suggestion split the Church Meeting, and led to an impasse, and now the children are less involved in communion services than before. In fact there was an all-round deterioration in the situation.

There are several equally important people in the events and the case could be analysed from each of their perspectives. As it was written by the minister from his perspective we examine it in relation to him and his thoughts and actions. Examining it in relation to one person (or one centre of co-ordinated activity such as a partnership) is very important. It reflects the realities of life: we are only ever one person; we can exist and act only from the being of one person; we work to change complex human systems from our own complex human systems; the greatest control and influence that we have, therefore, is over one person—ourselves. Analysis and action-plans must take this fact of life seriously if it is to be of any consequence. Even so, people are inclined to talk as though others can be moved around at will in human affairs. "He should do that. She will do this. They must be made to do that...." That is to treat people like chess pieces and they are anything but that; it is to turn the story of the case into a fairy story. We will stick with reality, with one non-exchangeable centre of being and doing, the minister, the worker.

Many different groups of people—women and men, ordained, religious and lay from all the main denominations and working at different levels—have at various times discussed and analysed this case. They all identified with the essential dilemma of the minister, including Roman Catholics whose eucharistic tradition is so different. In what follows I am drawing on the principal points made in these discussions.

The discussion of the case is set in the period a month or so after the Church Meeting.

2. The Diagnosis

There are two aspects to this diagnosis: an assessment of the way in which the minister contributed to the deterioration in the working situation and relationships; and what is still "going for" him. Sometimes when we are diagnosing cases we can see what was not helpful without knowing what else could have been done. Indeed we may feel that what was done is just what we would have done. Alternative and better possibilities invariably emerge from considering such incidents. And it is seeing the kind of action we think would have been more likely to achieve the desired objectives that shows up the inadvisability of what was done or not done. So diagnosing is as much about discovering what could or should have been done as about what should not have been done: discerning and defining the one helps to discern and define the other. Generally speaking, people are more prepared to make constructive critical judgements of what a worker did/did not do when they see a better way in which s/he could have acted. Up to that point they are inclined to sympathize with the worker and resist any adverse judgement upon the action taken and its effects with statements like, "But s/he could not do anything else!" "What else could s/he have done, for goodness sake?" Therefore, where necessary in the diagnosis that follows, the critical assessment of the minister's action, given in emboldened type, is followed by notes about action more likely to have had good effects.

An Assessment of What the Minister Did
What was it then, that the minister/worker did or did not do which in our judgement contributed in any way to the *undesirable* outcome?

His Initial Response
He did nothing about the feelings of which he was fully aware of dissatisfaction with the arrangements for children being present at the communion and the nature of their participation until his hand was forced by his wife and the teachers. Then he made an immediate response to a

particular solution suggested at a teachers' meeting from which the one teacher who opposed it was absent. In that response he sided with the teachers and their proposed solution and inferred lack of sympathy with any who might oppose the proposal. He colluded with them in planning a course leading up to Easter Communion.

By allowing things to drift he lost the opportunity to define the problem and to work out how best to get the theological issues and the practical implications of such a sensitive subject considered and resolved. One of the consequences of this was that he had to make his initial move in response to the problem through his response to a solution suggested at a teachers' meeting. This prevented him from making his response freely after careful thought about the situation and the full range of options which would have been open to him. Moreover, he had to make his response under considerable pressure from his wife and the teachers to accept their solution—circumstances not conducive to deciding just how to tackle such a difficult issue. It is not surprising that he sided with the teachers and that he did let them act as though the outcome was a foregone conclusion—but that is a provocative act in an organization in which some members cherish their privilege and take seriously their responsibility to make decisions freely on all such matters.

So he had lost the opportunity to approach the whole situation freely and independently. Possibly his preoccupation with the "radical proposal" meant that he simply had not had time to give to this issue. Nonetheless he could have responded by saying that, as the matter was a weighty one about which people would have deep and conflicting convictions, he needed to think how best to get all the ideas on the subject and the theological and practical issues considered. Also he could possibly have assured them that he was very deeply concerned about the issues they had rightly raised and that he would be in a much better position to act in relation to them when the decisions had been made about the "radical proposal". Meanwhile, he could have suggested they discuss their ideas with the absent teacher. Thus he would have identified with their concern, taken them and their suggestions very seriously, got them to consult their colleague and got himself into a position from which he could decide how best to act in relation to the whole situation and for the common good.

At The Church Council
He brought the matter to the attention of the elders. He was party to a recommendation going to the Church Meetings advocating that the church try out the idea for a Family Communion on Easter Sunday; i.e. carry out an experiment.

Taking the idea to the Church Council himself meant that he personally became more and more closely identified with the idea. This made it difficult for people

34

to question or oppose the idea without feeling they were taking sides against the minister. The communion issue became a personal issue, even if by default. Moreover, the recommendation that it be tried out meant that several issues were now in the discussion: that children take communion; that there be a family communion on Easter Day; that this be treated as an experiment. All too easily these issues were confused, not least because of the emotions associated with the substantive issue and the feelings raised by the way in which the suggestion had been processed. The experimental method seems inappropriate. It is irreversible: once children have taken communion they have taken it and crossed the line of conviction that they should not take it until they are older; and people suspect it because they see it as a subtle pseudo-scientific way of imposing innovation, "the thin edge of the directive wedge."

Then there is the question of the ministers taking sides. Clearly, theologically and liturgically he favoured children's participating in family communions. To feign that he was neutral would be wrong and unhelpful but he could have refused to take sides. The stance that would have enabled the minister to be most helpful was one in which he declared his interests and said that he wanted all views, including his own, to be properly considered and respected in the search for ways of resolving the differences which would enhance sacramental worship for everyone. Such a stance was implicit. That is where he wanted to be. He never quite got there. Three things could have helped him to do so: greater clarity of role and function in relation to this issue; not taking sides; making explicit the stance he was taking and that he was taking it because it was the position from which he could best minister to the church as a whole on this issue and to each theological/liturgical faction within it.

At The Church Meeting
He was party to such a vital subject being brought to a meeting without a proposed way of tackling it and to placing it on the agenda before an item known to be of great importance which presumably was expected to be discussed at length.

Presumably he had to bring it to that meeting because of the timetable he had accepted from the teachers. All other things being equal, it might have been better to give notice of the subject and ask how and when they could give it the kind of consideration it warranted. If this were not possible, he could have suggested that they consider things in some order and in relation to purpose, belief and their two-denomination context: the nature and importance of communion to us; children and communion; experimenting with different kinds of services; the family communion on Easter Day. That would have given a framework, order and shape to the discussion. During the earlier stages the emphasis could have been upon building up understanding and acceptance of each other's views as a basis for finding a mutually acceptable way forward.

He did not get them to consider their differences in relation to what they had in common.

He trivialized the issue and caused offence, however inadvertently, by suggesting an orange-squash/biscuit love-feast compromise.

What they had in common was a high doctrine of and reverence for the communion service. The enormous spiritual significance of it for them led them to two quite different convictions: that children should have access to this vital religious service as soon as possible; that they should have access only when they understood what it is about. He did not make this point. Establishing areas of real agreement and common ground is of enormous importance in working where there is faction or the possibility of it. The suggestion about biscuits and squash was sacreligious. Equally he did not get them to draw out in an objective way the differences between them.

He used his position as minister and chairman to take "control" of the meeting by making strong definitive interventions when he just did not know how to handle the deadlock, viz:

— he would not allow a vote;

— he quashed the idea for a family communion at Easter by telling them that with feelings running so high it would not help any of them;

— he himself accepted the first positive suggestion (that he preach a series of sermons about communion) without testing it out for acceptability and seeing what other ideas members might have;

— he closed down the discussion by saying that it would have to be reopened at a later date and by moving on to the next item on the agenda.

There are times when it is right for ministers and and those in the chair to take directive action of this kind. It is required and expected of them. They are often the only person in a position to do so. But was it right for him to do so in this situation? I think not, even though I can see myself doing it in panic and desperation. There are times when it is right to mask uncertainty, but there are considerable dangers in acting as though you know what you are doing when you do not. What else could he have done? He could possibly have said something like this: "I just do not know what is the best way to resolve these issues. One idea is that I preach a series of sermons as a basis for further discussion. There may be others. I do not feel that we should take a snap decision by voting. That might make things worse. Clearly we are considering a very important issue about which we all feel deeply. I feel that we need to find a time when we can do justice to the issues that have emerged and decide what to do about the suggestion for an Easter Communion. What do you think/feel?" Such an intervention changes the focus of the discussion from children and communion to how are we (people and minister, not simply the minister) going to resolve the deadlock. It legitimizes not knowing what to do and gives everyone a chance to work at it together. It invites them to make decisions about process as well as content and the process by which they resolve the issues will profoundly affect, positively or negatively, the spiritual interplay between their life as a communion and sacramental acts of communion. Making such points could introduce new theological dimensions to the discussion. Of course, all this is with hindsight. But then had the discussion been postponed there would have been time to prepare such an input. What glorious theological possibility in this encounter!

After the Church Meeting
He lets things drift again: he does not preach the sermons; he tempts providence by allowing handicapped and other children to take communion; he does not arrange for further discussion; he rests uneasily in what one or two said about the "fret and fever" having been for nothing.

History seems to be in danger of repeating itself, that is up to the point of his writing up the case and seeking help with it.

Throughout
He **tried to work out everything in public.**

Some private discussions about the issues and how best to get them considered openly and constructively could have led to better discussions in the Council and the Church Meetings. But possibly he had no other choice simply because of the sheer pressure of events and of his work load! In fact he did not let things drift as some suggested; he had no option but to let some things drift and this was one of them! That meant he had to deal with them in public and that brings us to the next points.

He was not able to "steer" the proposal through the turbulence of the public discussion and he did not get others to help him to do so.

It was the combination of these that created difficulties: if he had done the second, the first would not have had the same effects. An argument for collective effort.

He did not get people testing out and working on the possible positive and negative effects upon the church community as a whole of considering the proposal for a family communion and of having one at Easter.

The discussion was child-centred, child/teacher/parent-centred rather than church-communion-centred. The following question could have set the discussion in the wider context: If the proposal was implemented, what good and bad effects do we think it would have on different members and parts of our church community in relation to our purposes in general and our common desire that children really feel that they are part of the church family? Follow-up questions could be: Can we reduce the bad effects to a tolerable level? If so, do we want to implement the idea? If not, what can we do in relation to the continuing felt needs that led the teachers to make the suggestion?

What is "Going For" the Minister
First reactions after such an assessment is that there is not much "going for" the minister! This mirrors feelings generated by such incidents. They are deceptive. In fact there are many things going for him, some of which are as follows:

• The minister is making a very serious attempt to resolve the impasse. He has written down the story in an open and manageable way in an honest manner; not an easy thing to do when the events evoke strong emotions and possibly self-rebuke. He has sought help to think through what he should do next. He is not defensive—yet! And there is time to think and act.

• Members of the Church Meeting have strong beliefs which they can articulate and the communion is very important to them.

• Things have calmed down. The church and the minister and his wife have been able to take the event and contain the argument: immediately after the fraught discussion about communion the Church Meeting acted unanimously in relation to a radical proposal; no one has resigned office or left the church; the teachers are still teaching; subsequently handicapped children have communicated without further argument.

• The inititative is with the minister and he has two possible openings: sermons and a further discussion.

• The minister has opportunities to promote discussion on what could be highly significant issues: the sacrament and ways and means of discussing and deciding about such things most likely to build up the church communion. Such discussions combine the pragmatic (procedures and processes) with the theological.

• The minister cares—cares about *all* the people, adults and children. He wants to do the right thing and build up the good relationships. He now knows more about the church and their feelings and about himself as a worker. He is honest and resilient.

3. Towards redeeming the Situation

But what can the minister do now to redeem the situation? Precisely what does he need to do with whom, in what way and to what end? Amongst the proliferation of ideas that have emerged from the analysis there are some that are persistent.   Only the minister, of course, can say what he could do and what he thinks would work. Our suggestions must be tentative. Then again, whilst objectives, approach and first steps can be planned in some detail, second steps will be influenced by what happens during the first round of action.

Do Some More Homework

Those who analysed the case agreed that the first thing that the minister had to do was some more homework. (A surprising number of them, however, only saw the significance of this when others had mentioned it.) Privately, on his own or with consultancy help from an independent colleague or consultant, he needs to work at several things.

First, he needs to work out his overall objective for his next phase of work on the family communion saga. Creating a better atmosphere could be very much on his mind: a "conspiracy of silence" is not a good ambience in which to minister. Achieving this is necessary and desirable, but not at any price. There are other things to be done. Those who differ need a better and more sympathetic understanding of each other's beliefs and convictions and their common ground (a high doctrine of the communion). Then they need to bend their minds and wills to find a way forward to which all can commit themselves and which contributes to making and maintaining a fellowship conducive to communion. Getting a better atmosphere is an integral part of that. Internalizing this objective so that it really does guide thought-out action is important: it is so easy to be deflected from it. Formalizing it in the following way could help him to do so:

> To get all concerned to so work at the theological and practical issues that they understand and love each other more and find mutually acceptable ways of resolving their dilemma which help them to achieve their purposes for adults and for children in the church.

It took quite a bit of effort to clarify this—and I am not emotionally involved.

Second, sorting out his own thinking would help him to give himself more freely to helping others to sort out their thinking. (His thinking, that is, about communion and the optimum human conditions for it to be effective.) This leads into a third thing: his stance in these particular discussions and what his main job is in relation to them. Earlier we touched on this in the assessment of the case. Whatever else he does, he will need to make significant contributions towards "facilitating" the subsequent thinking and deciding. To do this he has to be non-directive. Some felt that an independent facilitator was called for. Others saw the advantages of minister and people "facilitating" each other.

Fourth, he needs to decide how he is going to cope with any residual feelings he may have and just what apologies he needs to make to whom about what.

To assume responsibility for things for which he was not responsible reduces the significance of his own apology and trespasses upon the responsibilities others properly had for what went wrong. Blanket apologies are to be avoided: on that everyone spoke with some feeling. There is much more redeeming and reconciling power in specific apologies than in general apologies.

Fifth, he needs to think out what action he is now going to take with other people (what has been suggested already in this section is action of an energetic kind!). Many suggestions were made as we speculated about the possibilities. These are discussed below.

Clearly, hard thinking, reflection, prayer and much courage are required to do all this homework as working through these issues makes heavy demands upon the soul, the mind and the will.

4. Action Suggestions

There was strong support for the minister starting by discussing things with his wife. The idea of doing his homework with his wife did not seem to be a realistic possibility because of the way in which they had been involved. Much is at stake for both of them as husband and wife, as parents, as a ministerial couple, as teacher and minister. The problem is how to ensure that any discussion that they might have is creative. Here we mention two of the many things that will determine whether or not it will be. Timing is the first. He will know the conducive circumstances. It is up to him to create them or to seize the right moment when it arises (the preparation that he has done means he is in a good position to do that). The second is the use to which he puts his own thinking. He could share it with her fully or summarily or he could think through the events from her perspective—as we have done from his—and then from their joint perspectives or he may start with what he proposes to do and why. The minister alone has the information to decide which of the many permutations is most likely to work. Attention needs to be given to both these points—timing and the use of prior thought—in all the encounters.

After that there was a proliferation of ideas about those with whom he ought to discuss the situation—members? parents and children? teachers? the Council? the Church Meeting?—and about the order and manner in which he ought to do so. Setting these out as possible alternatives and considering the pros and cons of each of them enabled members to refine the various approaches and to settle on the one which they thought most likely to be effective. But, again, they realized that their suggestions must be tentative because they did not have the knowledge of the situation and the people which would enable them to make a situational judgement about them being a "fit". A possibility that emerged from all the suggestions was that the minister open up the discussion again with the members of the Church Meeting. Some thought that he ought to start with people informally, others with the teachers or the Council. But it was to the members of the Church Meeting that he said that the discussion would have to be reopened at a later date. Starting the discussion elsewhere could be misunderstood and resented as another attempt to force the issue. The idea was that he make a statement to the Church Meeting saying that he has been reflecting on what happened and has seen that they had been united in their high doctrine of the communion and divided in what that means in practice, that he believes that much could be gained by working together at the theological and practical issues; that as that is no easy thing to do they need to consider carefully whether or not they want to do so and, if they do, they need to think carefully about how they could do it so that the outcome is most likely to be positive and not to proceed until they were agreed how to go about it and how they would approach any difficulties that occurred. He could underline this last point by saying that he did not want to spring this matter on them, nor did he want them to drift into a discussion. So what he was saying was by way of notice of a discussion to be held at a future meeting to be determined by them, i.e., a discussion about discussions. This would provide opportunities for people, individuals and formal and informal groups to reflect and come prepared for the discussion. This would be the point at which he could make his apologies. If the meeting agreed with his suggestion he could say that he was concerned to get all points of view considered and taken into account. Would the meeting appoint a small group representative of various ideas and groups to meet with him for the sole purpose of working out how best to get the issue discussed?

Leading the discussion about taking these steps could be tricky. He needs to generate and maintain an objective, emotionally sensitive but low-key atmosphere. Two of the possible dangers are: that they drift into an unhelpful discussion of the issues; that in attempts to prevent this he frustrates one of those moments when much is transacted in a short space. Awareness, vigilance and judgement are called for.

Should he give notice of this discussion on communion or not? A bald statement of the item on an agenda sent out in advance could cause people to come prepared to fight their corner again. A full statement could be helpful. If this is not normal practice possibly the best thing is to introduce it at the meeting.

There may well be officers of the Church Meeting or the Council or the Teachers' Meeting with whom it is normal practice for the minister to discuss business in confidence before bringing it to any or all of these meetings. If this were so, he could discuss his plans and ideas with them and seek their advice. They could then help to promote the kind of discussion required.

So far we have been considering procedures most likely to promote processes of development. As suggestions are put to people their attention will focus on the subject-matter. They will be trying to assess the effects of working on the issues: Will it improve things? What's it all about anyhow? What do I/we/others have to gain or lose? Will I gain or lose? Will I/we be able to avoid trouble? Will it be worth all the effort? So they will want to know just what they are being asked to work on. Basically it is about how to meet the spiritual needs of children through communion services in such a way that the adult members feel good about what happens and therefore generate a human and spiritual atmosphere conducive to all concerned receiving maximum benefit and blessing from the services. So it is about building up the communion of the Church through communion services. Doing that inevitably involves considering all kinds of questions about liturgy and theology, growth in faith and Christian education. It could be an education for all concerned. It also raises questions about how the church members discuss and decide things, especially tricky questions to do with differences in faith, belief and practice. Consequently the agenda concentrated in "Family Communion" is of enormous importance to the well-being of the whole church.

Assuming that the members need more information and time to make informed decisions, they may want from the minister or the working group a description of what they would need to consider, in what way and to what end, i.e. information about content, process and objective. Also they may want to consider the possible effects of not tackling the issues in relation to their responsibilities for the spiritual needs of all concerned and implicated. It might help to know at this stage under what conditions the members of the Church Meeting would consider working at this subject-matter. This would help the minister/working group to try to work out ways and means of meeting the conditions. There are important aims implicit in all this. They are for the minister to get the Church Meeting to take more effective control of its affairs and to accept and discharge its responsibilities for the spiritual well-being of the church, to build up the confidence of its members and to build up the working relationship between the Council, the Teachers' Meeting and itself.

If and when it comes to working out the next steps it would be necessary to consider amongst other things: the aims of discussions; what use if any to make of the analysis or the means of analysing used here; the kind of specific questions to be asked and in what order; the time-scale.

II. WHAT ARE WE LEARNING FROM THIS CASE STUDY?

Examining what workers have done/are doing in specific situations through case studies serves three purposes at the same time. Foremost of these is to discover what action the worker should now take in relation to the specific situation. The second is to clarify things in the working situation which just have to be taken into account when working for development, what Batten calls the "authority of the situation". The third is to discover how the worker could do things better and become a better worker.

The first of these is the explicit purpose and the one to which we have devoted ourselves so far. Much emerged related to the second purpose, for example the consensus about the importance of communion and the significant differences

42

about children's attendance. In relation to the third purpose, the case shows how easy it is to trip up and to be tripped up! The minister was experienced, highly committed to working with people and keen on participation. He needs to avoid using trivializing words such as "squash and biscuits", which are so emotive. He needs to make alliances rather than "hidden coalitions".[1] He needs to determine how he can work with people who are expressing different opinions strongly and emotionally and taking up opposing positions, and to do so when he has a complex of relationships with the people concerned and the discussion is fast, furious and penetrating. As chairman, minister, husband and father he experienced a bewildering confusion of pressures emanating from several sources: the loyalties he had to his wife, to the teachers and to the elders, to the children; the theological and practical complexities involved in considering the pros and cons of children at communion; and the responsibility he felt to help the meeting to decide on a course of action mutually acceptable to the factions. What are the basics of an approach which help him to deal with such situations? He needs to know about working with groups in faction[2] and what is involved in taking things from one group to another so that there is accumulative creative participation. This brings us to the importance of "private" and "public" work and the interplay between them.[3] The quality of thinking on one's feet in meetings is related to the quality of one's thinking on one's seat in the study. These things are considered in the other parts of this book.

III. ESSENTIALS IN WORKING ON CASES[4]

Now we turn from the study of a particular case to the study of the essentials of the process of examining cases in order to help readers to make a critical assessment for themselves of the value of the approach for them and their work, to reject, adapt or adopt it and to put it into practice in their own way.

To use this case-study method to best effect on the actualities of church and community work it is necessary to have a firm grasp on the essential stages. They are:

Stage 1   Getting a clear statement of the case story.

Stage 2   Defining the overall change for the worse and for the better that has occurred.

Stage 3   Diagnosing what went wrong from the worker's perspective and assessing what action the worker could have taken to influence the course of events for the better.

Stage 4   Assessing the strengths and weaknesses of the current working situation and determining the implications for the worker.

Stage 5   Thinking out precisely what action the worker can now take.

Stage 6   Learning as much as possible from the experience in order to inform and improve the way in which the worker goes about things in the future.

Stage 1: Getting a clear statement of the case story. Cases are descriptions of things that have actually happened. They are about situations in which workers are not achieving what they set out to achieve. They are about workers who find themselves in situations and relationships that are debilitating and distressing. They are stories told from a worker's perspective. To work on them constructively the case story needs to describe several things: the initial situation and the worker's objectives; the key events in the order in which they occurred; precisely what action the worker took and why; details of the significant responses made by others; an assessment of the final situation; and a statement of the worker's dilemma, concerns or difficulties. Generally speaking it is better to write the case in the first person: "I wanted to. . .", "I did not...", "I aimed at", "I thought/felt/said/did". Sometimes I find I gain objectivity by using the third person and describing myself in different ways: "George said" or "Lovell did" or "The minister/chairman/worker felt". It all depends upon how I am feeling about myself and whether I am looking back over my actions with sympathy, disappointment or anger.

Writing the story down in this disciplined and structured way is no mean achievement, especially when doing so recalls strong emotions and a sense of failure. However, it is healing and helpful to put it on paper no matter how painful and costly it might be. Emotions are released and new energy begins to flow as workers feel that they have put things in a workable shape, they have got a hold on the situation and they are working at it in an orderly way. All too easily and often, however, these feelings can be eclipsed by feelings that the situation is hopeless. What buoys me up when that happens is that I have found something good always emerges from working at these cases.

Stage 2: Defining the overall change for the worse and for the better that has occurred. Overall changes for the worse and for the better that have occurred can be assessed by contrasting the situation as it was at the outset of the case with what it was at its conclusion; by comparing, for example, changes in relationships, attitudes, morale, willingness to effect change. The aim is to get a realistic view of "success" and "failure" (especially when the worker feels "a failure") and of positive and negative side-effects. Analysis and remedial action must take these actualities into account.

Stage 3: Diagnosing what went wrong from the worker's perspective and assessing what action the worker could have taken to influence the course of events for the better. Stage 2 defines what went wrong. Stage 3 makes explicit what the worker contributed to things going wrong. This involves being precise and specific about the when, where, how and why of his/her contributions to the bad effects. And, as we have seen, it involves exploring alternative actions likely to have avoided the undesirable outcome and to have achieved the desired objectives: a painful process, but one which reveals much of value for remedial action and future practice. This part of the analysis is best effected by making a series of statements beginning with either "S/he did..." or "S/he did not...", each statement being about an action or lack of action that contributed to the bad end-effect. The diagnosis is, in fact, based upon a behavioural analysis.

Stage 4: Assessing the strengths and weaknesses of the current working situation and determining the implications for the worker. Stating what is actually "going for" the worker alongside the difficulties in the situation helps to restore his/her morale and reveals firm ground on which to build.

Stage 5: Thinking out precisely what action the worker can now take. Being specific and explicit about the action to be taken is of the essence. Amongst other things this involves being specific about: the objective of the action (why? to what end?); about the situation, setting and context in which it is proposed to act (where? with whom?); about the manner and method of acting (how?); and about the timing (when?). Success can depend, for instance, on whether a worker writes a letter, telephones, calls unexpectedly or meets by appointment. Each of these is appropriate or inappropriate, depending upon people, situations and circumstances. Of course, the decision could be to take no action.

There is a propensity for people and workers to presume the outcome of the first round of action and to plan accordingly, instead of planning for the range of possible outcomes. This tends to reduce their freedom to work with people. Good designing and planning foresees the possibilities and prepares for them: it does not foreclose.

Ideas that work in one situation do not necessarily work in another. Similarly, what one person can do others cannot. So the solution must fit the worker and the situation. To aim for that is imperative.

This stage moves from the past to the future, from analysing to designing and from designing to planning. Choosing between the ideas for action involves analysing the pros and cons of each possibility in relation to purpose, beliefs, situations, circumstances and people. This kind of activity is discussed later.

Stage 6: Learning as much as possible from the experience in order to inform and improve the way in which the worker goes about things in the future. Drawing out conclusions or learning which would help workers to be more effective in future helps them to build up their own theory and code of good practice.

IV. USES OF THE METHOD

Case studies rarely fail to galvanize interest. People participate with an unusual degree of freedom; orderly discussion frequently gives way to excited interchanges as people struggle to articulate what they have perceived and grapple with conflicting views about what the worker did or should have done.

Frequently so many ideas and thoughts are produced in a short time that chaos reigns temporarily. The structured approach helps to give order and shape to the ideas and discussion. All this, and the intensive learning that accompanies it, seem to be related to the case being "real" and the tasks set being specific and concrete. Consequently it is inherently more difficult (but not impossible) for the discussion to become abstract (to "sky"). Everyone can contribute because they are drawing upon knowledge and experience in which they have a great emotional and intellectual investment, not least because it was gained in hard schools.

The potential in this method and its variations is great.

First, it focuses on workers and their perspective. As we have seen, it avoids and corrects discussions in which workers mentally move people around like pieces on a chess board. To be realistic we must focus on ourselves and what we can do to evoke the responses from others which engender creative action.

Second, it is a way of formulating experiences either in a verbal or written form which of itself:

— helps workers to objectify and order complex situations often highly charged with emotion and sometimes by feelings of guilt;

— can be therapeutic;

— is a way of getting real help from others because it makes the information available for them to work at the case.

Third, it can be used by individuals or groups. And as it draws upon knowledge and experience of human nature it can, suitably adapted, be used by people of any group or culture regardless of their formal education. Consequently it enables and encourages all to participate on equal terms; it promotes constructive co-operation rather than competition.

Fourth, it can be used formally or informally, as a mental exercise or a verbal or written process. Going through the stages rapidly when it simply is not possible to give more time to them puts some order into what would otherwise be frenzied thinking and gives at least a "first approximation" to the solution.

Fifth, it helps all concerned to "take hold of situations", to face up to them, to work through them and to decide quite specifically what they are going to do or not going to do. Thus it enhances their sense of being in control and "on top of things" and reduces the danger of their being panic-stricken.

Sixth, it is as applicable to "religious" case-study material as it is to that which is "practical". In fact such divisions are arbitrary because studying cases is as much a theological or ideological exercise as it is a pragmatic one.

Seventh, it is a way of analysing and profiling work situations.

Eighth, it is a way of self-training. Working on a number of cases, drawing out the learning points and classifying them helps us to profile our good and bad points as workers and to evolve our own codes of good practice. It also informs our intuitive responses and makes us more alive and alert to critical factors in our working relationships. Thus it helps us to be more effective in situations that call for spontaneous responses and action.

What I have written here draws heavily upon the vast amount of work that the Battens have done on case studies. They have written extensively about them.[5] They have grouped cases under subject-matter such as "working with groups" and "working with leaders" and "dealing with faction". Having studied a cluster of cases they draw out the implications for workers. Workers who do this for themselves build up their own codes of good practice and the body of knowledge upon which it is based.

Someone with whom I worked felt that one of the most important things about studying cases was that it builds up a psychological profile of the worker. So the training can be related to work behaviour, the psychological and spiritual traits of the worker and the profile of the essential characteristics of the work situation: a vital triangle.

V. REFLECTIONS ON THE METHOD

One of the common responses to such an analysis is excitement about the learning from the exercise and amazement at all that there is to consider in such situations. It shows up the awesome business of working with people for human and spiritual development, the enormous potential, the frightening dangers and number of trip-wires. It opens out on many fields of understanding and knowledge about the human and the divine. It is the world of thought, theology and action in microcosm. It is packed with the kingdom. Consequently thinking about it is mind-boggling. How dare I do anything with people again?

Another common response is that people say that they simply cannot find the time to do such analysis on all the situations in which they are involved. The discussion described above took a group about two hours. So, adding the time to write the case, there is almost a day's work involved. My suspicion is that as much time had already been given to it to much less effect. (Coming to terms with the situation and facing up to doing anything constructive about it involves going over and around what happened almost in circles. It is not always possible to go straight into a systematic and penetrating analysis, we need "explanations" as to what happened with which we can live.[6]) However, the basic point is accepted. It simply is not possible to analyse all our work in this way. But it does not follow that we should therefore not examine any of our work in this way. If it is imperative that we do examine some of it for reasons that follow, and if we cannot examine all of it, then it is vital that we select carefully that which we do examine.

We need to examine it for several reasons: to tackle difficult problems to best effect with an economy of effort and emotional energy; to increase our understanding and knowledge; to develop our practice theory and to enhance our practice in general; to be able to assess and analyse situations more systematically, accurately and quickly. My colleague and I can use this method as we walk round the block to do a first approximation. It is not as carefully considered as the above analysis but it is better than an unstructured examination would be. We simply go through the steps and stages. Doing this builds up the facility to think in this way on our feet, as they say. So hours of practice has many benefits for work beyond the case, for situations yet to be encountered.

Clearly we owe a great debt to the Battens for developing this case-study method and for describing and illustrating it so thoroughly. However, there are two assumptions underlying their writings on case studies upon which I need to comment, although they may now have revised them.

First, the assumption that much more is learnt from things that go wrong than from things that go right i.e. from "failures" rather than "successes". Undoubtedly much can be learnt from "failures" and from this method of analysing. That I have proved from my own experience and that of others. Much can also be learnt from "successes", i.e. from what workers are doing well. Getting out the essentials of practice-theory from what people are doing well is vital for the development and transfer of skills. All too often the success is put down to the person having unique gifts. This feeds the pride of the person concerned, makes others feel inferior and does nothing for the development of the work. Getting out the basics enables many more people to practise. This is what happened in Avec in relation to situational analysis and work consultancy, described later. I was doing it intuitively. After a group had analysed with me what I was doing and why, my own practice improved and many others were able to do it as well.

The second assumption is that Batten says if the worker does everything right he will achieve his purposes. "If he (the worker) fails, he fails because of some misjudgement or mistake that he has made".[7] Workers could do "everything right" and still fail to achieve their objectives. I say this because I experience sin and human perversity in myself and in others. In fact in some circumstances the worst is drawn out of us by those who do everything right! But beware that this is not used as an excuse. Amongst other things it means that studying cases is a theological exercise as well as a social/psychological one. It also means that remedial action involves spiritual matters; for example how we deal with our guilt, how we forgive and seek forgiveness. Also the development of ourselves as church and community development workers involves our growth as Christians. It is not only a matter of developing skills and insights.

NOTES AND REFERENCES

1. John Haley distinguished between open alliances for something, denied coalition against somebody. Cf. *The Hidden Games of Organization* by Mara Selvini Palazzoli (New York: Pantheon Books, 1986) chapter 8.

2. Cf. Batten, T.R., with the collaboration of Batten, M., *The Human Factor in Community Work* (London: OUP, 1965) pp. 126–149.

3. See pp. 193–196, below.

4. I have prepared some notes on the case-study method for those using it on courses. They are: "An Introduction To The Case-Study Methods", "Some Notes on Using the Case-Study Method in Church and Community Work" and "Discussing A Case in A Group". They are available from Avec, references Z1, 2 & 3.

5. Cf. Batten, *The Human Factor in Community Work*. These cases are set overseas but they are pertinent to work with people in any country. See also Batten *Training for Community Development: A Critical Study of Method* (London: OUP, 1962), pp. 39–40 and 113–120; Batten, *The Non-Directive Approach in Group and Community Work* (London: OUP, 1968), pp. 96–100. Batten, *The Human Factor in Youth Work* (London: OUP, 1979), is relevant to work with other age groups. In one way or another, these cases are highly relevant to the work of the ministry. Further, the classification of the cases and the conclusions the Battens draw are relevant to anyone working with people. Unfortunately the first three of these books are out of print but they can generally be obtained from libraries. Also see Avec Occasional Papers Z1, 2 & 3 referred to earlier.

6. David Smail in *Illusion & Reality: The Meaning of Anxiety* (London: J. M. Dent, 1984) says that "For everyday purposes, it seems that reality *is* the best description I am able to give myself of it" (p. 64).

7. Cf. *The Human Factor in Community Work*, p. 3.

CHAPTER TWO

Working on Problems

Problems of one kind or another stand between us and the achievement of anything of value in church and community work. Avoiding them contributes to their destructive power; owning them begins the process of controlling them; tackling them starts to give us power over them; dealing with them purposefully enables us to seize the opportunities they block off. Moving from the avoidance of problems to dealing with them is releasing, creative and satisfying. This is illustrated in the first part of this chapter by an experience I had of helping a group of people to get on top of a problem which, after a prolonged period of avoiding it, they had decided to face. This will lead me to examine the generic approach to working on such problems and some of the factors involved in using it. Lastly, I shall consider the nature of problems and what is involved in orientating ourselves to them in the constructive way to which I point in this paragraph.

I. A PROBLEM: COPING WITH A PERSISTENT SENSE OF FAILURE

A four-hour seminar on "coping with failure" held in Liverpool attracted an ecumenical group of twenty people who had not previously met. Most of them were working in areas of acute need and deprivation in Aintree, Dawley, Liverpool, Oldham, Runcorn or Telford.*

A discursive discussion in the full group showed that everyone agreed that *the* problem that the members of the group wanted and needed to tackle was how to cope with continual and persistent feelings of failing and being a failure. Having got that clear, we discussed how we were going to examine this problem. There was agreement that we should identify and work on the issues that emerged from our various experiences of the problem rather than focus on one or two specific examples. By doing this and using sub-groups we would draw upon everyone's experience and insights, including those of the three seminar leaders. At this stage I stimulated a discussion about whether in our analysis we should try to pursue the historical sources and causes of the

---

* The members of the seminar comprised one Anglican lay person and four priests; one Baptist minister; three Methodist lay people and three ministers; two Roman Catholic lay people, three religious and one priest; two YMCA staff members—five women and fifteen men.

problem *or* concentrate on the things that sustain it as a problem in the present. (I discuss these distinctions later in the chapter.) We were of one mind that we should concentrate on their experience of the problem in the present and what was making it a problem for them now—unless, that is, our examination of the problem showed that it was necessary to consider the initiating as well as the sustaining causes. We felt that the changes we wanted were more likely to come through this approach than the other. Turning from approach to method, we felt that tackling the following questions in the given order would help us to work at the subject systematically and a little more objectively than we would otherwise do.

(a)   What is the failure with which we have to cope?

(b)   How and why do we classify it as failure?

(c)   What effects, positive and negative, does this have on me and my work?

(d)   What are the specific changes that would help us to cope better?

(e)   Have we tried to make these specific changes and if so with what results?

(f)   What can we/I do towards making these changes?

(g)   What are we learning about coping with failure?

We worked at the first six questions in sub-groups and considered the findings periodically in the full group. The final question was tackled in a full group with buzz sessions, i.e., people talking for a few minutes to those sitting beside them.

(a)   What is the failure with which we have to cope?

(b)   How and why do we classify it as failure?

Responses to these two questions were intertwined. Five different areas in which the members of the group felt that they failed were identified. First, they felt that they failed to comprehend the situation in which they were working. An intellectual grasp of it eluded them. They knew that they were not getting at the heart of things. Consequently they were not clear how to work for change. They found this frustrating, confusing and demoralizing. Second, they said that they failed to contain their work load within manageable limits. This led to their not being able to cope and allowing quantity to compromise quality. Then again they said that they were failing to make realistic evaluations of the changes in people and their environment that could be attributed to their interventions. They worked on impressions and crude indicators. They simply did not know whether they were achieving their objectives—nor did they know how to find out. Consequently they could not tell whether persistent feelings that they were "not getting anywhere" were reliable guides or not. Understandably, these feelings depressed and drained them.

52

Relationships were the fourth area of failure. They had failed, they said, to achieve and sustain the kind of working relationships which they knew that they and others needed in order to be able to do the difficult work in which they were engaged. They had got people involved in programmes that undermined their self-confidence, already low, and broke down trust between people and workers. They felt that they had failed to build up the confidence of the people to do the job and to make the relationships to support and care for each other in times of difficulty. Finally, they said that they had failed to live up to their expectations of themselves; for instance they said they had become insensitive. And they had not been able to deal with the unrealistic expectations others had of them.

(c) **What effects, positive and negative does this have upon me and my work?**

The compound negative and positive effects of these failures - the failure to comprehend, to control, to evaluate to build up working relationships and to live up to their expectations were considerable. Negative effects were that they:

— doubted their ability;
   ("I failed to do what I set out to do." "Am I really any good at all?")

— became alienated, vulnerable, lonely, disorientated and ambivalent;
   ("Can I face 'them' again?" "Who can I turn to?")

— became drained, frustrated and angry;

— became cavalier;
   ("I bash on regardless." "I case-harden myself, which helps my equilibrium but I become insensitive.")

— became complacent and cynical;
   ("It's all a waste of time anyway." "What the hell?!")

— felt guilty;

— lowered their targets and "became emphatic about insignificant achievements";

— blamed other people and the system indiscriminately;

— engaged in diversionary activities that were more satisfying.
   ("I escape to my books." "I take too much time doing things that I can do to avoid the things I cannot do.")

On the positive side, they said that, provided that they drew out the learning soon after the events, they learnt more about themselves and their abilities and about how to do their work from their failures than from their successes. They felt that they were becoming more gentle and tolerant with others and possibly with themselves. And, in spite of all the negative effects, they were determined to do better and to organize themselves better and get more resources—and these were their reasons for attending the seminar. Also, they were becoming clearer about what really mattered to them, namely the spiritual growth and development of people, individually and collectively.

(d)   What are the specific changes which would help us to cope better?

(f)   What can we/I do towards making these changes?

In the event members considered the changes and how to make them at the same time, i.e., (d) and (f) rather than (d) and (e). But, as will be seen below, a profound action insight came later. By now the problem was being expressed differently: "How to break the hold of a persistent and debilitating sense of failure so that our sense of satisfaction is enhanced and our sense of failure reduced whatever progress we feel is being made or not". Members of the group were now beginning to see that the problem had to do with distortions in the interplay between subjective and objective realities. Work performance affects feelings and vice versa. Clarifying the problem* helped to identify the changes required and to think how to make them. They badly wanted to be better able to maintain their psychological and spiritual poise, or as they said, their equilibrium. It was too easily disturbed. They wanted to overcome the oscillation of mood and morale which they found so painful, disorientating and dysfunctional. Kurt Lewin's[1] concept of low- and high-force equilibrium helped the members of the seminar to understand what was happening to them. Low-force equilibrium is when people are kept in balance by low internal and external forces; high-force when they are high. Lewin represented it as depicted in Figure 2:1.

The disturbance of low-force equilibrium leads to mild adjustments, whereas the disturbance of high force leads to violent change because the forces released are so much greater. A familiar illustration of high-force equilibrium is when a barrier holding people back is suddenly released and they surge forward out of control. Ireland is experiencing a high-force equilibrium on socio- religious issues; England, Wales and Scotland a low-force equilibrium. Members felt they were in situations of high-force equilibrium so they were easily disturbed by small changes in their energy levels or their circumstances such as the loss of one local voluntary helper.

The forces are dynamic, not static as the diagram might suggest, so the

---

* Definitions of problems often contain solutions. That is why defining problems accurately is progress towards solving them. Care has to be taken because definitions can point to non-solutions. A simple example is: how to get "x" to do "y". Getting "x" to do "y" is a solution to some problem or other. But "y" possibly should not be done and even if it should be done "x" should not do it. And if "x" should do "y" perhaps we should not try to get him/her to do it. Definitions of problems can beg all kinds of questions.

54

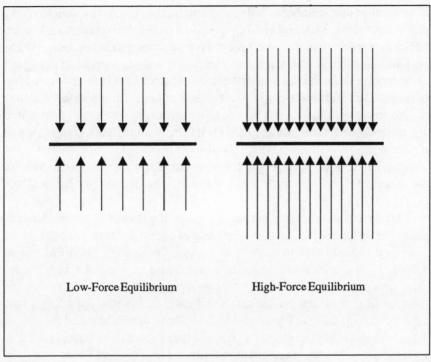

Low-Force Equilibrium   High-Force Equilibrium

FIGURE 2:1. LOW AND HIGH FORCE EQUILIBRIUM

equilibrium required has to be dynamic rather than static—more like riding a bicycle than holding a dead weight. Support, they felt, from individuals or groups independent of them and their situations who could offer disciplined and rigorous work-consultancy help of the kind that they were experiencing in this seminar would help them to maintain their equilibrium. Such support would introduce a counterbalancing force.

Several other changes, they said, would help them to maintain their equilibrium. Concentration was one of them. No matter how busy they are they need to give themselves to people and events and to slow the pace down so that they can concentrate: telling others that they are losing their concentration could help to regain it. The way in which we describe our experiences and feelings affects our equilibrium. Statements express feelings but more importantly they engender a particular frame of mind which can break people down or build them up. For example any one of the following responses could be made to several unsuccessful attempts to do something: "I cannot do that." "I have failed to do that." "So far I have been unable to do that." "I wonder why I cannot do that?" "How could I do that, I wonder?" "I feel I have failed." "I am a failure." Some of these statements are factual, others judgemental and self-condemning. Some make one feel bad and ineffectual, others help to explore the experience creatively. To say that one is a failure, as some members felt inclined to do, inhibits a proper understanding and evaluation of the situation.

Even an indefinite number of failed attempts do not necessarily indicate that a person is a failure. Many other things need to be taken into account, such as the difficulties inherent in the task, before even beginning to define ourselves as failures—and in any case what is the reason for and the purpose of doing so? To be precise about the reasons for the failure contributes to the proper analysis of the problem and obviates spurious feelings of guilt. Members felt that they needed to change the way that they describe and explain failure to themselves and others because this critically affects its power and effects. They saw that it also helps to accept the inevitability of some degree of failure without being complacent in work with people for human and spiritual development. An awareness of it is necessary: a sense of failure is not pathological, a total lack of it certainly is.

This discussion, essentially about understanding the situation and therefore about the first area of failure, took up much of the time. Other changes can be described more briefly in relation to each of the areas of failure identified earlier. With reference to the need to **comprehend**, they said that they needed more time for relaxed reflection on their goals, beliefs and the subtleties and nuances of their situations *and* analytical tools such as the ones used in the seminar that would enable them to search out the critical factors that they might otherwise miss. With reference to **control** they focused on establishing more realistic goals and on accepting work only when they had made a realistic assessment as to whether they had time to prepare for and follow through the face-to-face work involved: all too often, they said, they took on work only on the basis of the face-to-face commitment that it involved. With reference to **evaluation**, they said that they needed to define more precisely what constitutes "failure" and what constitutes "success" over a given period and to agree this with those with whom they worked and also to agree on ways of assessing them. With reference to **relationships** they said that they must do all that they could to be open with people about jobs and to ensure that they take up work freely and willingly—and especially when they are asking them to do jobs that they themselves hate doing! (Job dissatisfaction has bad effects on working relationships as well as on the work done and can be a major contribution to failure and a sense of failure.) Also, to make sure that everyone has the moral, spiritual and technical support they need. Combined, all these things helped to establish more realistic **expectations within and between people**.

(e)   **Have we tried to make these specific changes and, if so, with what results?**

This question, a *non-sequitur* by the time that we came to it, enabled members of the seminar to say that the problem of failure had been a constant source of worry to them but they had not previously faced it as they had in this seminar. They had tried to escape from it or to harden themselves against its effects. Some said that they talked to themselves about it and determined to do better next time. One person said that she tried to restore her equilibrium by making promises to herself. Such devices had enabled them to survive but they were no solution. Indeed, they contributed to the problem and strengthened the hold it had upon them.

(f) What can we/I do towards making these changes?

We turned to this question even though much had been said in response to it. It was useful to do so. They said: "Give over wallowing in our failures. Internalize that I am not necessarily a failure because I fail to do something and that a sense of failure is required, it is not pathological. Assimilate all that I am learning from this diagnosis. Slow down. Establish criteria for assessing failure and success." But the idea that really got them excited emerged when we turned to the final question.

(g) What are we learning about coping with failure?

Spontaneous response of the whole group to this question was, "We must get this kind of discussion going amongst the people with whom we work!" A dramatic change occurred in the group. Everyone was most excited. The energy level soared. The emotional profile of the seminar shows the significance of this moment of disclosure. Tackling the problem had not been easy. Thinking about it again had had a depressing effect. It evoked memories of failure which cast doubt over the exercise on which they were embarking: Would this seminar be another failure and therefore compound their sense of failure? Thoughts and feelings raised by the very thought of the subject palpably debilitated them. To begin with they simply could not put their finger on what generated so much emotion, and intensified the feelings of failure. An important part of the problem was clearly coping with these feelings. If anything constructive was to be done about them it was necessary to identify their source and recognize the strong emotions they generated.

These emotions tended to strangle the ability of the members of the group to think straight. It took a lot of energy and persistence on the part of the staff to get the members thinking the problem through. Our assumption was that the difficulties were created by the working situation rather than by psychological inadequacies of the workers. What emerged indicated that this assumption was valid and our approach relevant. Morale of the members gradually increased as we worked systematically at the questions and structured and summarized the material as it emerged. We all felt we were getting somewhere. The insight about getting those with whom they worked using the same approach and method took us to another plane of feeling and doing. People were deeply involved in the discussion, totally engaged. Excitement was in the air. At first, I am bound to admit, I was a bit disappointed with what seemed an obvious idea, because I wanted to get out the criteria for success and failure! What they had seen was that the way we had tackled the problem together was a way of rising above it, taking a creative hold of it and generating the ideas and the energy to do something about it. The process was as essential to the solution as the product of their thinking. They analysed what had enabled them to have this kind of discussion, so different from anything they normally experienced, as though their lives depended upon it. They plied the staff and each other with questions as they examined just what we had done to facilitate the discussion and read off the implications for themselves. They wanted to clarify the questions we asked and particularly the one that led to the breakthrough; they wanted to discuss initiating and sustaining causes (see next section); they wanted to trace out just what had raised their spirits. All in all, it was a very rewarding seminar.

Now we move from a particular problem to problem-solving generally.

II. FACILITATING PROBLEM ANALYSIS

Problems encountered in working with people come in all shapes and sizes. No two are exactly alike even when they are in the same family of problems. So, dealing in set and standard solutions is a hit and miss affair. Each problem is unique and needs to be treated as such. The principles and procedures described below enable people to do that and to determine what action they themselves are going to take.

1. Cycles in the Life of a Problem

The life of a problem has three stages: the latent period when the difficulties are incubating; the active and disruptive period; and the post-active period. (The ecumenical group were considering the problem of failure in its latent and post-active stages but were drawing upon experiences of it in all the stages.) Each stage, differing as it does from the others, requires different treatment. My experience is that we all have a tendency towards ignoring problems when they are latent, in abeyance and temporarily resolved, and attending to them only when we have to, i.e., when they are active or as soon after that as possible. Some problems, of course, cannot be foreseen and have to be tackled and solved when they are active. Sometimes it is better and more effective to tackle human-relations problems when they are active than to store up a series of incidents for a future confrontation. But some problems cannot be solved when they are active, they can only be contained: tackling them root and branch is for another time. Therefore, watching for and acting upon early warning signals is an important part of problem-solving. Failure to solve problems when they are active often leads people to conclude wrongly that they are insoluble; they may be insoluble when active but soluble earlier or later. Workers need to follow carefully the life cycles of problems and seize the opportunities when they can tackle them to best effect and with least hassle. *This method and the six basic questions that follow are ways of tackling problems at any and all stages of their life cycle.* Working at and to all the stages in the life cycle of a problem multiplies the possiblities for containing, resolving, preventing and curing it.

2. Six Basic Questions

Six basic questions help workers to examine problems systematically and to decide what they are going to do about them. They are:

1. What is the problem?

2. What has been tried so far?

3. What specific changes are required and why?

4. What are the causes and sources of the problem that we need to examine?

5. What are we/am I going to do about it?

6. What are we learning from our study of this problem?

These questions relate to three activities: definition, diagnosis and action decisions. Questions 1 to 3 help to define but they also help to diagnose; question 4 helps to diagnose; questions 2 and 5 are action questions, respectively about what will not and what will work. The order is not invariable; 2 and 3 are readily interchanged. What matters is that they are all considered. Now we shall look in more detail at what is involved in working through these phases using these basic questions and subsidiary ones.

Basic Question 1: What is the problem? A clear and accurate definition of problems in concrete terms is crucial. Sometimes problems defined are problems solved. Too often we tackle and solve the wrong problem. As I have already indicated, more often than not "solutions" are implicit in statements of problems. Take, for example, the problem, "How do I get the church council to do a parish audit?" Doing a parish audit is a solution to some other problem; it may or may not be the right one. What is the problem behind the problem? Is it "How to get the council to examine the ministry of the church in relation to the realities of the parish community?" Or is it "How to get the council to consider things in a systematic and technical rather than a purely 'spiritual' way?" (And that could be about a conflict of approach.) Or is it to get the council to be in fashion? Tackling the "audit" problem, therefore, may avoid or compound the substantive problems. It is essential to get to the substantive problems and that is not always easy. One of the ways of getting to the heart of the matter is to approach the basic question from different angles through a range of supplementary questions such as:

— What makes this a problem for you?
— How often does it occur?
— How long does it last?
— How does it affect you, other people and your work?
— What does it do to you?
— What does it prevent you from doing?
— Why is it important?
— For whom else is it a problem, and why?
— What is the nature of the problem?
— How do you normally think and talk about it?
— How do you see it now?
— Is it one of a group of similar problems?

These questions clarify the nature, scope, effects, frequency, intensity, duration, and the context of the problem and those who suffer from it.

Gradually, answers to these questions make it is possible to define the problem, i.e., to answer the question, "What is the problem?"

Basic Question 2: What has been tried so far? Answers to this question can help to understand the problem by considering the problem of dealing with the problem. They reveal something more of the nature of the problem, its depths and its intransigence. It helps to list each idea that has been tried so far and what ideas have been thought of but not tried. Having done that, it is helpful to examine them in turn to identify how and why they failed and to draw out the learning. Supplementary questions that help to do this are:

— Why do you think the idea did not work?
— To what or to whom did you attribute the failure of the plan?
— How do you explain to yourself what happened?
— How do you explain your explanation?
— Have you had any ideas for tackling the problem which have not yet been tried?
— Why have they not been tried?
— What would have to happen before they would be tried?
— What would enable them to work or prevent them from working?
— Would you try them and if so why, how and when?

Investigating previous attempts to solve the problem before making any suggestions is a brilliant idea put forward by Watzlawick and others.[2] On many occasions I have got into an impasse when each suggestion I and others made was countered by statements such as, "I have tried that and it didn't work". "That would simply not work in my situation". "If you knew the kind of people I am dealing with you would know that that simply would not work". Almost always the replies were unconvincing. Sometimes, I felt that a parody of what was suggested had been tried and predictably found wanting; at other times I felt that they simply did not understand the suggestion and/or how to put it into effect. Suggestion-parrying builds up defensiveness which kills dead attempts to get any further. With hindsight I realize that much of this could be avoided by looking first at anything that has been tried or thought of, i.e. by starting at the point at which they had arrived in their experience and thinking. Amongst other things, this can give valuable clues about the nature of the working situation, what the workers are capable of, the intransigence and subtle dimensions of the problem, or the kind of suggestions that could be relevant and acceptable. Greater sensitivity in presenting ideas is needed so that they are most likely to be accepted if suitable and rejected if not.

However, important as all this undoubtedly is, dwelling on past failures can demoralize and impede the analytical process. A penetrating and profound analysis that leaves people devastated is highly undesirable. Maintaining or building up the confidence and courage required to tackle difficulties is an essential part of working to good effect on problems. People need to be affirmed by non-judgmental understanding and help. Sensitivity and judgement are required to keep morale and analysis in creative tension. In the seminar the morale increased as they saw that they were getting somewhere and this eventually led to a disclosure experience. As people gain confidence in the method it is possible to undertake a more searching analysis because people know that any drop in morale is likely to be temporary and that the process will lead to insights and possibilities that have good, genuine and trustworthy effects.

Basic Question 3: What specific changes are desired and why? This is another defining and diagnosing question. Stating the changes required involves contrasting the actual with the desired. It defines the nature and scale of the transition to be realized. It shows up the actualities of the undesirable state and therefore may throw new light on the problem. Statements about objectives, purposes and beliefs and needs are proper responses to the question "why?" Other reference points are discussed in Chapter 5. This helps to set the specific changes in a wider context and to check them out.

Basic Question 4: What are the causes and sources of the problem that we need to examine? This question takes us into the diagnosis of the problem.[3] A problem has causes and sources in the past (initiating causes) but it is kept going by causes in the present (sustaining causes)—these can be in the reactions, perceptions and emotions of those involved or they can be in the circumstances in which they live and work. The initiating cause may be what is keeping it going now. On the other hand the links between the initiating and sustaining causes may be more significant than those between the initiating causes and the problem. Indeed, the initiating cause may be irrelevant. I represent the overall pattern of causes and sources and their possible connections in the following diagram, Figure 2:2.

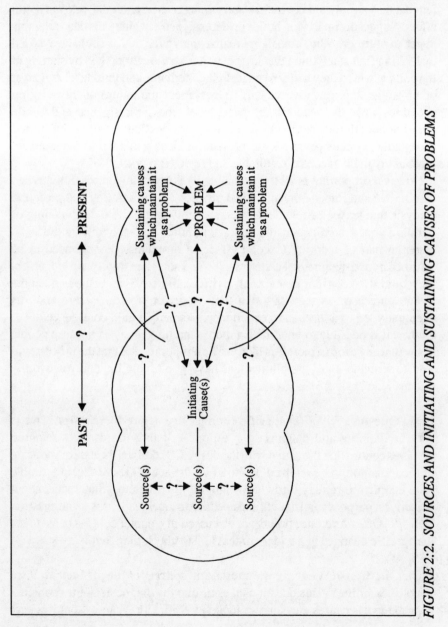

FIGURE 2:2. SOURCES AND INITIATING AND SUSTAINING CAUSES OF PROBLEMS

The respective effects of these various causes and sources will vary from problem to problem and their effects upon a particular problem could change from one part of the life cycle of the problem to another. The sustaining causes could be in some issue, difficulty or relationship otherwise unrelated to the specific problem—a rogue cause or source.

The Irish Troubles illustrate these distinctions: undoubtedly economic, political, cultural and religious aspects of the faction derive directly from historical events which are the initiating causes; present attitudes, feelings and actions of significant minorities kept the conflict devastatingly active and were therefore sustaining causes; those who sustain the problem are diversely influenced by historical causes (or, more precisely, by a historical "mythical consciousness"[4] of these causes). So in this case powerful historical, psychological and spiritual links between the initiating and sustaining causes and the present problems constitute complex problem-sustaining systems. In church and community development work in Ireland I have found it best to concentrate with priests, clergy and laity on analysing the sustaining causes in relation to their parish work and ministry and deciding with them what they can do about them.

Thus there are critical choices to be made in deciding how to diagnose a problem. Is it necessary:

— to examine the history of the problem and the initiating causes?
and/or
— to analyse the sustaining causes currently operative, and then, if it proves necessary, their initiating causes?

It might be that the problem cannot be eased without looking at its origins, or past attempts to overcome it, or both. If, however, the initiating cause is not what is keeping the problem going now, analysing it could distract, at times intentionally, from the search for answers, and inhibit fresh thinking.[5]

Watzlawick, Weakland and Fisch argue and demonstrate that the "why" of a problem, i.e. the explanation and understanding of causes and their source, is not necessarily a pre-condition of change. Indeed it can deflect one away from resolving the problem. (They claim for example that even a plausible and sophisticated explanation of insomnia usually contributes nothing towards its solution.[6]) In deliberate interventions into human problems the most pragmatic approach is not the question why? but what?: What is being done here and now that serves to perpetuate the problem and what can be done here and now to effect a change.[7] And one thing might well be to tackle initiating causes or myths about them. They claim that such an approach is extremely effective in promoting change, especially second order or transformational change. Their experience is in psychotherapy but what they say is applicable beyond psychological problems. I have found it to be relevant to the church and community development work in which I am engaged.

Some of the questions that help to examine initiating and sustaining causes are:

— What effects do they have upon whom and what?
— When are they most/least effective?
— What brings them into play? When? How frequently?
— What nullifies them?
— Where are they located in the scheme of things?
— What are the main links that fix them in the system?

So, diagnosis is greatly helped by differentiating between initiating causes and their sources *and* those that sustain it. Making a good diagnosis depends upon making an appropriate choice between (a) examining the initiating causes and their sources; (b) examining the sustaining causes and their sources; (c) proceeding directly to what action to take, i.e. to question 5. Sometimes it is clear which course to take. Choice (c) is appropriate when a solution has emerged from steps 1 to 3. Deciding, however, can be tricky. Prolonged consideration of which route to take can cause frustration. When there is an impasse it is often advisable to decide intuitively or at random to pursue (a) or (b) or (c), to get on with it and to review the choice if and when it is not proving to be helpful or at some other agreed point. Attempts to establish criteria that help to make the choice have not been very satisfactory. However, I find it is necessary to explore initiating and/or sustaining causes and sources when participants *either* feel intuitively that they must get to the "bottom of the problem" *or* find that route (c) does not take them to ideas for effective action.

Also, it is generally unwise to pursue (a) or (b) if doing so

— takes participants further and further away from the immediate problem into a self-contained historical exercise which is not yielding clues about how to tackle or solve the contemporary problem;
— takes the participants into unhelpful realms of speculative thought, into diversionary consideration of things about which they can do nothing and reveals work they cannot handle;
— engenders paralysis of thought and action.

Four questions that need to be kept constantly in mind are:

— Is looking at the history and initiating causes helping or hindering us from making progress with this problem?
— Is examining sustaining causes helping or hindering us from making progress with this problem? In what ways?

64

— Why is it helping or hindering?

— What must we now do?

Note: In the discussion about a sense of failure I gave a strong lead, which was accepted by the group, that we should concentrate on what in the here and now made it a problem for them, i.e., on sustaining rather than initiating causes because I believed that a historical examination of the sources and causes would not have been as profitable.

Questions, questions, questions...! But they are powerful tools!

Basic Question 5: What are we going to do about it? Now we are into the activity that we have called action design. Later we consider this in more detail. What is important is that the emphasis must be upon what *I* am going to do about this problem, what *we* are going to do. It is all too easy to discuss what *they* should do. That is a waste of time unless we decide what we are going to do that is most likely to lead "them" to do what they need do. (Even if we have the power to command it is largely irrelevant to the work being discussed here.) A cluster of questions such as those that follow can help people to inch their way towards realistic action decisions:

— What can I/we do about it?

— What are the choices?

— What are the pros and cons of each?
(It is vital to look at both. "Selling" things involves heightening the "pros" and minimizing or obscuring the "cons".)[8]

— Where is the balance of advantage?

— How can we ameliorate the disadvantages inherent in our choice of action?

— What action am I/we going to take, to what end, why, with whom, how, when?

Attending to minute detail and being specific is on the side of successfully completing this step, generalizing and vague decisions are on the other side.

At the end of the analysis the conclusion may well be to decide not to do anything. That is doing something of considerable importance. It is taking decisive inner control of the situation/problem. Revising the work on earlier stages in the light of the work on the later ones is quite normal. The use of reference points is discussed in Chapter 5.

Basic Question 6: What are we learning from this problem and our study of it? Addressing this question caused the group working on the failure problem to see just what they must do about it—engage others in the activity

65

in which they had been engaged. The question distanced them sufficiently from doing what they had been doing to be able to look at what they had been doing. From that perspective they saw the significance of the process, a significance that had eluded them whilst they were busily engaged in the process. By breaking the sequence of a closed analytical sequence, this question, which I discuss more fully in Chapter 5, enables people to come at things from a new angle—always, in my experience, with profit.

The basic questions are set out in Figure 2:3

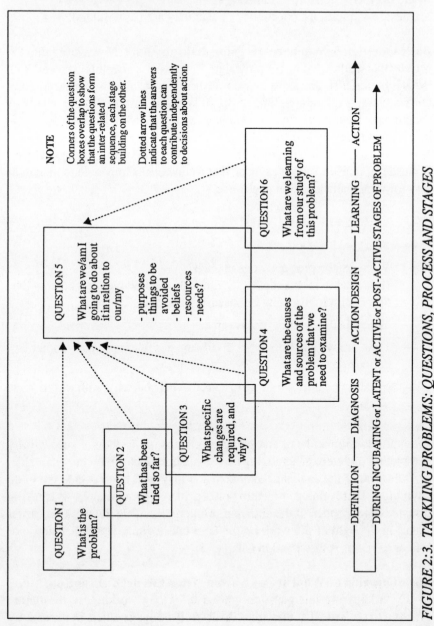

FIGURE 2:3. TACKLING PROBLEMS: QUESTIONS, PROCESS AND STAGES

III. PROBLEM-CONSCIOUS NOT "PROBLEM-CENTRED"

Tackling problems in this way helps to overcome attitudes and feelings that prevent us from approaching difficulties in the best frame of mind and working at them creatively. I have in mind particularly those things that predispose us to associate problems with failure and to be negative towards and fearful of them, to assume that people with problems are problem people, to be preoccupied with apportioning blame and inducing guilt. Several things in the nature and structure of the approach we are considering are antidotes to these things which debilitate us. Negative feelings and thoughts of failure are displaced from the centre of attention by the persistent thrust towards constructive action built up by pursuing the problem-solving procedure step by step. In analysis, the questions and methods focus on the nature of the difficulties, why they occur and what went wrong rather than upon culpability, blame and guilt. In designing future action, attention is focused upon finding things that work and making things work better and therefore upon success rather than failure.

Then again, the approach helps us to distinguish between different kinds or orders of problems by paying attention to sources and causes. One set of problems, for example, results from things in the past that have not gone to plan because of chance factors that could not have been anticipated, things beyond the control of those most involved or because of human error or sin. Yet another set of problems are the things we need to do but cannot yet do to achieve our purposes and to translate visionary thinking into creative action. They mark out the difficult ground still to be covered between the actual and the ideal. They derive directly not from our fears and failures but from our hopes and dreams. They are the unanswered "how" of our ambition.

Thus, the attributes of this approach mean that its use does not induce the kind of "problem-centred approach" that rightly receives much criticism. On the contrary, facing and tackling problems becomes an integral and constructive part of the process of development. The following things help to achieve this positive orientation through using this approach:

First, it is sometimes necessary to avoid using the word "problem" because of the negative feelings it can engender. On one occasion, whilst talking to a Parish Church Council about the ways of tackling problems described in this chapter, the Vicar, who was in the chair, a man of commanding presence and well over six feet tall, sprang to his feet in a small crowded room, towered over me and bellowed at me, "Dr Lovell, we do not have any problems in this parish", and, addressing the members of the Committee, he added "Do we?" They meekly agreed. I made conciliatory gestures and said, "But do you face any difficulties?" "Yes", he said, and for the next hour or more he and his council spoke with deep feelings about one difficulty/problem after another!

Second, it can help in trying to face up to the challenge of difficulties to realize that the scale of the problem is a measure of the disparity between us, our ideals and the actualities and complexities of the situations in which we want to achieve them. It is increased or reduced by the material, human and spiritual resources available to us and the kind of opposition we encounter. Another critical factor is the climate of opinion within which the problems have to be dealt with—it can support or undermine. (Sometimes, of course, a negative atmosphere can engender very determined action—but at what cost?) Putting all this in a different way, the problems of climbing Everest are of a different order from those associated with climbing Ben Nevis. It is one thing to climb either when you are healthy, well-resourced and supported; it is another when you are unwell or handicapped, ill-equipped and unsupported.

Third, whilst problems seem to have a life of their own, they are intrinsic parts of complex systems with many initiating and sustaining causes. Moreover the same factors create different kinds of problems for people located at various parts of a system. For instance, the sense of failure experienced by the workers in the problem discussed in section one creates different but no less acute problems for their spouses, the people with whom they work, their bosses, and their spiritual directors. Realistic action results from accepting the complexity and working to as much of it as possible.

Fourth, notwithstanding what has been said above, analysing problems inevitably leads to making judgements about human culpability. We are inclined to judge and blame ourselves and each other, struggle with feelings generated by our incompetence, look for scapegoats, try to excuse ourselves. One thing that helps me to work at such feelings constructively is to remember that failure is relative: there is simply no way in which people who hold to their beliefs and to high purposes and continue to struggle with seemingly impossible circumstances can be said to fail, no matter what the outcome of their endeavours might be. Another thing is that apportioning individual and collective responsibility and "blame" for problems in human affairs is an extraordinarily complex business—sometimes necessary, but often unproductive in tackling problems. It is all too easy to take more or less responsibility for problems than it is right for us to do. Identifying, facing and accepting our own proper responsibility as far as we are able to do so is necessary and productive. Blanket acceptance of culpability and responsibility may appear to be helpful in the short term; it is never so in the long term. Yet there is a widespread propensity to see problems as *my* failure or *their* failure. And, as we have seen in the problem discussed earlier, a sense of personal failure easily becomes confused with feeling a personal failure.

What has been said above about the complex causation of problems not only helps me to apportion blame more accurately but also engenders in me a much healthier frame of mind about blame: I feel more objective and philosophical about it. Analysing problems, whilst it involves identifying what went wrong and who and what were responsible, is substantively a development task, not a trial. Securing this orientation is vital.

Fifth, I try to avoid the words "solve" and "solution" in discussing problems because whilst some problems can be solved, others cannot; some problems "go away" without returning, others do not. However, to say that there is no solution is not to say that there is nothing that can and should be done. Always there is something that can be done, even if it is to say, "I must live with this problem because there is no other way." Inasmuch as the analysis is correct, such a decision can have profound effects.

Tackling problems is, in fact, about finding ways of thinking and acting in relation to them which have good all-round effects upon people and the situations in which they live and work.

NOTES AND REFERENCES

1. Kurt Lewin was an experimental social psychologist (1890–1947) who developed a "field theory" of human behaviour. I first met this idea through a lecture by T. R. Batten in 1967.

2. Watzlawick, Paul; John Weakland and Richard Fisch, *Problem Formation and Problem Resolution* (New York: W.W. Norton, 1974), p. 110 ff.

3. The origin of the ideas in this section was in the book by Watzlawick and others quoted in 2 above and an article in the Journal *Human Development,* Vol. 1, No. 3, Fall 1980: Amadeo, Linda, and James S. Gill entitled "Managing Anger, Hostility and Aggression". The diagram is mine.

4. I am drawing upon the work of Grant, Henry, *Understanding Ulster* (unpublished manuscript, 1983), Chapters 2 and 3. He published an article on this work in *Studies: An Irish Quarterly Review* (Summer 1983) entitled "Understanding the Northern Irish Troubles: A Preliminary to Action".

5. Some of the thoughts here derive from unpublished notes by Peter W. Russell entitled "A Way of Approaching Problems".

6. *Ibid.,* cf. p. 86 and cf. Chapter 3.

7. *Ibid.,* cf. p. 83 f.

8. Cf. Batten, T.R., & M., *The Human Factor in Community Work* (London: OUP, 1965), p. 182, point 7.

CHAPTER THREE

Working on Situations

Periodically Avec organizes ecumenical consultations for people with regional and national appointments. Amongst other things each participant makes a study of his/her work. The first part of this chapter describes the one made in 1988 by a Suffragan Bishop of the Church of England who had been in post three years after a prolonged and distinguished ministry as a parish priest in England and Africa.* Brief observations on the substance of the work study are then given in part two and notes on the work-study process in part three.

I. WORKING WITH A BISHOP ON HIS SITUATION

In order to illustrate the work-study process I describe each of the stages and what emerged from them: the bishop's preparation; the analysis of his situation in a sub-group during the first week of the consultation; the work done between the first and the second week held a month later; the designing and planning done during the second week in the same sub-group.

1. The Bishop's Work Paper

Prior to the consultative sessions the Bishop wrote what we call a "work paper" based on the outline given in Appendix I. To encourage people to get at the essentials we suggest that they aim to make them about 2,000 words long. In this section I quote extensively from the four parts of the Bishop's paper because what he wrote greatly helps us to understand his perspective on his work—and in the first instance we must work to that.

Part One: My Working Life, Journey and Story
Looking back over his life as a priest in the Church of England he identified three landmarks.

> **Landmark 1.** After conversion to Christianity at University, and then ordination, I arrived in the centre of a large English city still full of the enthusiasm of conversion. In a centre-city/inner-city area, I found with some

---

*The Bishop generously gave permission for me to use the study for this book, which I deeply appreciate. For various reasons we decided to disguise his identity and that of his Diocese.

alarm that I only seemed able to share my spiritual experience with people of a similar background to myself—commuting church-goers, not those who lived locally. With those young people with whom I was particularly connected locally, there seemed to be a sheet of plate glass between us on any matters to do with the Christian faith. I was happy in their company in general, and I think they with me. Why the blockage?

Landmark 2. This was followed by my ministry in Rhodesia (now Zimbabwe) from 1960–1970. Because of seeing Christ through the eyes of people of another culture, race, and language, I had to dissect those things in my own faith that were essentially English rather than Christian. The Bible seen through African eyes reveals its deeply corporate understanding of human nature and the world. In the same mix was a rapidly growing political awareness.

Landmark 3. On return to work again in the centre of the same English city, I realised that the plate glass screen that I had experienced before was about cultural division between middle-class Christianity, and the people of that inner city. Its depth and importance was no less than the cultural and racial gap that I had met in Rhodesia. I began a continuing process of exploring ways in which the structures of our society mould people's perceptions of faith, and either block it off or open the door to very attenuated forms.

During the third of these phases of his ministry he was influenced by the approach to urban mission by people such as David Sheppard, Neville Black, Jim Hart, and Roger Dowley, all members of the Evangelical Urban Training Project. They helped him to grapple with the question: "How is the Gospel communicated to communities that are not middle-class and professional, who can read but don't, whose style is much more corporate?"

Part Two: My beliefs and purposes
The Bishop expressed his beliefs and purposes in this way:

I became a Christian part-way through doing a degree in modern languages, then went to a theological college at which were many students with absolutist views of scripture. I found my new faith (with many old roots to it) articulated in two evangelical emphases: the uniqueness of the scriptural revelation, and the experience of justification by grace through faith. I found myself equally sceptical of the fundamentalism of other students and the various forms of biblical criticism to which we were introduced. The Church did not figure very much in my thinking, and I had difficulty in taking various "religious" activities seriously. Since then I have been concerned with the corporate aspect of the Christian faith, through ministry in Africa, and in exploring how far the Christian faith has been imprisoned by European culture and concepts. The Old Testament has become more and more important to me, both in my own understanding and in preaching and teaching. I have come to respect "religion" in a way I found difficult at first, but usually folk-religion rather than the religiosity of the Christian Church.

I have had to face my own pragmatism, in the sense that most of the thinking I have done since becoming a Christian has been retrospective. My instinct has always been to do a thing in what seems to be the most immediate practical way, and it is then hard work to conceptualize or think in long-term strategies. I have been relieved to discover a lot of theology is (like mine) retrospective thinking (at its best), and self/Church-justification (at its worst); that, however, does not let me off the hook of having to work hard to stop myself being satisfied with hand-to-mouth practicalities.

I spent the 1960s, so strong in their secular drive in the U.K., in a highly religious society in Rhodesia. I found the only way I could cross the culture gap there was in attempting to do good "in minute particulars", as Blake so clearly saw. Generalities like "God is everywhere" seemed little different from "God is nowhere"; Anglican inclusiveness, "God bless everybody", seemed little different from not caring about anyone. If God did his work in the minute particulars of the life and death of Jesus Christ, then communicating that faith came from amidst the minute particulars in people's lives. "God bless everybody", in a nation where power was so unjustly divided between black and white, meant getting involved in things that were a very long way from "blessing". From that experience came a new struggle with the meaning of justification by grace through faith: I have become increasingly convinced that as a Church we seek to be justified by decency and trying to live a good life, and no independent observer would ever believe we were justified by grace through faith. How can we bear a truer witness to what to me is at the heart of the Christian experience?

Here, too, lies the key to the corporate questions. Until we discover the depth and reality of our corporate responsibility—i.e. the impossibility of disclaiming our share in the destructiveness to others of things which benefit us—we will never know how much and how desperate is our need for justification by grace. The main thrust of my ministry in this country since 1970 has therefore been to interpret these facts to the powerful and the wealthy, through known and observable alliances with those on the wrong end of things (embarrassingly, the dispossessed in this country are usually folk religious but not Christian—in Rhodesia they were often Christian). I believe whatever happens that is creative must come from a real sense of justification by grace, ridding us of the guilt that is often the motivation for doing almost the same things.

Part Three: My present job
Becoming a Bishop involved changing dioceses to work in another English city, one of the largest. He described the job and his feelings about it in this way:

In the 1980s the Diocese was divided into three areas, and I was given the eastern block, which covered three local authority areas give or take a bit. The area division meant that the diocese was not to be lumbered with three synods, three office centres etc., but to work as one in those respects, while giving area bishops, with two archdeacons, full responsibility for the care of clergy and full-time lay staff, relationship with the parishes concerned, replacement of staff in vacancies, relations with secular bodies.

I find the framework a satisfactory one in that it does not over-burden us with triplicate structures, but does give considerable freedom to act within the area and in the context of an episcopal team. It so happens that I find the present team one which is very easy to work with, that we have an area of agreement which is essential for co-operative work, and yet we are widely differing personalities and outlooks.

It is necessary for the diocesan-wide bodies to be divided out between the four bishops, and this means chairmanship of boards. This is a much more difficult part of the work to handle in a diocese of over 300 parishes, and a massively dense population area. My brief is the Board of Social Responsibility (B.S.R.) and an ad hoc policy group on ministry issues. The B.S.R. has grave difficulties in communication with a large diocese, and considerable frustration in how the considerable abilities of a number of the delegates (representing six archdeaconries) can best be deployed. There is no full-time officer, but a number of agencies which relate to it from a very independent position. Under social responsibility in this large city, the issues are many and vast, and raise the question of the best use of very small resources.

Community and Community Issues in the Area: In a diocese in which a third of the parishes are urban priority, my area has over 100 churches with fifty-six UPA, and sixteen marginal UPA parishes. It is heavily inner city and council estate. Just over two-thirds raise all the issues of deprivation, and the congregations are usually small, hard-pressed, and tenacious. Responses to the urban priority issues range from the exciting to the cataclysmically bad. I see my role as affirming, and standing with, small communities in such situations, particularly where exciting things are happening, but the style is totally contrary to the professional, middle-class style of the Church of England.

It was experience in urban work which made it seem good to respond to the invitation to come to this diocese. I find relationships with such people easy and their continuing lack of response to the Gospel a stubborn fact which goes on engaging me. I find contact with people in this area enjoyable, opportunities to preach and teach around a hundred-odd churches and congregations very satisfying, the wide range of people in the secular world who are ready to have contact with the bishop good. Particular difficulties are the enormous amount of paperwork, lack of immediate local community, pastoral pressures of an over-large organization (140 full-time staff). I want space for thought and experiment in evangelism, more resources to tackle social-responsibility issues, alternative styles of ministry to the parochial.

Ecumenical Relationships: I represent the diocese on the City Churches' Group (social-responsibility orientated), and attend the City Church Leaders' Group. The latter is the sponsoring body for ecumenical projects in the area, and handles a great deal of business with considerable difficulty. I groan at the cumbersomeness of the present procedures, but look with complete disbelief at the heavy load, in this respect, carried by other church leaders covering so many different ecumenical regions.

The Diocesan Organization: The Church of England carries within it uncomfortably two kinds of government—episcopal (monarchical in origin) and synodical (democratic in aspiration). As an area bishop I am part of the following structure: parish—parish priest—rural dean—archdeacon—area bishop—diocesan bishop (note this line has a distinct break between rural dean and archdeacon, reflecting to some degree the gap between shop steward and line management). In this line, I meet with the diocesan bishop and the other two area bishops regularly, with the bishop's staff meeting (diocesan officers, and all archdeacons), with my two area archdeacons, and with the area rural deans. At present there is no other area meeting, although we propose a meeting of deanery synod lay chairpeople, together with the rural deans as an expression of the area identity.

The second line is parochial church council—deanery synod—diocesan synod—bishop's council—diocesan bishop, and in this line I am a member of the diocesan synod and the bishop's council. Historically there is a direct link between the bishop and the churchwardens in each congregation, which looks like part of the democratic line but is part of the older episcopal system. Today, the churchwardens or other parish representatives have got the final say in all clerical appointments.

The four bishops have recently been using a business consultant to help in facilitating their own meetings, and he has pressed consistently for more strategic thinking and less time spent on nuts and bolts. The fact that we do not meet daily in any one building, and relate to the two differing governmental processes, means that we have to do a lot of business that others would do during the morning tea break.

One of the astonishing obstacles is the lack of processes of communication in the diocese. The bishop can make statements in synod, which is really only heard by the delegates present, and rarely communicated to anyone else. The diocesan newspaper handout (four times a year) is a newly created means of communication, but many are left in church porches unread. The monthly notice paper that goes out to all clergy is but rarely made available in any effective way to lay people. This (typical of the Church of England in general) means that congregations are still struggling with "new" pressures upon them, i.e. the necessity of paying clergy from weekly offerings, and the need for co-operative ministry—both of which have been obvious and harsh realities for the last two decades.

Members of the Board of Social Responsibility recently drew diagrams of the diocese as we see it, and the most typical picture was of a large circle symbolizing the parish, an arm to a small circle standing for the deanery, and an arm to a tiny dot in the distance called the diocese. The Church of England as a whole did not get into the picture, and this is both the strength and the problem of the parochial system—everyone outside the parish being "them", and many inside!

My Place: I work very happily in two *primary teams* of four bishops, and myself and two archdeacons. I see these as both working relationships, and supportive ones, in shared worship, discussion and mutual concern. This has taken some while to develop, and it was a shock to my personal system to leave the primary community of the parish after thirty years and enter this kind of role. It has also been a problem for my wife, who has tried to solve it by belonging to the local parish where we happen to live.

In analysing a year's work, relations with the clergy and the working of the *parochial system* occupies a very large percentage of my time. I seek to meet all clergy and full-time lay staff (together with the archdeacons), for appraisal/support annually, and try to visit each parish for two days on a five-year cycle. I meet clergy for many other interviews on particular issues, and all who are in training. Parish groupings help to reduce the load of Confirmation services, and are about a third of some ninety liturgical occasions (including ordinations and the licensing of new appointees).

As an evangelical bishop, I am part of a number of national networks, especially those dealing with urban issues (Evangelical Coalition for Urban Mission, and Evangelical Alliance urban group). I feel a particular responsibility in this, as evangelical churches of all denominations have not been notable for urban involvement, so many being suburban and/or pietist in style. I am actively involved in the Evangelical Urban Training Project, which, while inevitably managerial, has also got considerable input from shared vision and fellowship.

My Working Relationships: My relationship with the local area authorities has been considerably helped by the "Faith in the City" report. Each of the three local authorities with which I am involved took the initiative in organizing conferences, assuming automatically an ecumenical basis, and bringing together people in all the churches who had never met before. A traditional left-wing suspicion of the Church has been set aside, mainly because all three local authority areas are desperate for allies. It has, however, enabled much more speedy confidence to be built up both with party leaders and with the executives. Relationships with MPs are reasonable, surprisingly four are conservative, in contrast to the local authorities. Four out of the nine affirm specific Christian commitment, which cuts across the political divides sufficiently to establish confidence.

Relationships with the police are on two levels—through the City Church Leaders' and Anglican bishops' meetings with the city police and locally with the consultative groups. I was deeply involved in trying to resolve the breakdown in relationships between the local communities and the police. Relationships with the city police, however, are considerably more difficult than my previous experience with the police in another metropolitan area.

Part Four: My Aims for the Consultation
The work paper concluded with a statement of what the Bishop wanted to get out of the consultation. These are described in the next section.

2. Studying the Situation Over the Period of the Consultation

Writing the paper involved the Bishop's thinking, reflecting and writing about his ministry personally and in private in a way he had not done previously. The paper was circulated to the members of the consultancy group with whom he was going to work on his situation: a Chairman of a District (subsequently the first woman President of the Methodist Conference); a Church Army officer with national responsibilities; two provincials of R.C. religious orders, one male and the other female, and the President of an R.C. lay community of women; and two staff members, an Anglican and myself a Methodist. (The members of the group were not previously known to the Bishop and they had no experience of his diocese.) The Bishop had a one-and-a-half-hour and a twenty-minute session with this group during the first week exclusively on his situation and the same in the second week: no anecdotes or references to other situations were allowed during these sessions. Also, he had private consultations with me before and after the longer group sessions to prepare for them and to follow them through. A member took notes for the Bishop during the group sessions. After each session the Bishop wrote and shared notes of any developments in his thought. Each participant took a turn in acting as observer to the group and fed in their observations on process or content before the end of the session. Their observations on content are subsumed in this section, and those on process in Part III.

The consultancy process took various twists and turns: it was discursive and focused; it was bemusing and exciting; it eventually led to a most important disclosure about the Bishop's theological approach. Quite deliberately, I have described the process stage by stage so that the reader might sense and feel the realities and messiness of it.

The Bishop's Aims for the Consultation
In his work paper the Bishop had said that he would like to get the following out of the consultation:

1. Help in balancing a pragmatic temperament with the need for analysis and strategy.

2. How to handle the vast range of relationships in which anyone in my position is now involved—perhaps the best example being the difficulty of the ecumenical relationships in the city Church Leaders' Group.

3. How to handle the vast quantity of paperwork which passes through my hands—nothing can be addressed without proper research.

4. How to give space for my personal pilgrimage in relation to this role (I have not gone into this aspect, as it is not the prime purpose of the consultation—the issue of how to give space for it, however, seems to me to be relevant.)

The process in which we were engaged made contributions towards achieving Aim 1. The third aim, a problem members of the consultation had in common, was dealt with in a plenary session. We approached the two other aims via an analysis with the Bishop of his situation: quite deliberately we did not tackle them as problems; we used them to help us to understand the Bishop and his situation and to discern with him just what was needed to promote development.

The First Consultancy Group Session

Studying the paper and the Bishop's aims for the consultation before I met him led me to an hypothesis which was very much in my mind as I entered the consultations: the Bishop's capacity for reflecting, conceptualizing and thinking out long-term strategies would improve and he would have more time to think and experiment *if* he were able to work to the diocesan system as well as he could to the parochial system *and* if he worked primarily to the diocesan system.

We, the group members, committed ourselves to three tasks in this session. The first was to understand how the Bishop saw and felt about his work and situation—to see it through his eyes; to stand in his shoes; to empathize with him. The second was to analyse the underlying dynamics of the situation with the Bishop to discover what made things work and what prevented them from doing so. The third task was to help the Bishop to determine the action most likely to promote overall development. Wide-ranging discussions led us to explore the following three aspects.

(a) **The Parish Perspective:** Two principal concerns emerged from exploring with the Bishop his experiences of working with the parishes. First, he was finding it very difficult to get the parishes to take seriously what he saw to be their responsibilities for social issues and concerns. Generally speaking, he said, they did not engage with what emerges from diocesan and national social-responsibility boards and committees no matter how much he tried to get them to do so. He felt bad about this because the needs were great and because the time he spent on the parishes (he estimated 85 per cent of his working time) prevented him becoming as involved as he would have liked with various non-church people who wished to explore social issues and concerns with him. The second concern was identified by considering the hypothesis I had formulated. In fact the Bishop did find that once he was in a parish the parish perspective would take over. Similarly, he said that when he was working with other units their perspectives took over. Empathizing with them in this way was important. (It was what we were doing in relation to him and his work.) But, we saw, he had also to work to another perspective because these sub-systems together formed a complex system in its own right, the Area of the Diocese for which he was responsible. Essentially this was his working entity and a sub-system of the Diocese and other contingent systems. He had a unique perspective on his area which in turn was an important part of the context of the parishes and other sub-units.

It became evident that the Bishop needed to be clear about his own overall perspective, the perspectives of the people in the sub-units and how the two related to one another.

(b) Justification by Grace through Faith: Members wanted to understand just what it was in the experience of "justification by grace through faith"[1] that led the Bishop to attach such importance to this aspect of Christianity.* He said that the more that he had got involved in the messiness of life, the more important justification by grace through faith had become to him. Essentially it pointed to inner transactions between himself, God and others which made unique contributions to restoring all his human and spiritual relationships.+ These transactions were based on grace.++ Attributing and accepting culpability can take us only so far. Getting our moral sums roughly right does not of itself bring reconciliation; it can have quite the opposite effect. Christian grace is required. This released him from trying to justify himself publicly and privately through works and through demonstrating and proving himself to be in the right. It was an effective way of dealing with debilitating residual guilt—the guilt that lurks around even when you have done all you can to make amends for your failure and sin. It helped him to acknowledge his culpability openly and with dignity rather than smoothing things over with superficial apologies and casual "forgiveness", and to avoid self-righteousness and defensiveness—all things that inhibit human and spiritual well-being and development. In short, the continuing experience of justification by grace through faith gave him the freedom to get involved with people even though he knew that no matter how much he tried, his behaviour and that of others would be flawed. Many people with whom he worked, including police officers, valued the doctrine for similar reasons.

Protestant privatized Christianity, he felt, emphasizes the restoration of relationships between individuals and God through justification by grace through faith but neglects its application to collectives. He wished to see this imbalance corrected. He wanted to get people to see the relevance of the doctrine to their work in church and community for development as well as for their own personal spiritual well-being. The group was aware that this doctrine could be corrupted into an easy "spiritual" way of avoiding accepting responsibility for our actions and culpability. For the Bishop, as with the New Testament, it is quite the opposite: it is a God-given way of taking our failure and sin so seriously that we wish it to be dealt with radically. What the Bishop was aiming for was for workers and people, individually and corporately, to be living out this aspect of the Christian faith.

---

* They were also very interested in the relevance of what the Bishop was saying to them and to their work: they had not previously thought about it in the way in which he was presenting it. The Roman Catholic members were particularly intrigued. But they held to the discipline and stayed with the task of studying the Bishop's work with him.

+Somewhat confusingly justification by grace through faith is about restoring relationships rather than making people just.[2]

++ "Justification is that immediate getting-right with God which God himself accomplishes by his grace when a person has faith".[3]

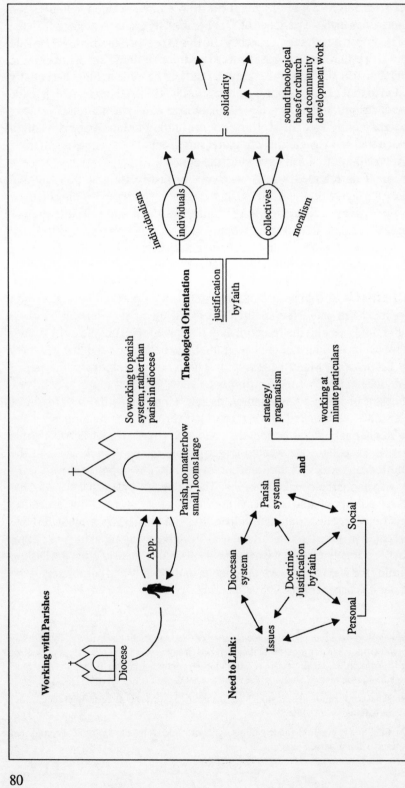

FIGURE 3:1. SOME DIAGRAMS FROM THE FIRST CONSULTANCY GROUP SESSION

(c) Strategic Thinking and Planning: Members of the group turned their attention to the kind of strategic thinking and planning that was going on in the Diocese. The discussion led to a chart which showed the various groups with whom he worked on a general continuum from those who were most effectively involved in strategic planning to those least involved. From the most to the least involved it read: the four Bishops, the National Evangelical groups, his area team, the Diocesan Social Responsibility Board, the police, the parishes, ecumenical teams and groups. Making this explicit led the Bishop and the group to a deeper understanding of the situation which provided important information for development planning—and it generated much excitement.

Roughly equal amounts of time were given to discussing these three subjects. Constructing diagrams on large sheets of newsprint helped us to work at them. Copies I made of some of them after the session are reproduced in Figure 3:1 by way of illustration of the use of diagrams. They do not communicate as effectively in their final form as they did to those engaged in the discussion.

Settling on Development Tasks

A few days after the analysis session the group met the Bishop again to consider with him what he felt he needed to do in order to develop his work. By way of preparation for the meeting the Bishop had let us have a note of his subsequent reflections. Sharing the reality of justification by grace through faith, especially its corporate aspects, was, he said, a primary thrust of his ministry because it affects all we do: for instance guilt-free use of "personal space" and participation in social responsibility depended upon it. But he saw real difficulties in sharing the reality because of the "extreme individualism of the dominant suburban culture", the practice of "many other forms of justification", the difficulty of communicating justification on a broad front. Thinking about these things led him to list the contacts he had with people in his Area, the different ways in which he communicated with people and the roles he performed. (As we shall see, this information triggered off a sequence of thought which eventually led to Figure 3:2 and the chart in Display 3:2.)

Mulling this over in the light of what had happened in the first session led the Bishop and the group to settle on the following tasks to be tackled in a session a month later:

1. To discover ways in which I can better express my theological orientation to ministry (justification by grace through faith), apply the doctrine and pursue my purposes in the parishes.

2. To test out the relevance of this doctrine to parishes diverse in theology and in different kinds of social areas.

3. To determine the theological and practical implications for my ministry to the parishes of any conclusions that I reach.

1. *Personal qualities in regard to my work connected with the parochial system (85% of my workload)*
   - 29 years' experience as parish priest
   - people use me as a leaning post
   - slow to react to people (not sharp)
   - give people plenty of space (which some experience as lack of direction)
   - instincts about people fairly accurate (gut, not reasoned)
   - people can understand what I am talking about
   - *but* I do not show my hand, I can be devious and assume others are.

2. *What effect does the reality of justification have on me in these relationships?*
   - reinforces a natural tendency not to explain myself
   - allows me to risk getting my hands dirty and allows me to "free wheel" on both doctrinal and moral issues
   - leads me into alliances of a corporate kind (political, minority group, issue-based) which opens door to criticism/alarm/embarrassment at parochial level (e.g. photographed in protest surrounded by banners saying "Get the Fuzz!")
   - makes me under-estimate/underplay what significance is placed on a bishop's presence/doings.

3. *What do parishes want of me?*
   - affirmation—especially struggling urban congregations, or strongly aligned groups in churchmanship terms (catholic, charismatic, evangelical)—often feel that nothing else is wanted!
   - shared experience in parish problems which leads to sympathy
   - understandable preaching—which affirms them as part of something much bigger, and of God
   - speaking with and for them in diocesan, secular and public settings
   - seeking all possible resources that can encourage the life of the parish—primarily staff
   - being a "focus" personality, with whom to identify.

4. *What do I not want to happen?*
   - to affirm the parishes in conservative and individualist stances justified by my own tendency to let people lean, give space, not react sharply, have parochial sympathies
   - to create ever more "churchy" dimensions in people's lives which become means of justification - either ecclesiastically or morally
   - to find that upset in the parishes (about bishops who do not exercise discipline over deviants, and are perceived to be engaged in societal change) removes the very open possibility which flows from justification.

DISPLAY 3:1. A NOTE PREPARED FOR THE GROUP BY THE BISHOP

It was suggested that the Bishop could prepare for the session by noting anything that occurred to him in relation to his felt need for a "strategy for the parishes" and the other points made in the first consultancy-group session which concentrated on the analysis.

Working on the Development Tasks
We orientated ourselves to this phase of the work study by agreeing that our dominant activity would now be designing and planning; analysis would be restricted to that which we had to do in order to do the designing. Our job was to help the Bishop to decide what he must and could do. Ideas and plans must fit him and what he could do and what would work in his situation.

Private Preparation
Reflection on the work done so far and the agreed tasks led the Bishop to write and circulate to the members of the group the note presented in Display 3:1.

As part of my preparation for the work group session on the development tasks (a month after the first session), I found myself classifying and cross-referencing the different forms of interaction between the Bishop, the clergy, full-time workers, church wardens and parishioners in his area and the three principal contexts in which this took place:

— **parishes** (during "pastoral visits" and when sharing in special local occasions such as confirmations and patronal festivals);

— **church meetings** (councils, consultative and training sessions);

— **ad hoc consultations** (dealing with things like appointments, human and spiritual problems, major policy matters).

Significant differences between modes of interaction associated with these contexts struck me as important to the task. The geographical location of the first is the parish, the second and third can be sited anywhere. The first is open to anyone, the second and third are open only to those who qualify to be present by virtue of their office or status and are mainly clergy, full-time workers, church wardens or lay workers. The first has generally to do with joyous liturgical events, the second with business and with training (routine and special), the third with important events in the lives of clergy, workers and churches, extraordinary business, critical events and pastoral crises. The first involves churches, congregations, preaching and visiting homes; the second involves committees and councils and formal and informal training sessions; the third involves face-to-face meetings with one person or small groups, interviews, pastoral counselling sessions. Events associated with the first and the third contexts are extraordinary and special to the people whilst they are part

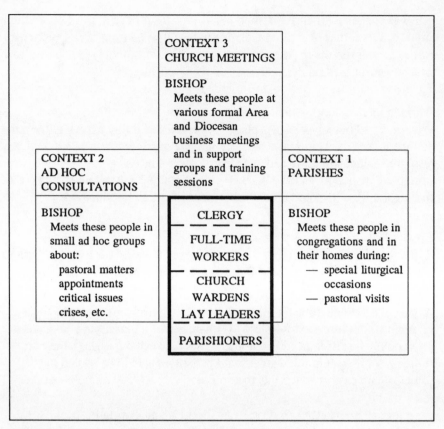

FIGURE 3:2. THE BISHOP'S WORK CONTEXTS

of the Bishop's normal round of ministry. Roles, functions, responsibilities and the form and the nature of the exchanges vary significantly from one context to another, as do the abilities required. I modelled it in Figure 3:1.

I shared these ideas with the Bishop in a private consultation to prepare for the next session with the group on the development tasks. He found the distinctions helpful and suggestive of other categories and so we decided to share them with the group.

The Consultative Group's Work With The Bishop on the Development Tasks
As I entered into this session I felt I ought to keep the following things in mind:

— What could be the implications for the Bishop of the different work contexts as he pursues his work generally and his concern about "justification" in particular?

— Is there any danger of the Bishop appearing to justify the doctrine of "justification" and, if so, how can it be avoided?

Context & Features		People		Setting
1. Bishop in Parishes				
official		clergy	**in**	groups of
festival	**with**	full-time workers		varying sizes
liturgical		lay leaders		one-to-one
		congregation		
2. Critical moments in Parishes				
face-to-face consultations	**with**	clergy full-time workers church wardens lay leaders	**in**	small groups
3. Meetings				
(a) UPA Parishes:				
conferences	**with**	all clergy and lay representatives in diocese	**in**	large groups(?)
(b) Deanery Clergy Chapters:				
business meetings	**with**	clergy	**in**	medium-sized groups
social events	**with**	whole deanery		groups of 10-20 people
(c) Area Leaders' Meeting:				
weekly	**with**	2 Archdeacons	**in**	groups of three
3 times a year	**with**	various transparochial officers and rural deans	**in**	groups of various sizes
4. Appraisal Interviews:				
interviews	**with**	clergy	**in**	one-to-one
annually		full-time workers		relationship

DISPLAY 3:2. THE BISHOP'S WORKING RELATIONSHIPS & SETTINGS

— I am clearer about the application of "justification" to individuals than to collectives.

— How can the dangers intrinsic to the use of a dominant theological model be avoided?

The group noted the tasks already agreed and proceeded to work towards them from what had emerged so far about the working situation and the Bishop's ideas about it and his approach to it.

The members found the notes that the Bishop had written between the sessions (cf. Display 3:1) most helpful because they took the thinking forward and enabled them to start closer to the position to which he had now moved. They were struck by the inner freedom that the Bishop had gained through living and working by "justification". Nevertheless, they noted that, misunderstood, this aspect of Christianity can weaken moral effort and responsibility—people can substitute justification indiscriminately for effort they should have made and use it to cover moral lapses they could have avoided. That is a perversion of the doctrine. Pursuing the Christian faith seriously involves working assiduously for the truth in human and spiritual affairs knowing that we are justified, not by works but by grace through faith. Continuing in a state of "justification" is hard work.

The presentation of my classification of the different working contexts animated the group. Quickly the Bishop and the group extended and refined the classification of context 3 and produced the chart presented in Display 3:2.

This classification led the Bishop to see the significance of the distinction between what he referred to as "UPA" parishes (urban priority area parishes, 65% of his Area) and "BUPA" parishes (i.e. more affluent parishes characterised by people belonging to British United Provident Association). UPA parishes get more of the Bishop's attention than the BUPA parishes because they are the majority and they need it; because of the developments following *Faith in the City*;[4] and because of the Bishop's deep commitment to them. Some in the BUPA parishes feel that the Bishop gives an unfair amount of his time to the UPA parishes and that he is more sympathetic to them. This had created tensions. Examining this classification led us to see that most of the work with BUPA and UPA parishes was done quite separately. BUPA and UPA people did not meet; clergy met only at the Area Leaders' Meeting (context 3(c)). Consequently the Bishop, the Archdeacons and the Diocese were the main unifying forces holding the two sections of the Area together. The Bishop and the group felt that creative interaction between clergy, church workers and people in these different kinds of parishes could break down the divisions between them and lead to holistic development. (Meetings planned for deanery, synod, lay chairpeople, and rural deans might help to promote such interaction.) The Bishop said, "clergy and full-time workers are a critical group if anything is to happen" and that a primary need was for them to think together about their theology and its implications He said that he had not had formal discussions with them about "justification" because he had not so far felt he could without causing theological faction through people taking up church-manship and doctrinal positions in relation to each other and to him.

The group started to think about how he might get this doctrine over to others. Gradually we saw that getting clergy and workers to think about the Bishop's theological thinking was a one-sided process. What was needed was to get them to think about their own theological ideas and about each other's as well as about the group's. At best such many-sided theological exchanges would affirm everyone, and lead to multi- rather than mono-theological modelling. It would reveal the other theological realities to which the Bishop needs to work from his own theological position and give others the chance to do the same. It could build up collective effort. But it could cause theological confusion, faction and suspicion.

All this convinced the Bishop that the tasks must be changed from discovering ways of expressing, testing and determining the implications of *my theological orientation* to ministry to discovering ways of expressing *our theological orientation*: a radical change which involved taking risks but avoided dangers already foreseen.

Attention then turned to the kind of approach most likely to gain the advantages and minimize the chances of falling foul of the dangers. The Bishop and the group felt that it was necessary to adopt a non-directive approach because it helps people to think about their own ideas and those of others, to give proper weighting to all views regardless of the status of those who hold them and to examine ideas and beliefs non-judgmentally. Discussions of this kind, it was felt, need to take place formally and informally. Alongside this the Bishop and the group saw the need to create opportunities for clergy and full-time workers from UPA and BUPA parishes to meet together with the express purpose of exploring their theology. Groups in which there could be genuine affirmation of people and their thought were seen to be essential because the ability of clergy and workers to sustain their involvement in a critical theological exploration would be related to the quality of the affirmation they received.

Soon after this consultancy session a two-part plan of action which he felt could make generic contributions towards the development of his work and that of his area was forming in the Bishop's mind. The first part involved considering appropriate ways in which he could, formally and informally, share the reality of justification by grace through faith in the areas of work outlined in Figure 3:2 and Display 3:2. Each context called for its own approach. Basics of the other part of the plan he outlined as follows.

1.   If anything is to happen the 120 clergy/full-time workers are a *critical group*.

2. Therefore gather clergy and full-time workers:
   — in *borough* groupings?
   — in ways that give reasonable-sized groups and theological variation (prevents forming theological cliques and blocks).

3. *Task*: each of us to articulate our central theological conviction/thrust which determines/moulds our work.
   Caution: must be structured to avoid sterile, fixed-position conflict and to release clergy from threatening/competitive relationships.
   Possible method: people who differ theologically pair off; each explains to the other important aspects of their beliefs/theology; each articulates the beliefs of the other to the satisfaction of the other. This engenders deeper mutual understanding.

4. *Within shared tasks*: my own central conviction is able to emerge non-threateningly; likely to be a number for whom similar convictions are important; some general theological shape may well emerge which allows us freedom to re-examine the theological under-girding of our work.

The objective was to discover ways in which Bishop, clergy and church workers can better express to each other their theological orientations to ministry, examine them critically and determine the implications for them personally and collectively.

II. NOTES ON THE SUBSTANCE OF THE WORK STUDY

One of the striking things about this study is the centrality of an aspect of Christian theology and experience rarely discussed in relation to the church at work in contemporary society amongst the most deprived: justification by grace through faith.* It was tempting to ignore or dismiss it because it was not our common theological currency and because we had to think quite hard to see just what it contributed. Significantly, it was our commitment to the non-directive approach that led us to accept the Bishop's theological thinking and to work at it with him (cf. what the group said about the need for the non-directive approach). Essentially the Bishop presented to us the story of an evangelical minister of great integrity who had found "justification"

---

*I have thought much about it in relation to church and community development because my experience and understanding of both justification by grace through faith and of the non-directive approach convince me that they are linked because they share the same nature and quality of acceptance, people being accepted as they are, for what they are and for what they can become. Both are about an acceptance that establishes egalitarian relationships which enables, stimulates and facilitates growth and development.

indispensable to a long and distinguished ministry for justice and the common good in the church and in society.* True to what he said about his pragmatism, he valued and argued the importance of this aspect of Christianity from the practical contributions it had made to him and his ministry.

From his own experience, he was convinced that the quality of church and community work and of the lives of workers depended upon their embracing this doctrine. For several reasons I believe we were right to stay with his concern. First, because it was his concern. Second, getting at the theological heart of our approach to our work in church and community, keeping it in view and reviewing it is very important because of the positive and negative effects it can have upon us and our work. Third, there was no point in questioning the obvious value and importance to the Bishop of "justification", but there was every need to explore how he was going to share his experience and convictions. Doing that led the Bishop quite naturally from a programme based on sharing *his* theology to one based upon people sharing *their* theologies which he "owned". This was a substantial shift in orientation from communicating "my" theology to doing theology together, which had more development potential. (I illustrate and discuss these design models in Chapter 6 section V.) It also led to differentiating and classifying work areas and their significant characteristics and to seeing the dichotomy between UPA and BUPA parishes and the need to promote creative interaction and also finding ways to do so. The classification has many uses. It helps, for instance, to establish programmes that fit the different parts and the whole. Thus it helps the Bishop to think strategically and it helps him to help others to do so.[5] (Having written this up I can see how useful a chart of all the Bishop's work situations could be. I am tempted to try to do it!)

It is intriguing to see how the different lines of exploration and aspects of the analysing and designing came together and looped back to development tasks and aims which once established tended to be in the back rather than the front of our minds: we started from them and returned to them but we did not work at them face on, as it were. In this way progress was made towards the objectives the Bishop had for the consultation particularly in relation to:

— balancing a pragmatic temperament with the need for analysis and strategy—he sustained the analytical process over a period of several months;

— handling the vast range of relationships—we enabled him to differentiate them in ways which helped him to handle them;

---

*The biographical outline and the notes about the Bishop's beliefs helped us to see that his experience of "justification" was a powerful thrust in his ministry, a well-established theological trajectory central to his vocation. This longitudinal discussion informed the cross-sectional analysis of his present work.

- reducing the tension and bridging the gulf between UPA and BUPA parishes because of the time he spent on the former—the theological programme had potential to do that;

- improving the theological foundations on which members of the Diocese were building individually and collectively—the theological programme had potential to do that;

- creating more "space" for the Bishop—I think that the approaches will create more work and therefore less space for him, but it will give him the opportunities to experiment that he wanted;

- applying "justification" to collectives—this was not worked out but arrangements were suggested for people to work on it together.

The analysis, systemic but partial, provides a basis and much information for further analytical and design work.

III. NOTES ON THE WORK-STUDY PROCESS

Basically the processes used in this situational study are: a written presentation; exploration and analysis leading to establishing what we were going to work on; designing and planning action programmes which the Bishop felt he could and wanted to carry out. (The process is examined in some detail in Chapter 5.) It involved working throughout to the Bishop's perspective on his area of work and using our perspectives on his analyses and design. This meant there was a creative interaction of perspectives. A primary reason why these consultancy processes were effective was that the Bishop gave himself to them eagerly, openly and industriously.

The process is one of putting things in order (in papers and notes); exploring and taking things apart and putting them together again in a new shape.

Progress was made through the interplay between several kinds of work: the work done personally and privately by the Bishop and other members of the group; the private consultations I had with the Bishop and the group work; writing and talking. The Bishop's work paper was indispensable. Writing notes after each phase of the process gave a creative dynamic to the consultative process. Preparing notes stimulated the Bishop himself to continue the thinking process and enabled the group to start at the position to which the Bishop had moved. My reflections and my thinking had similar effects. What both of us did enabled members of the group to make their best contributions. Writing up can, of course, be a bit unnerving because it exposes weaknesses and gaps in the work done. (I have experienced this as I have written up this study as honestly as I could!) Of itself, this is, of course, a strong argument for writing up studies in some detail. Such records check out analysis and design and can lead on to further analysis and improved design.

An important part of my preparation was working out things that would act as foils to my thinking when I got caught up in the discussions. One example of this is the systemic hypothesis that I formulated entirely from the Bishop's work paper; I had not previously met him. It proved to be a reliable analytic tool and guide. Another example is the dangers I noted part way through the process. The dangers of appearing to justify justification and of making it the dominant theology were avoided. The question I noted about working to contexts was answered satisfactorily, the one about the application of justification to collectives was not. Diagrams and charts were important thinking tools.

Studies of work situations always reveal more things to do than can be done. The art is to identify what needs to be done at the particular time and especially those things that are the key to widespread developments—and the discipline is to stay with them even when there are other things to do that are more attractive to us.

Even though it is not possible to determine accurately the time given to this process (people did not keep accounts and the time given at odd moments is difficult to quantify) it is interesting to make an estimate. The actual time that the Bishop (the principal person) gave to the formal discussions was four-and-a-half hours. Treble it for reflecting and writing up and we get thirteen-and-a-half hours. It was of course supplemented by the time of the staff members (twenty hours) and that of the group (say six hours to reading papers, attending sessions and reflecting). In total some one hundred hours of people's time. An economic use of the Bishop's time: overall an efficient use of time because everyone is learning things of value about process and working with people for development.

IV. SUBSEQUENT DEVELOPMENTS

After reading this account in August 1992 the Bishop wrote:

Lastly, long-term effects. I have no doubt that the consultation has coloured the way that I have done my work ever since. I have faltered in working through the precise strategy which we identified, both by the impact of new and urgent pressures (particularly financial), and by trying several different shapes in which to enable clergy to articulate their theological insights and bring my own together with theirs (i.e., using borough groups, diocesan training staff, deanery clergy groups, diocesan conferences, lay and clergy). None has worked as well as I would have hoped, but on the other hand, there is little I do that has not been touched with the insights I gained from the consultation.

NOTES AND REFERENCES

1. Cf. Paul's Epistle to the Romans: Chapter 3 and especially vv. 24, 26 and 28.

2. Snaith, Norman H., "Just, Justify, Justification" in *A Theological Word Book of the Bible,* ed. A. Richardson (London: SCM Press, 1950). Snaith says, "The verb *dikaioo* (justify) does not mean 'to make just', and indeed is not so much an ethical word as a word which belongs to the vocabulary of salvation. On man's part, the essential condition for justification is faith in Christ. This involves a complete trust in him.... On this condition every repentant sinner is brought by God into fellowship with him. This is the working of his grace, the undeserved favour with which God welcomes all who truly turn to him.... Justification is the first step in the process of salvation, that first reconciliation to God which is the beginning of a steady growth in grace and the knowledge of God (II Peter 3:18)".

3. *Op. cit.*, p. 119, I have substituted "person" for "man".

4. *Faith In The City—A Call for Action by Church and Nation: The Report of the Archbishop of Canterbury's Commission on Urban Priority Areas* (Church House Publishing, 1985).

5. Another example of this is to be found in Lovell, George and Catherine Widdicombe, *Churches and Communities: An Approach to Development in the Local Church* (Tunbridge Wells: Search Press, 1978, reprinted 1986), p. 60.

CHAPTER FOUR

Designing a Project

In 1980 three prominent Jesuit priests of the Irish Province decided to live alongside people in Portadown, one of the most deprived communities in Northern Ireland. They deeply desired to put their commitment to the "preferential option for the poor"[1] into effect. Ecclesiastical relationships and politics had prevented them from developing work in the North for a long time. They felt bad about this. They wanted "to be with people in the North in their suffering".

The priests decided that two of them, Fathers Patrick Doyle and Brian Lennon, should attend an Avec work-consultancy course in 1980 to think about this idea with an independent ecumenical group. (The commitments of the other priest prevented him from attending as well.) The course was very much like the one described in Chapter Three. It had two work study groups. My colleague, Miss Catherine Widdicombe, worked with Father Brian Lennon in one group and I worked with Father Patrick Doyle in the other. Other members of the group were: a Church of Ireland priest; a Presbyterian minister; and superiors of two Roman Catholic religious orders for women. Between times they discussed the consultancy sessions with their colleague and fed anything that emerged into subsequent consultations with their respective groups. (This arrangement has always worked well. Members can explore their own thoughts freely, more ground is covered and more people are consulted. Sometimes staff members talk to the team to consider what has emerged and especially any mutually exclusive ideas that arise—strangely this has rarely happened.)

The group and I worked with Father Doyle on the design of the Jesuits' Portadown project. This chapter describes aspects of the design that evolved and how we arrived at them: the story-line, therefore, is the design process rather than the consultative procedures. It concludes with an evaluation of the design by the Team five years later and a comment in 1992 by Father Doyle.

I. DESIGN INFORMATION

Using as starting points papers* written by Fathers Doyle and Lennon,

---

*In order to meet their circumstances the papers were based on a different outline from the one used by the Bishop in Chapter 3. The titles of sections were: looking back—what I have learnt about working with people and its implications; looking forward—aims, the new situation, opportunities and difficulties, ideas, initial objectives, beliefs; hopes for the course.

members of the group first built up a picture of the thinking behind the project, the orientation of Father Doyle to it, the nature of the working situation, the difficulties anticipated and the action already taken.

1. Father Doyle and the Project

Father Doyle had trained and practised as an industrial scientist. Gradually his interest in philosophy and theology had led him to become a Jesuit in 1954. For fifteen years he had held positions of responsibility: the headmaster of a boarding school (two years); the superior of religious communities (four and three years); the Provincial of the Jesuits in Ireland (six years). He said that being placed in these roles had always surprised him because he did not regard himself as an administrator or an authority figure. Through these experiences he said that he had learnt much about the personal care and support of individuals and had accepted in principle the vital need for planning and consistent implementation of programmes for groups but had not utilized properly or sufficiently the necessary processes involved in the latter. He said he had no personal difficulty in devolving responsibility and that he could live comfortably with a high level of uncertainty. However, he did not allow sufficiently for the effects of this on groups depending on his decisions for action. Currently he was between jobs: the clearly defined post as Provincial and the experimental project which was at the negotiating and planning stage. He expressed his beliefs and aims in the following ways.

Beliefs: My central belief is in the inseparable unity of all persons and the unique contributions each individual makes to what it is to be human. I do not become myself fully until all people become fully themselves and so this life and the next are a continuous growth and a final reconciliation of evil by the overwhelming goodness to be discovered in persons, in Christ and in the loving divinity he opens to us. Thus nobody, of whatever belief, background, race or nation can be excluded from our personal concern and love. We have to learn to relate and grow through our immediate contacts but our meaning and concern have to embrace even all those we do not know and cannot meet until the next life. There we meet, understand, forgive and love in union with Christ in the mystery of the Divine Life. This is a very condensed statement of what I think motivates my life and guides what I try to do. It is also the ground of the guilt and pain I experience as I try to avoid its implications through selfishness and general sinfulness.

Aims: I would wish people to be more aware of their uniqueness, personal worth, and capacity for continuous growth; of their unity with all people; of their need for others and the vast opportunities for co-operation and mutual support; (for Christians) of Christ as being for all people and not narrowly for church members; of Christian unity as a sign of the greater and fundamental unity of all peoples; of the loving presence of God in all lives.

2. The Team's Ideas for the Project

With the "received approval of the Cardinal Archbishop of Armagh"* they hoped to have the freedom to operate in counselling, adult education, community development, ecumenical action and similar areas of work within and beyond the Portadown Parish. They would not engage in established parish work other than to a small degree and only then by mutual agreement with the parish priest. The most valuable opportunities should arise, they said, from the fact that they would be a new and relatively free agency for undertaking new initiatives.

Initially they were concerned "to settle into the area quietly and to begin to learn from the people there." They wanted to have the time and means to learn about the real needs that the people experience in their lives. They wanted to find out what they should do by living there and by promoting friendly acceptance and mutual trust. Two questions were in their minds: "Have we resources which could be useful? How do we make these available to people?" The "Avec approach" they said, seemed appropriate to this kind of activity.

3. Difficulties foreseen

At this stage the basic difficulty that the Jesuits faced was effecting an entry into Portadown and establishing creative relationships with all those with whom they wished to live and work. This difficulty had several inter-related and compounding aspects.

First, as Jesuits had been *personae non gratae* in the Province for a century, a lot of mistrust had to be overcome for the Team to be really accepted by the bishop, priests, religious and laity in the diocese. This was in addition to the traditional tensions and rivalries between diocesan (secular) and religious clergy. Over the past few years some Jesuits had been active in the North and done some distinguished work which had been generally well received ecumenically, but without official permission and somewhat clandestinely, as the Roman Catholic hierarchy had not agreed to a formal presence and groups of priests in the North. This was an undesirable situation because it could so easily adversely affect relationships.

Second, they would need to overcome the widespread assumption that they could not understand "the problems" of Ulster and feel the fears that accompanied them because they were "outsiders".

Third, there were considerable difficulties in getting alongside the people in the deprived areas of Portadown where they intended to live and minister and establishing genuine and equitable relationships of mutual respect and acceptance. They were priests, Jesuit priests, not laity. In stark contrast to the local people they had distinguished academic careers, they were widely travelled, they had held positions of high status and they were people with

---

*The Cardinal was the Bishop of the Diocese in which Portadown is situated. To save confusion I refer to him as the Bishop.

influence. Father Lennon, for instance, was a lecturer in the Irish School of Ecumenics, an author and broadcaster. And, whilst they had wide pastoral experience of people with more formal education and ecumenical sympathies, they had no experience of pastoral work with the kind of people who lived in Portadown.

Fourth, because of differences of theology, ecclesiology and ecumenical stance they saw considerable problems in getting local clergy and laity to work with them according to the insights of Vatican II to which they were deeply committed.

4. Action already taken

Official agreement of the Irish Jesuit Province had been obtained through the person who succeeded Father Patrick Doyle as Provincial for the three priests to try to develop this work in Portadown. The bishop, priests and curates of the diocese in which the project would be situated had agreed to the project in principle. But it had yet to be inaugurated.

II. DESIGNING-ACTING-DESIGNING

In this section I describe a design-action-design sequence which occurred over a period of eleven weeks: getting out the basics of the design of the project related to the overall pattern of working relationships during the first week of the course (November 1980); the Jesuits going to live in Portadown; getting at the essential design and redefining purposes during the second week of the course (January 1981). Once the basics of the design became clear, effective action followed at a breathtaking speed.

1. Entering The Diocese

Aware of the critical importance of the entry into the diocese upon the viability of the project, members of the consultative group questioned Father Doyle closely about the nature of the negotiations. Whilst he was the Provincial, Father Doyle had tested out the idea of the project with the bishop of the diocese concerned personally in order that he could respond freely and privately. The bishop was convinced of the value of the Project; had he not been, the Jesuits would not have pursued the idea further. He was also convinced that the priests and curates of the diocese should be given an opportunity to decide freely and privately whether they wanted the project. So the bishop himself tested out the idea with them. They were in favour of the project but did not want to make a final decision until they had met the Jesuit team and discussed it with them. A meeting was arranged. The bishop introduced the Jesuits and withdrew to allow the discussion to take place. The priests and curates decided for the project and the Jesuits accepted the offer.

Members of the group explored thoroughly the entry into the diocese because they could scarcely believe that the negotiations could be done so thoroughly, sensitively and non-directively and because they were concerned to ensure that the project had not been imposed on the priests and curates. Three things became clearer from this exploration.

First, in this instance initial resistance of the official church to the Jesuits' presence in the North had been overcome. Opportunities to develop new relationships had been secured. Second, the project was now set in a powerful matrix of free acceptance from "below" and "above" in the diocese and in the Jesuit Province. Third, important as this was, it was only the ecclesiastical gateway into Portadown; there were other things and relationships equally as difficult to negotiate. Father Doyle said that the next one was the physical entry into the parish—and he felt that that would be a tricky operation. At this stage we differentiated between approach, entry, work and withdrawal and this helped us to think more realistically about the initial stages in relation to the later ones. Father Doyle found this particularly helpful.

2. The Overall Pattern of Working Relationships

The next stage of the discussion in the same consultative group session was one of the most exciting, intensive and productive in which I have engaged. As the discussion proceeded I built up an untidy version of the following diagram, Figure 4:1. Doing so clarified, facilitated and honed the discussion and the ideas that emerged thick and fast. Afterwards we realized that what we had produced was a project design which modelled working relationships.

A running summary indicates the twists and turns of the discussion and how we worked on first one and then another aspect of the design and put them together. It started by members of the group asking whether the Team had any contacts in Portadown which might be growth points for creative caring and community building. They had: Father Lennon was meeting with a group of parents in an area of deprivation and had good relationships with brothers teaching in the area and some local parish clergy. At this point it dawned upon us that, not surprisingly, so far the focus was entirely upon the Catholic community: the Jesuits were Catholics going to work in a Catholic setting facing Catholic entry problems and the needs of local Catholics were great. But the purposes the three Jesuits had for Irish society and the church could not be achieved through working only with Catholics. They knew that. They needed and wanted to work with people of all denominations and none, for the benefit of both Protestant and Catholic poor and everyone else (see the diagram as a whole and seven o'clock in particular). Establishing good working relationships with their fellow Catholics had temporarily overshadowed the need and problems of doing so with Protestants!

Three other groups now came clearly into focus with whom they needed to work: the poor, Catholic and Protestant (seven o'clock on the diagram); the

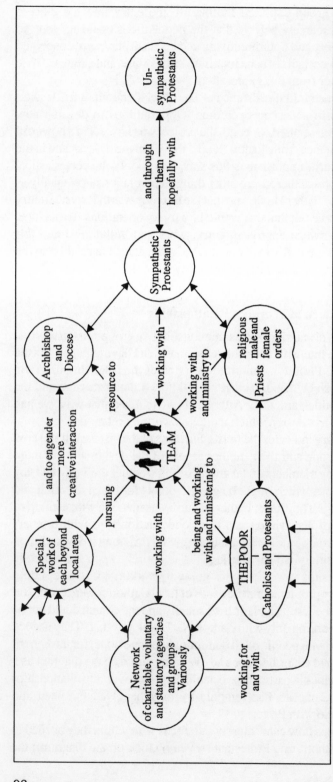

FIGURE 4:1. PATTERN OF WORKING RELATIONSHIPS: FULLY ASPIRED; PARTLY ACHIEVED

Notes:

• The team is put in the centre of the diagram because our focus is upon it, and because it best enables the points to be made diagrammatically about the working relationships. I was tempted to change the diagram to show the team alongside and to avoid the accusation of being hierarchical. I resisted because that is how we produced the diagram and because there is a hierarchy.

• During the sessions we produced three diagrams quite separately: one was the right side; another the middle and the bottom left; and the third was the remainder. Then, in a moment of enlightenment, we put them together!

network of charitable, voluntary and statutory agencies already working for and with the poor and deprived (nine o'clock); and the Protestant churches, ministers and laity (three o'clock). Examining what was involved in establishing comprehensive relationships led us to see that the whole constituency, including the Roman Catholics, comprised those sympathetic to the Jesuits and their project and those unsympathetic and antipathetic. All too easily they could find themselves working with the sympathetic and consequently, by default, reinforcing faction between those sympathetic to ecumenical developments and those not. These were developments they would regret.

Considering all this reinforced the desire and intention to work *for* the whole and *with* as many people as they could from the Catholic, Protestant and secular communities for the common good and holistic development. But we acknowledged that it would be quite impossible for the Jesuits (or members of other religious or secular groups) to work directly with some of those who were unsympathetic or antipathetic to them. Facing this led us to underline the need for those who can work together to do so for the common good and holistic development, not simply for their own good. In the long term this strategy can gradually break down mistrust and build up trust in communities where sectarian groups have blatantly "looked after their own".

Then we started to look at the bridging and mediatorial roles that people from the different factions could play when they are working together for the whole. Our attention focused particularly on the Jesuits and the Protestants. Protestants working with the Jesuits live and work with Protestants who are not sympathetic to the Jesuits. Clearly the sympathetic Protestants could be mediators between them—provided, that is, that they are not marginalized because of their associations with the Jesuits: a real possibility. An important part of the development work that sympathetic Protestants and Jesuits could do together, therefore, would be to think out how the sympathetic Protestants could avoid being marginalized and how they could act as mediators. The Protestants could do the same for the Jesuits. In fact this could be a feature of all the working relationships. (This led to the three o'clock part of the design!) As we discussed all this it struck Father Doyle that the women religious would make good intermediaries.

Attention then turned to the network of charitable, voluntary and statutory agencies and groups working with and for the poor (Protestant, Catholic and neither). By default they could easily induce bad relationships with such people and be played off against them if they started to work with the poor without making themselves and their purposes known to them. They would need to work for change with and through them as well as with the poor. (Seven and nine o'clock of the diagram represent this thinking in the design.)

Then there was the contribution, which is discussed later, that the Jesuits could make to development through action in relation to, but beyond the project area (eleven o'clock on the diagram), and the other contributions which they were making through their not inconsiderable scholarship and their

99

status in the Church. They were keen to continue to make these.

Reflecting on the diagram helped us to see that this pattern of working relationships could develop a wider and deeper sense of community between the Team, between workers of different denominations and agencies, between organizations and churches, and between people with different needs.

Towards the end of the session we felt that the project Team members needed to consider what had emerged and to determine the implications of any conclusions they might reach. We also felt that they needed to establish criteria that would help them to decide where to live and to work out the steps to be taken during the next phase of the project.

All this was done in just over one-and-a-quarter hours by a newly formed group!

3. Entering Portadown

Events moved fast once the Jesuits had agreed that they wanted to establish the pattern of working relationships depicted in the model above. Entry into Portadown was their next objective. They worked out their criteria for the house in which they would live and checked them with local clergy. The principal ones were that the house enabled them to live alongside a Catholic area of extreme deprivation in accommodation indistinguishable from that of local people; that Catholics and Protestants alike could visit them freely; and that it provided accommodation for three priests to live and work. Then they worked out how best to move into such a house. They thought about it from their own perspective and they tried to stand in the shoes of their new neighbours and to speculate on the possible effects upon them of three Jesuits moving in next door. Through looking at in this way they really saw and felt that their entry was a dramatic event which could have positive and negative effects.* Three Jesuit priests moving in to a closely knit homogeneous community of deprived people was indeed a serious discontinuity! Some would welcome them and be glad to have such neighbours. Others could feel intimidated, that they had lost some of their freedom to be themselves and that they faced censure from what was normally hidden from priests. The Jesuits got very excited about approaching their entry in this way and the challenge to make it a dramatic event of a positive kind.

Against this background they drew up these entry guidelines: establish neighbourly relationships as priests gradually and gently; invite people in as opportunities present themselves; keep a low profile; establish a parish role

---

*The Jesuits got the idea of considering their entry as a "dramatic event" from a session conducted during the first week of the course by a Jesuit of their own order who was on the staff, The Revd Dr Henry Grant. He was presenting an analysis of the "Troubles" that he had made for a doctoral thesis. As part of the analysis he had traced out the socio-religious effects of what he called "dramatic events of a divisive nature" e.g. bombings and sectarian murders. He has since published an article on this entitled "Understanding the Northern Irish Troubles: A Preliminary to Action" in *Studies: An Irish Quarterly Review* (Summer 1983).

through helping with liturgy; explain who they were and what jobs they were doing outside the area and that they wanted to be part of this community; avoid making people feel deprived or inferior (this had profound implications for the way they furnished the house and their standard of living); get to know families; prepare people for the coming and going of priests and Protestant clergy and people to their house.

Less than eight weeks after the discussion on working relationships they were living in a house they had rented in Portadown in a block bricked up because no-one else wanted to live there which met their criteria! Settling into the community had gone well. The Jesuits said that the things which helped most were the sensitivity engendered within them by thinking of the move as a dramatic event and in the change of orientation from thinking about it as "our entry" into their community to conceiving it as "their reception of us into their community"—both things achieved by trying to stand in the shoes of the local people to see things through *their* eyes.

Now that they had successfully entered into the diocese and the local community they set about building up the working relationships they had with others.

4. The Essential Design

We now pick up the story nine weeks later during the second week of the course. Father Doyle said that he and his colleagues were following through the work done during the previous session on working relationships; they did not want any further help on that at this stage. They wanted the consultative group to work with Father Doyle on the "basics of the project" and particularly on its design and purpose. They felt the need for "crucial reference points in the surging seas of project work in areas of deprivation deeply affected by the 'Troubles'". They had now stated their overall purpose: to contribute to the reconciliation of the people of Ireland. We worked on the project design and then on their objectives for the project.

The Diagram on Working Relationships (Figure 4:1) helped us to identify the following basic groups of people:

Group I   The local people. (Almost entirely "working class" people.)

Group II   The Jesuits living in the area and working at all levels of the community.

Group III   Those who work in the local area but who live outside it. (They are mainly "middle class".)

Group IV   Those who live and work entirely outside the local area but who have the power to affect what happens to it and in it. (This is a vast number of people at all levels in politics, military and para-military organizations, government, industry, voluntary organizations and in the church.)

I contributed the following diagram (Figure 4:2) to show the interaction between these groups.

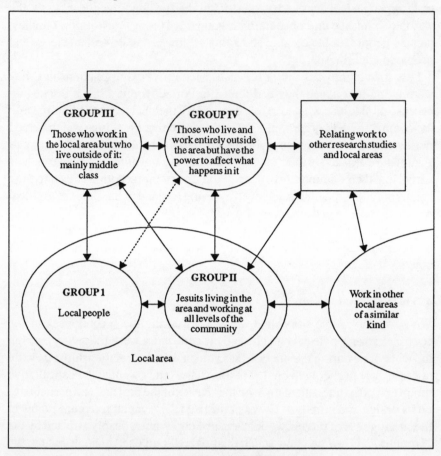

FIGURE 4:2. ESSENTIAL DESIGN OF THE PROJECT

For Father Doyle and the members of the consultative group this diagram powerfully depicted essentials in the structure and design of the project: we referred to it as the "essential design". It was a "disclosure model"[2] which animated us. Poring over it led us to make the following points.

- People in the local area have contributions which they alone can make to their own well-being, development and redemption no matter how deprived they seem to be. Nothing that others do is a substitute for these contributions. A primary responsibility of the Jesuit Team is to help them to make these contributions through their interaction with Groups, II, III and IV. For instance they could work with Groups III and IV to reduce undesirable forms of dependency frequently induced and encouraged by their interventions.

- Overall development is most likely to occur if people from all the groups are acting collaboratively. The Jesuit Team could help to promote this because they are both local and non-local workers.

- The Jesuits must work alongside the local people but, if they are to make their fullest contributions, they need to work with and talk to people in Group III (and possibly help people in Groups I and IV to do so); they need to relate their work to the wider debate about working for development in such areas; they need to report their experiences and educate others; they need to promote and support similar work in different local areas. This will tax to the full all their reserves and exploit their status, learning and contacts to work out their commitment to the preferential option to the poor. These activities beyond the local area are an integral part of it: they are not activities to compensate for the local involvement.

- The Jesuits were, in fact, ideally equipped and placed to make this design work.

- At the time we felt that this design model seemed to be the single most important thing that came out of the consultations.

5. Project Objectives redefined

Now we were in a position to redefine the objectives the Jesuits had for the project in this way:

(a) To promote human and spiritual betterment in an area of acute deprivation in Northern Ireland from a living/working base within the community by getting all parties (Groups of people I, II, III and IV) to make their contributions and, whenever possible, to work together for the betterment of the whole.

(b) To learn as much as possible about reconciliation and development in Ireland from the experience and to get as many others as possible to do the same.

Achieving these objectives, they felt, would make significant contributions towards achieving their overall purpose—the reconciliation of the people of Ireland.

III. OBSERVATIONS ON THE PROCESS

Now to some observations about this particular experience of designing a project; then, in Chapter Six, I consider the creation of designs for church and community work most likely to promote development.

1. Purpose and Objectives

It is interesting to see the ways in which the purposes and objectives evolved as the design unfolded. Father Doyle's expression of aims in his initial paper enabled us to carry out the first phase of the design. At that point he expressed his aims in terms of the things that he desired for all people—becoming more aware of themselves, their capacities for growth and their place in the overarching unity of all people, non-Christians and Christians. During the time of moving to Portadown they had felt the need for "crucial reference points". (During the plenary sessions of the first week of the course we had discussed reference points along the lines that they are discussed in Chapter Five.) They now stated their purposes as, "to contribute to the reconciliation of the people of Ireland". This enabled them to go on with the next phase of design. Then after they had got out the "essential design" they were able to articulate their objectives. These were: to promote betterment in an area of acute deprivation in Northern Ireland bedevilled by the "Troubles" and to learn as much as possible about reconciliation and development in Ireland and to make it widely known. One of the interesting things about all this is the creative interaction between the clarification of "aims" and the designing of the project. Successive statements of aims helped the Team to design the project and successive stages of the design helped to clarify aims. As the aims became more specific, so did the design, and vice versa.

2. Developing a Systemic Approach

The way in which the Jesuits had approached the Diocese showed deep insights into ways in which the inter-related parts work. What the design process did was to bring out the systemic nature of the activities in which the Team planned to engage and led to the project being seen as a systemic exercise.

First, they worked at the Roman Catholic aspect. Gradually they built up a more comprehensive picture of Portadown by putting together sub-systems which they had previously thought of separately. For instance they first worked at the Roman Catholic diocese as *the* system. It is in its own right a very complicated and important one. Then they saw it as a sub-system related to or adjacent to other sub-systems: the community in which they would be living; the voluntary and statutory agencies; the Protestant churches, etc. A systemic picture emerged. Then it became clear that the Team were introducing another sub-system, foreign to the host system because it was Jesuit and different in membership, approach and theology. As far as possible the Team and their project had to mesh in with as much of the system as possible. Making systemic connections avoided it being a top-down or bottom-up project. They had begun to do this with the Roman Catholic diocese without conceptualizing what they were doing in the way we have just done. Having conceptualized the process systemically they were in a better position to engage with the system as a whole and with its parts in a systematic way: they would, of course, encounter the system whether or not they were conscious of it.

Whilst they wanted to mesh into the Portadown system they also wanted, as an integral part of the project and their ministries, to mesh into the larger human and religious systems of action and research which affected the locale. They wanted and needed to be both local and non-local workers.

It was fascinating to see how, by concentrating on purpose and actualities, we moved from a single organizational (the Roman Catholic diocese) to a multi-organizational community development approach and from an expanding complexity to an essential simplicity of design.

At an early stage the Jesuits had been asking whether they would constitute a team or a religious community. These questions were not pursued in the consultative sessions. Looking back, I realize that designing the project helped to form the Jesuits into a working team and to get them working at their separate and collective functions. They were, in fact, being formed by their purposes, the context and the functions they would have to perform—quite a different process from that of forming a community and then implanting it. Other aspects of their community life would develop from within themselves and their personal, devotional and social activities.

3. Diagrams and Models

Diagrams and models were principal tools in this process. It is quite impossible for me to do this kind of designing or to see how to do it without diagrams, models and flow charts. I discuss their uses in Chapters 6 and 7.

IV. ASSESSMENT BY THE TEAM

This chapter is based on notes I drafted in 1985. I sent a copy to the Team and had this reply from Father Patrick Doyle.

> Your account was very useful to read especially as we are now reviewing our first five years in Portadown. The work has not been written up fully but progress is being made. . . . I bring out the notes and diagrams of the Consultancy Sessions at our various review and planning meetings. So the influence and help of the Avec course '80-81 has perdured. The Essential Design did in fact embrace most of the developments which have occurred. Clearly the depth and effectiveness of the different relationships have varied considerably. Also the sequence of their development has depended on many things outside our control. However, by now when one fills out the structure with actual named relationships it can look impressive! It is therefore still valuable in the process of assessment and planning.

In 1992 I sent Father Doyle a draft of this chapter. The following is an excerpt from his reply:

It might be of interest to add that the house we rented was in a Housing Executive Estate with endemic unemployment of 90 per cent and very run-down physically and in morale. The house we got was in a block, of many others, bricked-up because nobody wanted to live there. After one year we took the adjoining house because the whole block was being renovated for others now applying. Eventually the whole estate got a complete and effective renovation. The first Community Council Brian Lennon developed was largely responsible for this advance together with better relations we helped develop with Groups III and IV.

Fr Michael Drennan, SJ was in Portadown only for the weekends during the first year. His place was taken in the end of 1981 by Brother David Byrne, SJ, who is still doing trojan work amongst the people of the area. Fr Declan Deane then joined us and we were four for most of the time until 1988 when I came to Belfast to open another residence. My place was taken by a Fr Senan Timoney. Changes of personnel continue but Father Brian Lennon has remained for the twelve years the centre of great activity and initiative. Many local people have grown very considerably in confidence and skill so that even Brian could leave soon with the good hope that much community development would continue. Over the years after our first five the spiritual dimension flourished in ways we could not have more directly encouraged in the early years. Ecumenical contacts and co-operation in community affairs also grew but of course even now in limited ways.

NOTES AND REFERENCES

1. A phrase now in common use amongst Roman Catholics and particularly Religious. It was first used in the conclusions of The Third Conference of the Latin American Bishops in 1979 at Puebla attended by Pope John Paul II in a message to the peoples of Latin America as a main heading. Cf. Sheppard, David, *Bias to the Poor* (London: Hodder & Stoughton, 1983), p. 149.

2. Cf. Lovell, George, *Diagrammatic Modelling: An Aid to Theological Reflection in Church and Community Development Work* (an Avec Publication, 1980), p. 26.

Part Two

Approach and Method

The value of the modes of studying work discussed in Part One is proven. I have used them extensively over the past thirty years. At the same time I found myself adapting them in this way and that to fit in-service training courses and project and consultancy work. Gradually I realized that I was working to an underlying sequence which constituted a basic analysis-design process. Making the nature of this primary process explicit is important. It has helped me to work to it and to produce with greater ease and confidence various task sequences for different purposes and situations. I describe the underlying sequence here, discuss what is involved in using it and illustrate ways in which I have adapted it. Then I return to a much neglected subject, the design of work programmes with the potential to promote human and spiritual development, and I round off this part with a chapter on basic equipment.

CHAPTER FIVE

Process, Context and the Human Factor

The first part of this chapter presents a schema for studying all kinds of church and community work. The second part discusses some of the things involved in using this schema, such as coping with feelings and limited thinking time and workers being their own analytical instruments. The third part is about coping with contextual intimidation.

I. THE CORE PROCESS: FROM EXPERIENCE THROUGH CRITICAL AND IMAGINATIVE THOUGHT TO CREATIVE ACTION

Underlying the examples I worked through in Part One is a very important dynamic and thrust from experience through critical and imaginative thought to creative action.* I would represent it diagrammatically as follows in Figure 5:1 in order to suggest how thought, informed by experience, is earthed in action.

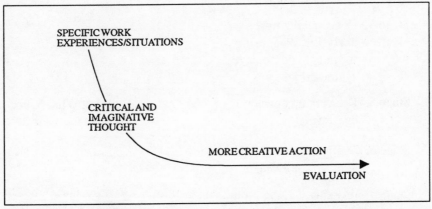

FIGURE 5:1. THE CREATIVE ACTION THRUST OF CRITICAL AND IMAGINATIVE THOUGHT

*To communicate about the experiential approach to Christian Education during the 1960s the late Douglas S. Hubery coined the phrase "from experience to experience through experience". Cf. *Teaching the Christian Faith Today* (A Chester House Publication 1965). This was the inspiration for "from experience through critical and imaginative thought to creative action".

This thrust is built into the structures used to work on problems, cases, situations and projects in Part One. It directs and eases people towards thoughtful action even while holding them back from precipitate action to enable them to think things through. Getting as many people as possible engaged together in this process is of the essence of church and community development.

1. Stages in Critical and Imaginative Thought

As Part One illustrates, our ability to think things through to a good conclusion improves when our efforts are guided but not dominated by a logical sequence of thinking steps. Reviewing all the examples and my experience I identify the eight stages in thinking critically and imaginatively about church and community work which are set out in Display 5:1.

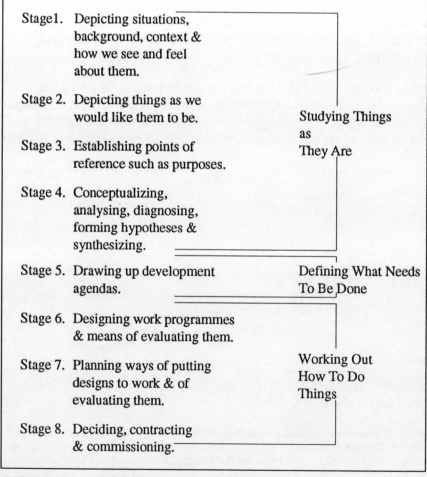

Stage 1. Depicting situations, background, context & how we see and feel about them.

Stage 2. Depicting things as we would like them to be.

Stage 3. Establishing points of reference such as purposes.

            Studying Things as They Are

Stage 4. Conceptualizing, analysing, diagnosing, forming hypotheses & synthesizing.

Stage 5. Drawing up development agendas.

            Defining What Needs To Be Done

Stage 6. Designing work programmes & means of evaluating them.

Stage 7. Planning ways of putting designs to work & of evaluating them.

            Working Out How To Do Things

Stage 8. Deciding, contracting & commissioning.

DISPLAY 5:1. EIGHT THINKING STAGES

Our aspirations and feelings are significant parts of "things as they are"; that is why Stages 2 and 3 are grouped with Stages 1 and 4. Whether people are satisfied or dissatisfied is, for example, an important part of any situation. Each stage has its own ethos. Looking forward and designing, planning and dreaming have an ethos quite different from that associated with analysing and deciding. The systematic movement in thought from what is to what is to be has a momentum and drive of its own which uplifts the spirit and stirs people to want to get on with things.

These thinking stages are especially helpful when we are overwhelmed by complex situations and issues, when we are daunted by the task, when our feelings tend to inhibit rational thought, when we just do not think it is possible for us to think our way to a good conclusion and when we are so eager to get on with things that we do not want to stop and think.

There is a logic in the order but the sequence is not invariable. Stages 2 and 3 could well precede Stage 1. Sometimes an examination of a situation or problem starts with what people are planning to do next, i.e. with Stages 6, 7 and 8 or in the evaluation of a programme of work. Wherever you start, some of the steps can be done adequately only when the others have been worked on: 2, for instance, can be informed by 4; 6 and 7 depend upon what people are prepared to do, and that comes out clearly in 8. In practice, each stage facilitates and refines the others, and Stage 3, points of reference such as beliefs and purposes, is a guide to them all. So it is good practice to summarize what is emerging in order to revise earlier thoughts in the light of later insights.

There are many ways in which this process can be sabotaged deliberately or by default. For instance some people make heavy emotional bids to "get on with the job because we all know what needs to be done, don't we?" They want to by-pass Stages 1 to 7 if not 1 to 8. Others are very happy to think and think again without acting on their conclusions. Maintaining the thrust towards action generates the distinctive ethos of a workshop in which people are engaged in purposeful, productive thought rather than in a "talking shop".

Pursuing this process in living situations in which you have invested a lot of yourself taxes your feelings as well as your ability to think critically and imaginatively. You can experience all kinds of emotions. We need to deal with these so that they help rather than hinder the thinking processes. Those helping people to use this process need to be sensitive and to offer the moral and pastoral support and care which enables people to think through things about which they feel deeply and to think about their feelings as well as their ideas.

Our ability to think things through also improves when the uses of these stages is accompanied by meditation, reflection and prayer and when what is being learnt through the process is articulated. Adding all these dimensions to figure 5:1 gives us a conceptual framework for analysing and designing all kinds of church and community work, a schema. This is presented in Figure 5:2 and described and discussed in detail in the remainder of this chapter.

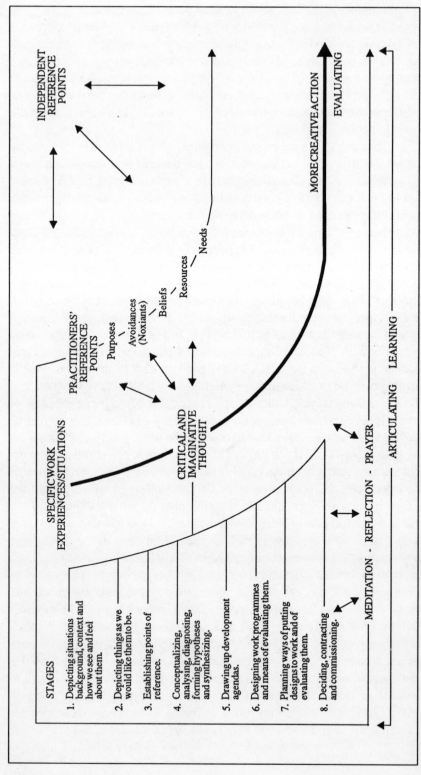

STAGES

1. Depicting situations background, context and how we see and feel about them.

2. Depicting things as we would like them to be.

3. Establishing points of reference.

4. Conceptualizing, analysing, diagnosing, forming hypotheses and synthesizing.

5. Drawing up development agendas.

6. Designing work programmes and means of evaluating them.

7. Planning ways of putting designs to work and of evaluating them.

8. Deciding, contracting and commissioning.

SPECIFIC WORK EXPERIENCES/SITUATIONS

PRACTITIONERS' REFERENCE POINTS

INDEPENDENT REFERENCE POINTS

CRITICAL AND IMAGINATIVE THOUGHT

Purposes

Avoidances (Noxiants)

Beliefs

Resources

Needs

MORE CREATIVE ACTION

EVALUATING

MEDITATION · REFLECTION · PRAYER

ARTICULATING   LEARNING

FIGURE 5:2. A SCHEMA FOR ANALYSING AND DESIGNING CHURCH AND COMMUNITY WORK

116

*Stage 1: Depicting Work Situations, Backgrounds and Contexts and how we
see them and feel about them*

Part One showed the importance of getting as accurate a picture as possible of
the work situation, the nature of the workers' involvement and how they feel
about it: the problem and the project were defined; the case set down
succinctly; the situation described. Subjective realities (feelings, ideas,
thoughts, hopes and fears) were differentiated and stated alongside objective
ones about place, programmes, numbers of people, finance etc: they are
equally material "facts". The examples I have given in Part One showed the
importance of working to the perspectives of those involved because how they
see and experience the realities conditions what they do. Clarity about this
facilitates creative interaction between their perspective and those of others.
The art in all this is to depict these various realities about workers and their
situations in ways that enable all concerned to grasp the essentials and to work
at them. I say "depict", rather than describe, because, for me, it conveys
portraying things through graphics and possibly paintings as well as through
the spoken and written word.

All but painting were used in the worked examples. The aim is to portray as
succinctly as possible the essentials of situations, the experience and dimensions
of problems, the story-line of cases. Descriptive economy is necessary in what
is essentially an exercise in profiling: too many words and fussy diagrams
obfuscate.

Stage 2: Depicting Things as we would like them to be

There are many reasons why it is good practice for people engaged in
development work to describe and share their visions, their ideas about how
they would prefer things to be. Actualities and visions are creative foils to each
other when they are depicted together and compared and contrasted. (A.N.
Whitehead said, "... progress in the right direction is the result of a slow,
gradual process of continual comparison of ideas with facts".[1]) Individuals
working privately and groups of people need to have both in view. What can
happen is that people in working groups who have shared their understandings
of their situations try to continue without sharing their vision. (It can happen
the other way round as well.) Working to public statements of the actualities
and private visions is a recipe for frustration and confusion: people are
assuming or guessing what others think would be ideal. Visions help us to
formulate some important points of reference such as purposes.

Stage 3: Establishing Points of Reference

Five reference points that help people to regulate this process are described in
section 2. They are purposes, noxiants or things to be avoided, beliefs,
resources and needs.

Stage 4. Conceptualizing, analysing, diagnosing, forming Hypotheses and synthesizing

Essentially this activity is about workers systematically conceptualizing, examining, diagnosing and analysing their work themselves and establishing their hypotheses in order to be better able to achieve their purposes, improve their performance and develop their abilities and themselves and to help those with whom they work to do the same. Others, such as consultants, may help them to do these things and may suggest analyses but workers need to "own" the analyses. Consultants must aim to help workers to analyse their own work and to become increasingly better at doing so: they should not do it for them. I would hope that workers would help those with whom they work to acquire these skills.[2]

Analysis is about taking things apart or "the resolution of anything complex into its simple elements" and "the tracing of things to their sources; the discovery of general principles underlying concrete phenomena" (S.O.E.D.). Part One shows that the kind of analyses we are considering are about what is happening to people and workers in complex collectives (groups, committees, churches, organizations and communities) as they go about the business of living, working and worshipping together. They are, for example, about patterns of interaction which facilitate and inhibit human and spiritual growth being achieved; they are about people and groups working well together; they are about clashes between people, workers and groups and faction; they are about elitist, autocratic, authoritarian and non-directive action. The analyses, like the patterns of interaction, touch the nerve centres of workers' and people's motivation, purposes, beliefs and sense of vocation. Clearly, such essential analytical work is as sensitive as it is intellectually demanding: those who help others to do it need to be pastors as well as analysts, who tread carefully on vocational ground because it is holy.

In this context, dealing as we are with living situations, it is particularly dangerous to take apart what subsequently cannot be put together. I have experienced it. To be health-giving, diagnosis must be followed by effective treatment. Similarly work analysis must be construed in a positive synthesis and used in the design of realistic plans as a prelude to creative action. Analysis and design must always be coupled: analysis is a means to an end, not an end. We return to this later. This underlines the importance of working at all the stages of the sequence so that analysis leads to synthesis, and to a purposeful movement from what was done to what is to be done.

Holland and Henriot, dedicated advocates of "pastoral social analysis" in the service of faith and justice, underline all this:

First, social analysis is only a negative instrument. By that we mean it has the destructive power to tear away the mystification of our social world and to unveil the deep structures that control it. Our response to that disclosure is often a feeling of powerlessness. We are overwhelmed and immobilized. (We experience the "paralysis of analysis".)

118

To move beyond this feeling of powerlessness, we need the creative resources of vision and energy.

Second, social analysis is a scientific effort; that is, it uses analytical tools to divide reality into separate and abstract parts.... However, if the analysis breaks a living body into its component parts, it risks destroying its creative life. If a social analyst takes away life, what will return it—at least in social terms?

That task falls to the artist—not only the artist of high culture (the great painters, composers, and authors of classical literature), but an artist whose roots are found in popular culture. We believe that the artistic impulse is the creative force in modern civilization. It is the spiritual source from which vision and energy flow. While we need to analyse society with scientific rigor, we must be wary of destroying that impulse.[3]

Stage 5: Drawing up Development Agendas

By "drawing up a development agenda" I mean determining just what needs to be done to pursue the implications of the analysis. This was done in working on the bishop's situation. Three tasks were identified, and others were added after further reflection. In the case study we speculated about the action that could now be taken.

Drawing up such agendas is a reflective phase which follows analytical probing and precedes designing and planning. It is a brooding mood stage and a standing back to take stock before going forward. For this stage to be creative the workers directly concerned have to experience a subjective synthesis which brings together several elements: intellectual and intuitive convictions that the analysis is sufficiently profound and the tasks essential; feelings, convictions and assurances that they can and must do the tasks and that their commitment, calling and integrity as workers require them to do so.

Sometimes workers simply cannot commit themselves to tasks that seem obvious and logical both to them and others. Enthusiasm can waver after the excitement of analyses which lead to disclosures. At other times what they feel in their bones is needed just does not seem to fit the logic of the analysis. Sometimes I have become impatient with myself and others over such dissonance. At my best I have stayed with it and had the great privilege of waiting expectantly whilst others search inwardly for the connections they need to make.[4] It has always been worth while. It has led to new insights and to key tasks being discerned which were previously obscured by other more obvious tasks.

Waiting and working for connections to be made by workers themselves between their inner and outer worlds is essential because these connections are a primary source of creative energy. It leads to what Eric Fromm calls non-alienated activity and that, he says, gives "birth to their own faculties and brings life to other persons and to things".[5] Genuine development agendas emerge from this process which is soul-searching rather than brainstorming. Mechanical listing can be a servant of, but not a substitute for, this process. At times it prevents reflection.

119

Stage 6: Designing Work Programmes, Projects and Programmes and Means of evaluating them

Designing the basics of human work programmes is one of those things it is easier to illustrate than to describe. The Jesuits' project described in Chapter 4 illustrates it admirably. Figures 4:1 and 2 are designs. It shows how it was intended that the Project would work. It sets out the structures and the working relationships that would hold the human parts together and facilitate the flow of creative effort in many different directions. It shows the kind of structures and relationships necessary; it does not show how to construct and establish them. Doing that, in the terminology I am using, is planning, contracting and commissioning. More often than not, people in church and community work act without overt reference to the designs upon which their action is based. This is a stage that is generally omitted. This neglected activity is considered in Chapter 6.

At this stage it is also desirable to design a system of evaluation, i.e. to decide just what is to be evaluated and in what way can it be shown that objectives have been achieved.

Stage 7: Planning Ways and Means of putting Designs to Work and evaluating them

This stage is about the steps to be taken to convert designs into reality. Thinking through these steps is a real test of the feasibility of designs and a prelude to the next stage. People often think quite wrongly that they are "designing" when they are doing this. It involves things like: deciding who to see, in what order and to what ends; convening meetings; deciding what to do and how to do it; setting up groups and organizations.

Stage 8: Deciding, contracting and commissioning

Generally speaking people give themselves more freely to the tasks associated with the first seven stages when there is a firm and genuine understanding at the outset that decisions will be made only when the implications are sufficiently clear for all concerned to make them freely and realistically. With this understanding, provisional decisions are made en route to facilitate the processes of analysis and design. At appropriate points these are revised or confirmed. When the information is available decisions and contracts are made and people commission themselves and others to do the work. Such arrangements help those who get so carried away by the subject matter and group processes that they over-commit themselves. At the same time they help those who hold back for fear of committing themselves prematurely. And they defend people from those who habitually think of things for others to do and leave them to do them!

Thus, in the early stages of this process, tentativeness engenders free, imaginative and creative thought that leads to well-informed decision making and action. The later stages lead to disciplined decision making. The process

120

opens out thought to lead on to action. This is an action-focused, not an open-ended, process.

2. Workers' Reference Points

To be most effective the use of this process has to result in activities which those concerned can sustain and which:

(a) give expression to their beliefs;

(b) are along the line of their purposes;

(c) make constructive contributions to the overall context in which they occur.

I would now like to show that these fundamental requirements can be used to produce overall reference points which can be used to guide, check and regulate the process and, if necessary, to adjust whatever emerges from it.

Formulating reference points and using them is an integral part of the process. There are several reasons for setting them alongside the process as well as within it.

First, they are rarely used consistently to check what is emerging from the various stages even when people are convinced of their importance and have taken the trouble to formulate them precisely. They tend to be polished, put on a pedestal and forgotten as people grapple with more tangible things. Setting them out separately alongside the process helps to remind people of the importance of using them over and again.

Second, in working on the stages it is all too easy to produce lop-sided plans through becoming preoccupied with one part of the analysis rather than the whole of it. This was a very real danger in designing the project described in Chapter Four. The design was developed piecemeal. Critical pieces would have been missed had we not compared the pieces of the design we had put in place with the Jesuits' beliefs, purposes, personal needs and critical features of the context in which they were to work. I have in mind the subtle and significant nuances of the relationships in the design between the Jesuits and people in other organizations working with the poor and in the way of relating to unsympathetic Protestants through sympathetic ones rather than directly. Without these refinements of earlier designs the project would have been seriously flawed. Clearly, the effects of errors multiply as one works through the stages.

Third, putting this process to work involves introducing a systematic and closely structured way of going about things into specific human activities with their own flow of thought and action and in which people have their own way of going about things. Sometimes it all comes together in a positive dynamic. More often than not, cross-currents of thought, beliefs, purposes, approaches and methods play on orderly processes and interrupt, deflect, resist and even swamp them. (This is my experience, but it is also my experience that the process invariably generates more productive thought and action than there would be without it.) Whilst all this is going on, clearly marked reference points are needed to keep our bearings and to help others to do so. Reference points, not visions, are needed. Pictures of places help us to recognize them. Reference points help us to discern whether our thinking and deciding is going in the right direction. They need to be sharp and readily available to help us, individuals or groups, when we are deeply involved in the kind of processes we are considering here.

Fourth, reference points relate to all stages so they need to be readily available all the time.

There are many different kinds of reference points. Those that I use are beliefs, purposes, things to avoid ("noxiants"[6]), needs and resources. (Hypotheses are another kind that keep alive speculative thinking. They are discussed in Chapter 7.) Reference points, like tools, are useful for different functions and some are in more constant use than others. Beliefs connect us with the ground of our being and doing. Purposes point to what we want or need to achieve and noxiants to what we want or need to avoid. Needs and resources earth us in our situation and context. Together they form a framework of reference. Mission statements, which are very much in vogue in secular as well as religious institutes, weave together these kinds of reference points in a paragraph or two.

There is a limited number of different kinds of reference points. The content of each kind and the way in which it is expressed is unlimited. Individuals, groups, organizations, churches determine them in their own way. This brings us to the need to formulate the content so that it really represents our thinking and is useful in the work place.

a. Purposes and Avoidances (Noxiants)

For many years I worked consciously and systematically to what I wanted to achieve (purpose and objectives) and subconsciously to what I wanted to avoid (noxiants). Occasionally I did work to noxiants but I was not aware of the methodological implications of what I was doing. Now I work consciously to both. I put down quite unashamedly what I want or need to avoid. For instance I might put down that I want to avoid compromising my integrity or that I want to avoid making a mess of a meeting and having to endure the inner pain that would follow. The sea-change was brought about by reading about a contrast that Professor Gareth Morgan makes between "goal oriented strategies" in organizations and "a strategy based on the avoidance of noxiants". The latter, he says:

> involves a choice of limits and constraints rather than a choice of ends, creating degrees of freedom that allow meaningful direction to emerge....

122

Whether we examine the Ten Commandments or contemporary legal systems, we find the principles of avoiding noxiants defining a space of acceptable behaviours within which individuals can self-organize.[7]

Morgan argues that "the process of pursuing a specific goal and the process of identifying and avoiding noxiants" are not simply two sides of the same coin, they "are qualitatively different modes of action that impact on organization and environment in very different ways".[8] That may be so but my experience is that both modes of activity have a place in the kind of work in which I am engaged. They go together, just as Jesus' great commandments to love God and neighbour and self go alongside the commandments not to murder, commit adultery, etc.[9] I find working to both purposes and noxiants releasing and creative. It helps me to steer away from the noxiants and to keep nearer to the fairly narrow purpose path.

Purposes and noxiants help to check in a positive and negative manner whatever is emerging from the process. A purpose, for example, might be to promote love and care in a neighbourhood; a noxiant to avoid mistrust. Using these to check ideas for action involves asking, "Will our plans help people to love and care for each other? Can they possibly lead to mistrust?" Each question has its own potential not possessed by the other for checking things out and faulting plans. Together they have a pincer checking effect.

Noxiants are sometimes better evaluative reference points than purposes. Attempts, for instance, to promote dialogue must aim to avoid defensive thought and behaviour which rings the death knell on all forms of dialogue and critical thought. There is a checking cutting edge in the noxiant that is absent from the objective, "to promote dialogue". Noxiants they might be, but avoiding things can be very positive. Much in the case study in Chapter 3 and the project design in Chapter 4 is about avoiding bad relationships: the minister with his wife, Sunday School teachers and church members; the Jesuits with the local priests and with people in secular, Protestant and Catholic agencies who are working with the poor. The noxiants were very much in the Jesuits' mind when they were designing the project. Things might have been quite different if the minister in the case had had in mind the things he needed to avoid, for instance one section of the Church playing him off against another. For these reasons I find it more effective to use purposes and noxiants rather than to transform noxiants into negative purposes and objectives as is some-times done.

Formulating one's own real purpose is often a difficult thing to do; but when achieved it becomes a signpost, directing and redirecting attention and effort to vital points. Doing so involves clarifying to oneself what is at the core of what one aims to achieve in and through every aspect of one's work. An objective[10] is also something one aims to achieve but, in the terminology I use, it is a sub-purpose, something necessary to the purpose but not equal to it. For example, to increase church membership is an objective; to get people to live in Christian love with people in the Church and in the community is a purpose. The former is not a purpose because it is not the core of what the church wants to achieve. To achieve the church membership objective may or may not promote the overall purpose. It will only do so if, as the result of joining a church, people live in Christian love.

Similarly, to build a community centre is an objective; to help people differing widely in belief and culture to use the Centre and to love and care for each other is a purpose because it is about developing Christian attributes. The building of a community centre provides opportunities for people to meet; the way in which it is run and the effects, good or bad, that staff and members have upon one another are crucial to promoting the purpose. So, again, good working relationships are an objective, not a purpose.

A purpose stated in terms of helping people in a specific church and neighbourhood to love themselves, each other and God and to care for one another is more useful as a reference point than one stated in terms, say, of bringing in the Kingdom: it is useful because it is possible for most people to assess whether or not specific action in a given situation is likely to promote loving and caring relationships; the same people may make gross errors in assessing whether the action will bring in the Kingdom.

Purposes are formed within us by complex intellectual, moral, spiritual and intuitive processes.[11] Elliott Jaques says: "It is done by touch and feel, by intuition, by hunch, by guess, by flashes of insight".[12] It is a conviction about what is needed to improve things substantially. These purposes influence what we do. They are primary reference points. They are inseparable from us. They are buried deep within us. They are generally available for us as reference points only if we dig them out and define them. (Note that the task is to describe and define purposes that already exist: it is not to construct them, although once defined we may want to modify them.) People are generally helped to get at their purposes:

- by expressing their intuitions and gut feelings about what is needed;

- by differentiating between objectives and purposes through asking "why?" or "what for?" of each successive objective until the most useful formulation of purpose is reached;[13]

- by stating beliefs and purposes separately;

- by formulating statements which make clear that objectives are subordinate to purposes (this can be done by adding to a statement of objectives an "in order to" or "for" clause. It can also be done by adding to a statement of purpose a list of objectives, each one prefaced with "by" or "through". The latter I find particularly useful in sorting out objectives from purpose and in classifying them);

124

- by stating purpose in terms of:
  —people and their relationships rather than things and their relationships,
  —the human rather than the material,
  —personal rather than the impersonal attributes,
  —specific situations and people;
- by expressing purposes succinctly and plainly.

Our motivation is always mixed. Clarifying and working to our substantive purpose and noxiants helps us achieve our highest motives and to steer away from our lowest. These reference points, therefore, perform moral and spiritual functions as well as pragmatic ones.

b. Beliefs

Our belief systems are intricate and complex. They are rational and non-rational. Some of our beliefs are fine, noble and well thought out; others anything but. Consequently each of us operates out of a qualitative mix of beliefs as well as out of mixed motivation. Sometimes our beliefs are fixed, at other times they are in flux. At other times we cannot make up our minds whether to adopt beliefs about the essential goodness of people or their sinfulness and end up confusing ourselves by alternating between them. To complicate things further, our awareness of our beliefs and our ability to get in touch with them and to articulate them varies enormously. Some beliefs are located in our head, others in our heart or gut. Head beliefs are more public and easier to get at than those of the heart and the gut; head beliefs are better organized and more rational (or rationalized) than our heart and gut beliefs, which are personal and precious and which have more profound, pervasive and hidden effects upon our character and behaviour. This is discussed in Chapter 10.

Exploring all this is a privileged and fascinating occupation. Nevertheless, there are many problems in establishing reliable belief reference points. We need to resist the temptation to abandon the task: the rewards are great. *What is required is as honest a statement as possible of any beliefs upon which we believe we are operating in relation to a specific aspect of our work at a given time.* This focus makes the task more manageable. A statement of this kind is as good a reference point as it is possible to get, provided that the beliefs are stated, as a friend of mine, The Revd Dr Michael Bayley, is wont to say, "without reference to merit". They should not be edited simply to match standards of acceptability. To be true to ourselves and others and to be effective in our work and ministry, what we do together and separately must be authentic expressions of our individual and corporate beliefs. If they are not, we need to work at beliefs, thought and action until they are authentic expressions of what we are and want to be.

The case study in Chapter 2 showed just how important it was for the Church members, officers and teachers to state just what they believed about communion and to examine the problem in relation to those beliefs as well as in relation to their objective of making the children feel part of the family—much of the difficulty stemmed from treating this objective as a purpose. An ecumenical group of people with whom I worked on a good neighbour scheme were unable to clarify their *purposes* until they had defined the *beliefs* that motivated them.[14]

c. Resources

Basically, the resources required to do church and community work are people and their mental, nervous and spiritual energy, their time, equipment, plant and money. Making accurate estimates of the material resources needed is not too difficult. Estimating the resources of time available is also not too difficult whereas estimating that which will be needed is very difficult. Quantifying how much mental, nervous and spiritual energy is available and will be required is impossible. Nevertheless, it is necessary to make the best possible estimates of what is available and what might be required. For one thing it helps to make realistic plans and contracts. Another reason is that it reduces the dangers of people experiencing "burn-out"[15] through being over-taxed. Purposes to which people are highly committed induce what I understand some psychologists call "traction", i.e. the power to draw the various threads of individual and collective effort, energy and objectives together and to pull people along.[16] (Acute human and spiritual need also induces traction.) Traction can cause people who are highly committed to advancing their purpose to give time and energy they did not know they could find and which can take them beyond their reserves and strength. This can occur when things are going really well and people are carried along with the momentum and excitement. It can also occur when enormous effort is required to make very little progress or to hold the line. People who possess purposes ("my/our purpose") can be possessed and obsessed by them.

Beliefs drive people on. Purposes and needs and a sense of vocation induce traction. Christians are urged to give themselves unreservedly to the service of God, Church and world. No matter how long or hard people work, church and community work is never completed; there is always more to be done. (A discussion I had about the implications of this obvious fact with a very intelligent person helped him to find immediate release from grossly overworking. He realized that subconsciously he had been working on the assumption that if only he worked hard enough he could complete the work. What released him was the realization that he could complete *his* work, his contribution, but not all the work associated with his purposes; that was not his responsibility.) It is essential, therefore, to regulate the input of energy. Work aimed at promoting the well-being and development of others must also promote the well-being and development of the workers. Working to resources as well as to beliefs, purposes, need and vocation is one way of ensuring that this happens.

126

There are dangers, however, in regulating our input. The work requires the willing, costly and sacrificial giving and sharing of self. Doing that responsibly, we have to tread a narrow path bounded by reckless abandon on the one side and cool, calculated and careful giving on the other. It is hard to remain on that path. Pseudo-professionalism and over-concern for our own well-being take us to one side and obsessive and insatiable commitment to the other. Everything must be done to keep workers on the central path for their own good and that of the work in which they are engaged. Resources are a down-to-earth reminder that the work is infinite; workers are finite and so is the work they can do. Resources are a very important reference point.

d. Needs

Programmes of church and community work exist because they provide opportunities for multifarious human and spiritual needs to be met. On the one hand they exist to meet the needs of people for places to meet for diverse secular and religious activities and the needs for help, counselling and mutual support and many other things. On the other hand they exist to meet the needs organizations and their workers have for opportunities to pursue their purposes and to put their beliefs into practice. Some of these needs are healthy ones, others are not. Healthy and unhealthy needs of people, organizations and workers are key reference points: the former point to objectives; the latter to noxiants. Keeping them in mind and submitting them to critical analysis helps workers to get at substantive needs rather than superficial wants.

Generally speaking, careful attention is given to meeting the needs of the people whilst workers are left to see to their own needs. One reason for this is that workers tend to give themselves spontaneously, willingly and genuinely to the needs of others; another reason is that Christians have been encouraged to forget themselves and their needs and to deny and sacrifice themselves.

As we saw in the discussion about resources, workers' needs are important. Critical and compassionate attention must be given to them. The purposes of the Church require it: the Church exists for its non-members *and* for its workers and members. Self-interest requires it. Meeting workers' vocational needs is health-giving to them and to those they befriend and serve. Some workers may well be using, albeit unconsciously, programmes to "satisfy" unhealthy wants and needs such as a lust for power or desires to be the centre of attention. They require help. The purposes of the Church require that they be given the help that they need to develop for their own sake and also for the sake of the work in which they are engaged. Giving such help is a tricky work-cum-pastoral task generally best tackled in private through counselling and consultancy.

One of the effects of taking such needs seriously is that workers and people attend to human and religious needs at a progressively deeper level—they address "real needs", which they are constantly seeking to do. Clearly not all the needs of the workers are of an acute kind. More of them than ever before are now being met through assessment, appraisal, counselling, consulting and in-service training schemes. Most of the needs can go on the development agenda. Discussions I had with one group of lay workers deeply involved in the organization of both church services and church social work identified three needs.

The first, and most important, was to experience for themselves the successful application of Christian teaching to social situations. They had heard so much from the pulpit about how it does work and seen so little evidence of its doing so in their neighbourhood. Second, they wanted opportunities to go to church without having any jobs to do so that they could give themselves to worship and prayer. Third, they wanted to enjoy each others' company socially.

Setting out all the needs—those of people and those of the organizations and their workers that aim to see that these are met—helps to tackle the tricky business of meeting all the needs concurrently through church and community work programmes. Focusing predominantly, if not exclusively, on the needs of the people out there engenders a patronizing approach. Unavoidably it gives the impression that the workers are people without needs engaged in helping those who have them. Trying to equalize things by saying that the work helps to meet the needs of the workers can cause people to feel they are being "used" for purposes to which they do not subscribe. The only way in which I know how to pursue both ways concurrently is through egalitarian programmes of inter-related development of all the people and secular and religious organizations concerned.[17]

3. Independent Reference Points

People who follow the procedures I have described are taking a positive grip on their own situation and their environment. They are doing everything they can to direct, control and shape their affairs from within themselves in accord with their ideas rather than being formed and directed from without by other agents according to their purposes and beliefs, although they will, of course, be influenced by them. Inasmuch as they succeed they are able to be autonomous and act accordingly. (They are in fact "autogenic" rather than "allogenic".[18]) By defining their own reference points, they are constructing the context within which they are going to think and work and which they have organized in such a way that will impinge upon them, their thinking and their action.[19] Clearly there are dangers in all this. For instance, individuals, groups, organizations and churches can end up in a little world of their own. They can fall victim to what has been described as "group think".[20] They can be locked in their own closed thinking circuits.[21] Being alert to this very real danger is one way of obviating it. Others are discussed below.

Such undesirable things are less likely to happen when as many people as possible who differ significantly are using procedures such as the ones I have described to work through things together at local level (within and between churches of different denominations, in community groups and other

128

organizations) and at regional and national levels. They are even less likely to happen when people from local, regional and national "domains" are working through things together. Overall development which is contextually located depends upon this kind of critical thought/action in all these domains and between them. Progress is being made in promoting critical and open thought within and between these domains: the latter is much more difficult than the former.[22] Open participation in collective thinking allows different patterns of thought and reference points to interact and new patterns to be formed. (This can also happen when individuals and groups work with consultants and facilitators.) It enhances the contextual awareness of *all* concerned and helps them, separately and together, to have the most profound effect upon their context.

Church and community development equips people to engage in, and to promote, this kind of open participation: its philosophy and theology argues for it and its approaches and methods facilitate it. I have illustrated this in Part One, especially in Chapters 3 and 4.

Anything, in fact, that gets people comparing and contrasting their own thinking openly with that of others is to be welcomed, provided that it does not paralyse them. There are infinite possibilities of doing this through books, the media, worship, Bible study, house groups, etc.

Two things I wish to mention here. One is worship. Over and again during the past twenty years, as I have struggled to explore this new field of work, worship, and particularly the eucharist, has helped me to put it in a wider context. In that environment I have faced and explored issues I could not have done in other settings. I much appreciate Robin Green's suggestion that:

Liturgy, which is the vehicle through which worship is expressed, creates an environment in which human beings confront those sides of themselves which under normal circumstances they dare not face.[23]

The second thing I wish to mention is the important function that churches can perform by offering an overall reference framework which can act as a catalyst to our own. An example of this which helped me greatly was a statement in the 1986 Methodist Conference Agenda.[24] It was entitled "A Context for Policy Decisions". It had been devised to help the President's Council to review connexional policy with particular regard to the uses to which we put our limited resources at a time when new opportunities and needs are stimulating a desire to respond in new ways. The Revd Brian Beck, the author of the statement, set out the reference points as "nine obligations which we must seek to fulfil. They are the dimensions within which we have to live. They are not set out in any particular order (as in the three-dimensional world in which we all live, all three dimensions are equally important, whatever the order in which we speak of them) and they are not numbered for that reason." I paraphrase the obligations because they are such a good example of the way in which we can help people to reconsider their own reference frameworks. The obligations are:

— A deeper rooting of the life of the Church. (Several concerns come together here: the quality of worship, including the use of the arts, the need for better theological knowledge and understanding, and a wider concern for and fostering of spirituality.)

— To develop and pursue the mission of the Church, in its many forms, evangelistic and socio-political.

— To take seriously the intellectual encounter with our society. (The engagement is in several theatres: scientific/technological, political/economic, religious/theological, in the encounter with other faiths and moralities.)

— The discernment, development and deployment of the gifts of the whole people of God.

— To ensure that we do not allow two experiences of disappointment in ecumenical negotiations ... to deflect us from our commitment to the ecumenical movement, co-operation with other churches, and ultimately (in whatever form) the reintegration of a divided Church.

— To ensure that we do not allow the natural insularity of the British Islanders to blinker us to our membership in the world church, with the obligations and potential which that brings.

— Priority is to be given to the poor.

— Priortiy is to be given to those activities which have a long-term rather than a short-term application.

— We must ensure that our procedures acquire enough flexibility to enable changes to be agreed and take place rapidly, and local adaptations to be encouraged.

These obligations have helped me. It is not difficult to see how they can be used to check and evaluate our plans for action and our reference frameworks.

The possibility of closed-circuit thinking cannot be entirely avoided. We select our circles of influence and we have a propensity to welcome that which confirms our thinking and resist that which challenges and contradicts it. But we can reduce the dangers of our thinking becoming parochial and seriously dysfunctional by comparing our reference points with those formed in environments other than those in which ours were formed. This induces "double loop learning" which enables us "to take a double look" at things and to question the relevance of our operating norms.[25] It also helps us to relate our work to the wider context of thought and need.

4. Articulating Learning

"What are we learning?" This question can be asked at any stage of the process.

It never fails to evoke significant responses—frequently unexpected, always productive. There is an example of its effectiveness in the study of the problem on failure in Chapter 2. Spontaneously, the whole group knew what they had to do to tackle this problem when I asked them what they were learning: "We must get this kind of discussion going amongst the people with whom we work!"

I use the question frequently, especially when I and those with whom I am working are stuck or struggling with a bad experience. Addressing it causes us to look at whatever we have been doing from a different angle. It distances us from direct engagement with the subject-matter and gives us a new perspective on it and our activity in relation to it. The analogy that comes to mind is of craftsmen or artists standing back from whatever they are doing, walking around it and looking at it first from this position and then from that. Viewing their work in this way helps them to assess it and to decide what, if anything, now needs to be done. Thus informed, they can return to close engagement with their material. Asking this question, therefore, frees people to change their mental and emotional perspective—a coffee break can, of course, have the same effect. It stimulates lateral thinking, it gets people to articulate feelings and part-formed thoughts generated by the activity. Establishing what we have learnt from a particular experience—and there is always something to be learnt—adds value to it. In fact, it can salvage bad experiences. It is a way of building up our own practice theory. It helps us to rise above circumstances.

Also, by directing attention to what we are learning about doing God's will in the church and in society, it reinforces the vocational education model upon which the approach advocated in this book is based. Were it based upon a therapeutic model, the question would be, "Are you feeling better?" Of course, this could well be a subordinate question, but the primary issue in this context is about what we are learning about ourselves as workers and the work in which we are engaged.

5. Meditation, Reflection and Prayer

As I said earlier, this process is most effective when it is used in close association with meditation, reflection and prayer. They are different but complementary activities. Analysis and design are in the active mood and mode of being; they involve the disciplined application of mind, inspiration and heart to the job of working things out systematically; they are carried out by logical dialogues informed by intuitions. Reflection is in a different mood and mode. It involves concentrating and waiting upon things meditatively, "listening" to what they might say. Prayer is a dialogue with God about things. Meditation, reflection and prayer allow the free association of mind and heart with all that is happening in the widest possible context. These different activities draw and feed upon one another. Working at things systematically and praying about them in a context of pastoral care integrates the activities, creates a spirituality of its own, generates and releases energy and enables people to work creatively for human and spiritual development.

6. Evaluation

The processes I am describing enable people to evaluate past experience through analysing it in relation to a cluster of reference points and through reflecting and meditating upon it and praying about it. Similarly, they enable workers to evaluate their ideas for future action. At the same time they encourage people to articulate what they are learning and thus to evaluate the processes in which they are engaged. The result is that continuous assessment is written deep into the analysis and design of church and community work. Thus evaluation is an integral part of the process of thinking things through, not simply a stage in it. Consequently wherever, whenever and however people use this schema they have to be able to handle continuous feedback. I consider that later.

Other ways of evaluating can complement that which is embedded in the analysis and design of work programmes. That is why in Figure 5:2 I have shown evaluation following through the action. Various systems are used to evaluate different kinds of change.[26] The one I use involves assessing change in relation to objectives and purposes - I call it a "directional analysis of change". And I use "behavioural indicators" to assess changes in things such as commitment which cannot be directly observed or measured. To pursue this further would be to go beyond the scope of this book.

II. USING THE SCHEMA

So far in this chapter we have presented a conceptual framework, a schema, for analysing and designing church and community development work and have explored some of the things involved in using various aspects of it. Now we turn to using the schema to promote human and spiritual development.

This schema can be used by individuals on their own to help them to think through their work. No area of work is too small or too large for these analytical methods. Colleagues, teams and groups can also use it. Workers and consultants, too, can use it to help individuals, groups, churches and organizations to think about and to plan their work. Clearly there are significant differences in using the schema in these different ways and settings. Those will be considered later. Here we will concentrate on things to be taken into account in using the schema in any way whatsoever.

1. An Art and a Craft

Presenting the schema in an orderly way as we have done could mislead people into thinking that they have to use it, privately or with others, in a rather mechanical and inflexible manner in order to put their thinking and that of others into precisely the same tidy shape. That is not the aim. The intention is that the schema will help people to organize their thoughts and ideas about themselves as workers and about their work in ways which will enable *them* to make *their* best contributions in *their* situations. Doing that involves promoting, within workers in relation to their work, creative interplay between the schema and

- the ways in which the people concerned naturally and normally think about things;
- the thoughts and feelings that the people have about themselves as workers and their work;
- the subject-matter under consideration.

The potential for variation in each of these three factors is enormous and the permutations of them are infinite. People, for instance, think in different ways and at different speeds. Many things alter the tempo and rhythm of thought. Some people want to think from the abstract to the concrete whilst others are only comfortable when discussion is earthed in actual situations. Some people want to work through things systematically, whilst others like to move at will or whim from one topic to another. Turning to the second factor, people may be preoccupied with a particular difficulty or an idea or something they want to do. And the emotional investment that people have in the subjects under discussion will vary enormously. Some will be very clear, others confused. Similarly, the subject-matter could vary enormously in content and complexity.

Clearly, whether we are using the schema on our own or with others, promoting creative interplay between so many human factors, subtly different and bewilderingly complex, is an art or a craft. It calls for self-knowledge, skills in working on our own and with ourselves and others, sensitivity to thoughts, feelings and situations, and the ability to choose appropriate ways of using the schema. Sometimes, for example, it is right to go through the eight stages systematically, or versions of it, as we did in the case study and the situational analysis (Chapters 1 and 3). But even then it is essential to have the freedom to explore, to revisit previous stages and to visit stages not yet reached. At other times it is necessary to start with the things with which we are preoccupied or which we fear: beliefs or action plans for example. Then, from that point, to work backwards and forwards through the stages until all the necessary analytical and design work has been completed. Or, again, when working with others, it may be necessary to get people to work at stages they are neglecting or avoiding.

Then there are other choices, whether one is working systematically through the stages or in a much more discursive way. These concern methods. When working on a development agenda, for example, it might be appropriate to do some hard disciplined thinking about the alternatives and their respective advantages and disadvantages as a prelude to making decisions. On the other hand, it might be much more creative to meditate or reflect or pray or state what is being learnt about making development agendas.

Then there is the choice of perspective from which to do the analytical work. Sometimes it is right to focus on situations, problems and cases in relation to one's own reference points. At other times it is right to consider one's own reference points in relation to a situation and/or independent reference points and set the work in a wider context. Choosing the most helpful perspective from which to analyse and design, selecting aspects of the schema and using them in the most creative way, is a matter of judgement, skill and style calling for the artistry of the craftsman in sculpting church and community work, the analytical rigour of the scientist and the systematic approach of the technician.

2. Working to the Whole and the Parts

The craft, therefore, requires the ability to work at each stage separately and to the whole process. Each stage can result in a completed piece of potentially useful work: a building block. A sound design, for example, is a considerable achievement even if it is not deployed for some considerable time. The value, veracity and viability of the product of one stage depends upon the reliability of the stages that have preceded it: decisions depend upon planning, planning upon designs and design upon analysis. Error at one stage flaws the next. Fortunately the insights gained from a later stage often reveal errors in an earlier one. But this does not always happen.

One of the ways of avoiding the cumulative effect of error is to review periodically the stages covered in relation to each other by summarizing what has emerged from them and looking carefully at the connections between them. Contrasting and comparing stages can show whether or not the stages are building upon each other in the most constructive way. Using the schema, therefore, involves changing perspectives between attending to the stages of the process and to the process as a whole and focusing variously on the people, their situations, the schema and the interaction between them.

3. The Dynamic

Working for development with people in church and community is as complicated, messy and difficult a business as it is exciting and absorbing. So is thinking about it. The processes we are discussing help people to think about their work and to go about it in a more orderly and analytical way. They are tidy tools to work on untidy material. Concentrating on the tidy tools could give false impressions: that using the tools is as tidy as the tools themselves; that the subject-matter is more tidy than it is; that the thinking will be functional only if it is as tidy as the layout of the process. The aim is to get and maintain the clarity of thought which gives life to the dynamic of creative activity within the people concerned. A bit of tidying up, to continue the metaphor, can sometimes do this better than a thorough spring-clean. It is a matter of doing the amount of thinking and clarifying with which people can cope; no more and no less.

It is easy enough to indicate the untidiness and complexity of the thinking process but I find it impossible to model it in still pictures and diagrams. For instance, thinking about an old experience is a new experience which can include new experiences of the original experience. As we think, act and evaluate, we continuously look back to former experiences to bring forward anything of use in the present which we can use in the future. "Layering" is one way of describing the process of adding to previous experiences new layers of analytical and evaluative thought about them which contribute to an evolving understanding and interpretation of them. This happens in the use of the processes we are considering. The linearity of the diagram denies it. The "pastoral spiral" which some people prefer gets a little nearer to it but misses dimensions of my diagram.

Another metaphor, the incoming tide, helps me to represent rhythms in the process. Withdrawing from the action to think, plan and evaluate is like the ebb of the tide. It enables workers to gather themselves for the next wave of forward movement. Action, like the tide, sometimes moves gently forward whilst at other times it surges. Some ground gives way quickly to the incoming tide, some resists it. What is important is that the action tide is incoming. It is not always easy to discern whether tides are coming in or going out when they are on the turn. In human and spiritual affairs the eddies, currents and endless to and fro movements of human beings in thought and action often make it difficult to determine the flow of things.

Several pictures of the processes of moving from experience to creative action are emerging. One picture portrays it in eight carefully differentiated and inter-related steps. Another shows the movement of human thought from the present to the past, backwards and forwards to the future which forms new layers to old experiences and is ever generating new experiences. Yet another shows it to be tidal. Certainly it has a pulse. These pictures are complementary. Together they prevent the process being seen as either formless or as an inflexible, closed, mechanical system. It is living and vital, at its most effective when it resonates with the rhythms of thought and action of people and enhances their creative dynamic.[27]

4. Using it with Other People

Basically there are two ways of using this process when working with other people. The first is to lead them through it stage by stage in a way which seems

135

appropriate to the leader or worker. The schema as a whole is not disclosed at the outset: the leader uses it as a personal mental map. The second is to get the commitment of those involved to the process from the outset by describing it to them and adapting or adopting it. The first is to be preferred when, for example, people are likely to be put off or overwhelmed by the presentation of all the stages. The second is to be preferred whenever possible because all those involved have opportunities to contribute to managing the process and this, in turn, maximizes effectiveness and learning. Shared understanding of the process engenders discipline amongst the participants and gives them freedom; the discipline to follow the process and to see that all necessary stages are covered; and the freedom to modify it as required.

5. The Human Factor

Workers and people are the make-and-break factor in these processes of thoughtful action. The processes will only work if they have the personal resources and the skills and the will to use them. The human factor is critical. Three aspects of this are considered in this section.

a. Workers as their own Analytical Instruments[28]

The processes work in and through the people who engage in them: the workers. They provide the data from their observations. Everything, including the perspectives of others, is processed through their minds, hearts and souls. The principal axis of the process is their perspective. Much vital data is provided from their experiences of the situation upon which they are working and what other people think and feel. Other data comes from research, surveys, published papers, etc. They interpret their own data and that of others. The information they work on is variously about places, buildings, details of events, money; experiences of people and God; ideas and concepts, etc. They use their beliefs and noxiants as reference points and they assess resources and needs. The human factor dominates. Human error is omnipresent. Workers are their own analytical, design, decision-making and acting instruments.

Most of their information comes through the workers' own observations as participants in their working situations. Participant observation[29] is the principal research tool used in community studies, anthropology and action-research. (The processes described in this section are action-reflection-action procedures and sequences which have much in common with action-research.) Members of these disciplines have put an enormous amount of effort into studying the theory and practice of participant observation and experimenting with its use in order to make it as reliable an instrument as possible. "Participant observation" has, in fact, become a technical term for all that is involved in this way of collecting and correcting data which helps towards a better understanding of human situations.

All of us participate and observe. We cannot help doing so. What I have learnt about "participant observation" from the three disciplines mentioned above has enriched my ministry. It has helped me to be much more effective as a minister in my work with people in church and community. It has helped me to take better account of the effects that my part in the scheme of things and the nature of my participation have upon my observations. (The kind of participation varies greatly from active leadership to a passive presence.) It has helped me to take into account ways in which I distort data and deceive myself. It has helped me to be aware of the ways in which data is distorted by misinformation, evasions, lies and "fronts" and the need to correct it. It has helped me to see the value of recording what I have seen and thought. The enormous value of participant observation is that it enables workers to study human situations from within, the changes and developments as they occur, the sequence of events which lead to changes for the better and worse, and the causes of change.

When working with people for human and spiritual development, some people hesitate about using anything that smacks of a scientific method. They feel that "studying people" with whom they are working in loving, caring relationships can affect their relationships with them adversely. I agree, but the processes described in this book are designed for workers and people, separately and together, *to study the work in which they are engaged.* People, of course, are involved in the work and processes but the emphasis is on thinking through critical aspects of our vocational work or apostolate in order that we may do it more effectively and with growing satisfaction.

This is not the place to explore this subject further. I have described elsewhere ways in which this method helped a group of ordinary people to solve problems connected with violent behaviour which had vandalized and closed our youth club.[30] Also some books are listed in the notes for those who would like to pursue this matter further.[31]

b. Feelings and Emotions

Part One illustrates how feelings and emotions of varying kinds are inextricably intertwined with ideas, thoughts, beliefs and concepts in the lives and working relationships of church and community workers. They can range from depression to excited anticipation. Generally speaking, problems and cases are associated with a sense of failure and all the pain that goes with it. Examining what has happened probes sensitive wounds. Workers can experience frustration because they sense opportunities have been missed and that they have lost the initiative. Not surprisingly, they tend to be defensive and apprehensive because they know healing will hurt and that there could be hurt without healing.

Quite different emotions are commonly associated with new projects. Workers are excited about the possibilities and promise of new beginnings, the challenge of exploring the unknown and of creating something. Getting people to take a hard look at difficulties they had not previously seen in a project that they are on fire about can all too easily dampen their enthusiasm and weaken their will to continue with the project. Working to feelings and within the emotional competence of people, therefore, is as necessary as working to thoughts and their intellectual competence. People simply cannot think straight when they are out of their emotional depth. Defensiveness prevents creative thought. Panic is the end of rational thought.

A vital question for workers, co-workers and consultants is implicit in all this: what helps people to work at feelings and to develop emotional competence? I venture the following suggestions, based on the things which I have found help the negative feelings of people to give way to positive ones and which enhance their emotional involvement in their work.

- Offer and honour confidentiality.

- Establish an understanding with the people about what they require of you should their feelings take over.

- Acknowledge and accept feelings of any kind as a legitimate part of the reality of the work situation but avoid inflaming them.

- Work to feelings and thoughts. (One way of doing this is to ask people "How do you feel?" as well as "What do you think?" Another way is to ask if any feelings are inhibiting their participation.)

- Work with people on their feelings with empathy but non-emotively. (At times I have found myself adding my feelings about, say, the injustice experienced by someone, to theirs and using emotive language. Generally speaking, this does not help, whereas controlled emotional involvement does.)

- Work at feelings specifically and with objectivity. (Working at feelings in relation to specific situations, people and events using expressive but non-emotive language helps to do this.)

- Help people to express feelings that they need to make explicit and help them guard against the danger of saying things publicly that they will subsequently regret having said. (Sharing thoughts and feelings is always a risky business. One of the things I do when I think people are about to take too big a risk is to hold them back for a moment and ask them to consider whether they need to share whatever is about to come.)

- Check out and take seriously how people feel about doing things. (Sometimes people cannot enter into a discussion about something because they cannot see how it can be done or they cannot see themselves doing it. It happens to a colleague of mine. They need some idea of how the thing might be done before they can discuss whether it should be done.)

- Plan for affective involvement.

138

Working with people affectively in these ways gives them emotional confidence, develops work programmes with which they are most likely to be able to cope and gradually extends their emotional competence.

c. Handling Feedback

In addition to the technical and conceptual skills required, the ability of people to participate creatively in the processess described in this chapter depends upon their capacity to handle positive and negative feedback constructively. They are likely to experience both kinds of feedback. My experience has been that, overall, the effect of working through the process is invariably positive: facing up to and working through negative feedback is releasing and renewing; moving from designing and planning can turn any disappointment experienced in the analysis to the hope and expectation that comes from new plans and knowing just what to do. Part One illustrates this. The objective of this section is quite specific: it is to bring this important but often neglected aspect of the process into full view in order to encourage and help people to prepare themselves for it in advance. As people think their way through these processes, feedback can come to them in four different ways: they will certainly experience the first and probably the others as well.

Self-feedback. This feedback is the inner response we experience when we are involved in some activity or other in private or in public or when we are reflecting on it. We feel whether things are going well or badly. It is immediate, unbidden and can be difficult to control. It is the response of our whole being to whatever is happening. Every part of us is affected by our feelings, our mood, our composure and our energy level. It can variously freeze or free us; it can affirm, confirm, confound, confuse and embarrass us. It changes our state of mind and being and our ability to think and act. Some of the worst experiences of negative self-feedback come when least expected and consequently are more devastating. It must be said that self-feedback is not an infallible or even reliable guide to our performance as experienced by others even though it is often a good indicator of what is happening and of our effectiveness. Our poise, well-being and performance depend upon being able to handle, in public and private, a range of feedback from that which flatters to that which devastates.

Unsolicited feedback from others. The supportive and evaluative value of unsolicited and other forms of feedback is dependent upon the perceived motives, insights and sincerity of those who give it. It can be the expression of joy at some success or support at a time of failure or loss. It can be a caring challenge. On the other hand, it can be an attempt to hurt or to curry favour. We need to be able to discern feedback that must be taken seriously.

Casually solicited feedback. More often than not it is when we are feeling battered or uncertain that we solicit feedback casually. Loaded rather than unloaded questions come more easily to our lips under such circumstances. We are more likely to say, "I did all right in that discussion, didn't I?" than "Please give me you honest opinion of my performance in that discussion". It is more difficult to give an honest answer to the first because the request is for affirmative support rather than an assessment.

Serious attempts to get reliable feedback. Various methods of evaluation and survey can be used to get reliable feedback. As we have noted, the process described here is evaluative.

Possible aids to handling feedback. What will help us to handle feedback especially that which hurts, deflates and erodes confidence? Answering that question helps us to prepare to tackle the process and the feedback openly and more confidently. Church and community workers with whom I have discussed this have found one or other of the following things have helped them.

(i) The Importance of Processing Feedback. It is important to work on the basis that the quality of the human processing of feedback, not the nature or quality of the feedback, determines the substantive long-term effects that it has upon those who receive it and those with whom they work. Even though research shows that the most common result is that success leads to greater efforts and failure to less,[32] the reverse does happen: "success can lead to taking things easy and failure to increased effort".[33] Success can also lead to conceit. Research also shows that "those high in achievement motivation appear to be stimulated to greater efforts by both success and failure".[34] This underlines the enormous importance of the personal preparation to receive feedback and guidelines for processing it.

(ii) Personal Preparation for Feedback. Some questions help to prepare to receive and work on feedback that comes in all four ways:

- What kind of good and bad inner responses and reactions do you customarily make when you receive feedback that is positive/negative?
- What responses do those with whom you work often make and what effects does that have upon you?
- What would you have to do in order to improve the way in which you process and use feedback?
- What kind(s) of feedback do you need from whom or what?
- Why do you need it?
- Are there any dangers in trying to get it?
- How can you get and receive it?

140

(iii) Guidelines to Processing Feedback. Remain critically open to negative and positive feedback; don't dismiss or quench it by denigrating the sources. In relation to feedback, however, the source may be wrong and you may be right. Several things can help:

- Make it usable and manageable by:
  —collating and condensing it to avoid the problems of feedback overload;
  —trying to de-personalize and objectify it possibly by writing it down, or talking to someone else about it. Look at it from different perspectives. Feelings are facts but try to avoid being preoccupied with them. Delay reaction when possible.

- Determine quite specifically to what the feedback properly relates: to you? your work? your beliefs/purposes? your organization? Or is it a projection of a problem that others have?

- Decide whether or not anything can be done about it and whether it is worthy of serious attention.

- Try to keep things in proportion by counter-balancing positive with negative feedback and vice versa.

- Avoid confusing qualitative with quantative feedback: one person may be right and the rest wrong and vice versa; the person who makes most noise may or may not be right!

- Evaluate feedback and determine its implications in relation to beliefs, purposes, needs, resources and your personal performance (not only in relation to yourself) *and* in relation to what you know of its source.

- Whenever possible seek help and support, not just one or the other.

- Think, feel and pray things through.

6. Using Appropriate Modes

Successful use of these systematic thinking procedures depends to a considerable extent upon selecting a mode of the process most appropriate to the people concerned and the task in which they are engaged. This variously involves *translating* the description of the stages and procedures into a language understood by and acceptable to those involved; *choosing* an appropriate mode; *designing* new modes when the available ones are not suitable; and *structuring* procedures to fit people and their circumstances. This is true whether we are working on our own or with others.

Translating. The language used here to describe the process is appropriate to those who are comfortable with formal and slightly technical language. I use it with some, but by no means all groups. Some people, for instance, I encourage to work through the process by using two groups of questions. The first is about reference points: What do you want to do? (purpose); What don't you want to happen? (noxiants); Why? (beliefs); What are your resources? The second group is: What is the situation like? What changes would you like to see? What works and doesn't work? Why? What needs to be done? How can these things be done? How will we know when we have done them satisfactorily? What has to be done and who is going to do what? People and their situation would determine the order in which these questions would be put. Translating the terms into appropriate language is vitally important.

Choosing. So far we have described the generic process and four modes of it related to working on problems, cases, situations and projects. The stages and sequences of the generic process are directly useful to help people think through things. I have used it in this way on a wide range of my own work and that of others. One example is work that I did over a period of two years with a large ecumenical team. We agreed the process. They wrote papers depicting the situation as they saw it and as they would prefer it. I collected their replies and drew out critical features. We gave a day to discussing it and analysing the situation and to establishing the development agenda. Some of the work on this agenda the team carried out, some of it we did together. I have worked through the same process with many individuals and groups in two hours or so.

Sometimes the mode is appropriately self-selecting through the focus of people's attention on a problem, a case, a situation, a project or a whole programme of work. Generally speaking the problem and case-study methods are apposite when they can be properly considered without surveying the situation as a whole. Situational and longitudinal studies of projects and programmes are necessary when overviews of the inter-related parts are required. Studying problems and cases can lead to, or clear the way for, situational and longitudinal studies. Studies of situations, projects and programmes can identify key problems and cases that would not have been identified by working on the cases and problems initially presented by people. Modes are not always self-selecting so it is prudent to check out which is appropriate.

One of the issues is whether to start with problems and cases or situations. A way to check this is to ask at an early stage whether people experience this kind of problem or case frequently. If not, the problem or case mode is probably appropriate. If they do, then it may be that there is in the people themselves, or in the way in which they work, or in the situation, a more basic cause of the difficulties. The nature of those difficulties/issues will indicate the appropriate mode.

Designing. Tailor-made modes have to be designed if neither the generic process nor the four modes is suitable. (There is, of course, considerable scope

142

for adaptation in all the given modes.) Designing appropriate modes is a fascinating and fulfilling occupation. A project upon which I worked illustrates this process.[35] It was entitled "Relationships in Mission". The aim was to promote deeper levels of interdependence and mutuality in the relationships between the Overseas Division of the Methodist Church (MCOD) and Methodist Churches in West Africa.

Three consultations were held between MCOD and the Methodist Churches in Sierra Leone (1984), Ghana (1985) and Nigeria (1986). The facilitating structure for these consultations was an application of the basic principles and processes we are considering. During the course of a week we worked through a seven-stage process: agreement about objectives for the consultation (reference points); establishing profiles of the churches (situations as they were); agreeing a programme of work to be done on issues of mutual concern during the consultation (development agenda); working on the agreed tasks in separate groups (designing programmes); sharing findings and analysing and reflecting on what was being learnt about being together in the Kingdom of God (theological reflection); ensuring that the consultations flowed into the life and work of the churches (putting ideas to work); and preparing and agreeing a report during the consultation (recording). There were three core strands to the process: theology, relationships and practicalities, including finance (key reference points). Versions of the chart in Figure 5:3 were used to explain and promote the consultative processes, which were set in a prayerful context.

Structuring. People not only differ considerably in their ability and willingness to think systematically but they are more capable of doing so in some circumstances rather than in others. Helping people, therefore, to work through things as thoroughly as they are able—and that is the aim, not working slavishly through a process in a doctrinaire way—involves finding structures which fit them, their mood and circumstances. Both over- and under-structuring can inhibit thought. Frequently I have had the experience of people saying in a group that they feel inhibited from contributing something they feel to be relevant because it does not fit into the pattern that is emerging. Taking such incidents seriously invariably leads to a revision of the process, to a correction of the structures and to new patterns of creative thought. Another frequent experience is of people saying things like, "I am lost," "I do not know where we are going," "I just cannot see where that fits." This can be an indication of lack of structure or the failure to build up the unfolding pattern of thought so that everyone can see how things fit and do not fit together. One of my reflex actions to such situations is to *summarize*—I do it whenever I get lost or stuck in working things out on my own or with other people. Summarizing is one of my most useful tools. It gathers up the thinking, and gives us a chance to take hold of it together and decide just what we must do next. We are most likely to get the structuring right if we:

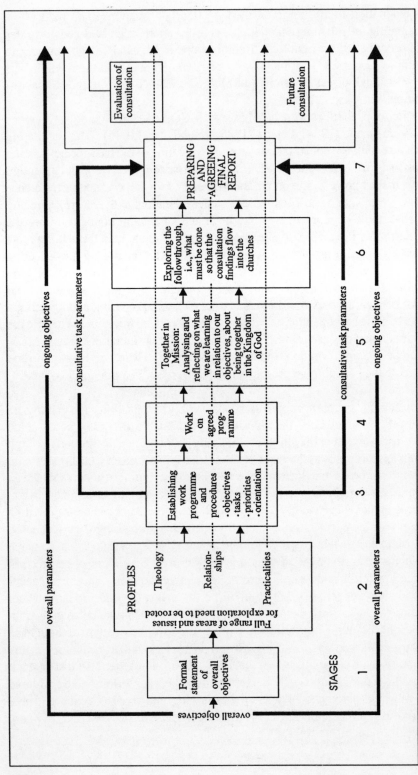

FIGURE 5:3. PROCESSES EMPLOYED DURING THE "RELATIONSHIPS IN MISSION" CONSULTATION

- have assimilated the essentials of the processes so that they are a natural part of the way in which we ourselves work at things;

- tailor structures to people rather than people to structures;

- work to the people, their thinking rhythms and their situation; (This is no easy thing when working with people who differ significantly, as I invariably do. I try not to leave anyone behind: working to those who can verbalize their thoughts most readily marginalizes the others and their contributions—and the best thoughts do not always come from the quickest thinkers! I find that this generates trust and mutual respect and understanding of each other's thought-processes. As trust and respect grow, people think together more deeply and more quickly. This does not, of course, preclude comparatively fast-flowing conversations between two or three people which others pick up in subsequent discussions and from which they learn.)

- stretch but do not overstretch people;

- keep a weather eye open for indicators that processes and structures are impeding thought; (Some indicators have been mentioned. Others are: the mechanical or/and desultory application of the processes; lack of creativity; the loss of energy; people not applying themselves; boredom.)

- check out from time to time whether or not people are happy with the way of working; (This can be done with a light touch. It does not have to be a ponderous evaluation!)

- strike a working balance between competing objectives. (There are several competing objectives in this kind of work related to: making critical decisions when time for thought is seriously limited; involving as many people as possible in the decisions and getting as many insights as possible; helping people to learn how to work things out more thoroughly.)

Such approaches to structuring formal and informal discussions help people to learn together as they work together. They give people clues about ways of promoting more creative thought through the informal conversations and gossip which are important parts of the fabric of human life. The grapevine and networks carry much of the traffic that promotes or undermines human well-being and development.[36]

All this is highly pertinent to an important issue in community development highlighted by Professor Roland Warren. He suggests that community development can be "seen as a process of converting the community or parts of it into a formal organization for problem-solving and action purposes".[37] One effect of this is that it converts the much-valued *gemeinschaft** (natural

---

**gemeinschaft* has three central aspects: "blood, place (land) and mind, with their sociological consequents of kinship, neighbourhood and friendship".[38] It is based on community sentiment, customs, commonly accepted norms and shared institutions and values.

community) to *gesellschaft** (organized society).

It has been commonly thought that the latter destroys the former. In part this is the case but more recent research demonstrates that they co-exist. The growth of *gesellschaft* does, in fact, lead to the growth of *gemeinschaft* as people seek ways of compensating for living in urban society by generating "community". However this might be, there is the possibility of community development that seeks to promote *gemeinschaft* actually converting parts of the community into *gesellschaft*-like structures and methods. This tricky issue from community development resonates with the problem of over-structuring analytical and design processes which we have just discussed.

7. Subject-Matter

These processes are used on various kinds of subject-matter: the actualities of working situations presented by the workers; what the workers think and feel about the situations; the beliefs, purposes, hopes, fears and aspirations of the workers; the understanding and knowledge derived from many sources that the workers have about themselves, other human beings and church and society. The processes are designed to help workers to gather this information; to shape and order it so that it is most readily available and useful; to supplement it; and then to work on it so that it is used in relation to the purposes of the workers.

In this way much complex information can be brought into consciousness. At times workers can manage to use it creatively with the help of the processes without too much difficulty. At other times the difficulties of handling it are further complicated by the cloud of unknowing that surrounds us when we are working with people: always there are so many things it would help us to know about what people really think and feel and how they will respond to this or that.

And there is another difficulty. On all sides the subject-matter opens out on to the disciplines of the social and behavioural sciences and theology and their endless literature. Seeking help from these disciplines in relation to specific work situations takes us into the complexities and contradictions of these disciplines. Not surprisingly, people stick to well-worn traditions and their habitual ways of working at things and are wary of new ideas! So much information can be overwhelming and intimidating. Several things can help, although the inherent difficulties do not go away.

First, my experience is that for the main part people, especially pairs and small groups, can be very creative when they work at the information and the knowledge that they already have in the ways I have described. The introduction of the process greatly enhances the use to which they put whatever knowledge and information they have. This is good because more often than not they simply have to get on with things and have not time to do any research.

---

gesellschaft "refers to the large-scale, impersonal and contractual ties that were seen by nineteenth-century sociologists to be on the increase at the expense of *gemeinschaft*".[39]

Second, when further information is needed the processes help to determine what is required.[40]

Third, to be most effective I need to work within my own discipline and to concentrate on my own work situation, paying particular attention to the interfaces between my situation and the contextual issues and between my discipline and that of others. Attention to those interfaces enables me to read off the implications of issues and other disciplines for my work and situations—and this, in turn, informs others working on the issues and in other disciplines. I have illustrated this later in this chapter from some work I did in Ireland.

This does not preclude my making excursions into other disciplines or working on critical contextual issues. On the contrary; it gives me a secure situational and professional base from which to make such excursions and many advantages accrue from doing so. For instance, I brought to the worked examples in Part One my experience and research into church and community development. But there are many difficulties and dangers in making these excursions apart from finding the time and the energy and selecting promising areas. There is the sheer number of disciplines that have so much to offer to church and community work through their study of things such as human and spiritual development, churches, organizations, communities and the ways of working with them. And one thing leads to another: I find community development useful and that takes me into adult education, community studies, anthropology, ethnography, social psychology, urban sociology.... All yielding useful information—and this is only one cluster of relevant subjects. Quite irrationally, I find myself feeling I must master these subjects. I get demoralized because I cannot do so. It is precisely at this point that the orientation described at the beginning of this paragraph helps me. My objective is not to master but to forage: to search for things which, once integrated into my own discipline (that of a Methodist minister engaged in church and community development work), will enhance my ability to do my work in my situation. So, in my foraging two important reference points—professional discipline and work situation—help me to find my way around the complexities of these disciplines and similarly around the complexities of the contextual issues.

A fourth thing that helps me is the realization that the substantive contributions of all the relevant disciplines can be made only through people from those disciplines working together. The processes described in this book and the non-directive approach make unique contributions towards making such multi-disciplinary partnerships happen and work.

Fifth, when people are approached non-directively they are more likely to share information about their thoughts and feelings which is highly relevant to promoting human and spiritual development—information, that is, which can be gained only through people themselves giving it. The use of these processes which are thoroughly non-directive, therefore, provides a sound body of knowledge and understanding upon which to build. Those who habitually take directive action are less likely to get into such privileged positions because they are inclined to overlay the thoughts of others with their own thinking and plans. However, in working with people there is always so much we need to know that we do not know but desperately want to know. Questions and hypotheses are, therefore, important tools when working with people (cf. Chapter 7).

The sixth point is the fact that we continually act to good effect in human affairs on the basis of a minute part of the sum total of human knowledge even when we are working at full capacity or overload.

So, having made the best possible use of the knowledge we have and that which we can bring into play through inter-disciplinary partnerships we can only commit the outcome and ourselves to God and his providence.

8. But there is limited thinking time!

Advocating this approach can all too easily give the impression that church and community workers should think about every aspect of their work in this thorough-going way all the time. Palpably, that is neither desirable nor possible. In one way or another we are thinking about things all the time. But at any one time most of us can think in depth about only a few things of importance to us. We are most free to do that when other aspects of our lives and work are running smoothly as a result of previous hard thinking, studying and training. Not being able to think in this thorough-going way about everything does not mean, as some suggest, that there is little point in trying to think about anything in this way. It points us to the vital importance of selecting carefully just what we should be thinking about in this way at any particular time. Discerning this with perspicacity can make heavy demands upon our thinking and decision-making resources. The processes described in this chapter help people to engage in this kind of thinking. Our effectiveness in promoting human and spiritual development depends upon doing this whether or not our thinking time is at a premium. Disciplining ourselves to do this helps us to encourage and enable others to do the same.

The task is a challenging one. There is not much difficulty in getting people talking and thinking quite hard about things of mutual interest. We all experience difficulties in thinking about things that we need to think about, but do not want to. Exploring why we are resisting may be a way forward.

My conviction about the need for this kind of thinking was reinforced recently when I reviewed in some detail the work we did over a period of six years in a church, youth and community centre. I was impressed by the breadth, depth and intensity of the thinking about fundamentals that went on. Ordinary people of all ages, Christians and non-Christians, engaged in it with me, using elementary formulations of the process described in this book. We had an enormous appetite for rigorous thinking about core issues that resulted in action. People's minds, as well as their hearts, were directing their action.

III. COPING WITH CONTEXTUAL INTIMIDATION

All aspects of church and community work from local to national and the disciplines we have just been considering open out on to pressing contextual issues such as poverty, deprivation, injustice, sexism and racism, conflict, faction and violence. When I focus on work of the kind described in Part One I have no doubts at all about the value of what I am doing and I am confident about the processes I am using. My feelings are less predictable when I focus on aspects of the context, i.e., the wider circumstances in which the work is set. Sometimes I am affirmed in what I am doing, and excited by the possibilities I see. This is especially the case when some of the acute contextual issues are being experienced and tackled in the situation upon which I am working. That is, when I am working on concrete effects of poverty, injustice, or racism: I have restricted myself to working at issues situationally rather than campaigning about them, important as that is.

At other times I am variously challenged, intimidated, overwhelmed, deflated and depressed by the puny contributions I feel I am making in relation to the awful vastness of human need; by new theories, approaches and methods which appear to invalidate the ones on which I am working; by the feeling I am dealing with symptoms rather than causes; by my inability to get to the heart of the matter which seems to be "out there" somewhere, and put things right at source; by the ever-changing climates of opinion in the economic and socio-religious spheres and the many disciplines which form important parts of my context. It is all quite disturbing. I cannot, and I know I should not, shut out the context, but there is a temptation to do so, especially when it is overwhelming.

What I believe I need is a creative tension between me, my work and my context with which I can live—if the tension is too high or too low it is disenabling. I am still struggling with all this and I know that that is my permanent lot! The modest aim of this section is to share some of the things that have helped me and those with whom I have worked to make the tension a little more creative and bearable.

1. Contextualizing our Approach

One thing I find helps me is to reflect on the contributions that the processes we are considering and church and community development are making and could make to tackling critical contextual issues. This reverses the process from thinking of the implications of the contextual issues for our work to thinking of the application of our approaches to the contextual issues. I have attempted the latter in Chapter Twelve.

2. Understanding the Dynamic

How I experience the overall context is one part only of the dynamic interaction that takes place. How others experience it could be significantly different. For instance, unemployment and its consequences will be experienced quite differently by the following: someone who is unemployed; employers with jobs to offer; ministers of religion with guaranteed employment ministering to congregations composed of a rising minority of people without jobs and a majority in secure well-paid jobs. The positive and negative effects of one or more contextual factors upon the interaction between these people is very complex. The following simplified version of the dynamics, Figure 5:4, helps to keep some of this complexity in mind and to work at it to better effect. It illustrates the ways in which contextual factors affect workers, people and the work in which they are engaged and the relationships between them.

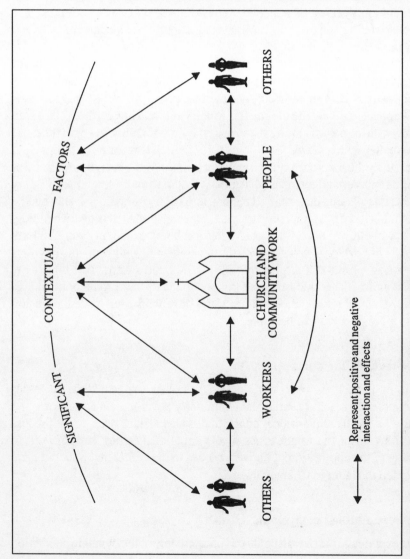

FIGURE 5:4. POSITIVE AND NEGATIVE INTERACTION BETWEEN CONTEXTUAL FACTORS, WORKERS, PEOPLE AND THEIR WORK AND RELATIONSHIPS

3. Relating to the Wider Context

One way of working at these things constructively is to consider what are healthy and what are unhealthy relationships between ourselves and our context. Those with whom I have discussed this say that healthy responses are those in which they accept and face up to the contextual issues in relation to their vision; listen to that which they do not want to hear; look for positives in what appear to be negative contextual factors and vice versa; keep calm and think of what they can do; collaborate with others and seek any necessary technical help to become properly informed; accept the pain, take risks and pray.

Unhealthy relationships, they say, are those by which they evade the reality by sticking to the status quo, burying themselves in *their* work, isolating themselves and rubbishing new ideas and those who propose them. Panic, they say, is a bad response because it paralyses them or drives them into inappropriate action. Examining these kind of responses helps people to determine the approach they wish to adopt towards contextual issues.

This can be followed by another thing I have found useful: tracing out the actualities of the patterns of interaction in given situations through flow charts or diagrams. This can promote mutual understanding and support between workers. Those who wish to pursue this more rigorously might find some work by Gareth Morgan helpful.[41]

4. Determining the Implications of the Context for my Work

During the 1970s and 80s I was involved in work-study courses in Northern Ireland. On the first course with an ecumenical group of twelve people, the work papers contained no references to the "troubles". (At that stage we did not ask them to write about the context as we did later: cf. the Appendix.) The situations described could have been anywhere in the UK; yet one person was working on the "peace line" and another in the Shankill Road and still another on the Falls Road! Understandable and responsible caution could explain the omission. They were taking considerable risks by joining an ecumenical group; to put things on paper about the "troubles" could have been dangerous. We raised this omission with them and after everyone had painstakingly committed themselves to absolute confidentiality they discussed it with us.

One of the things that emerged was that they desperately wanted to make contributions to peace but they felt that they could only contribute through becoming political activists. They did not want to do that.* They said that they

---

*Very interestingly some years later I read this comment by Professor Hywel Griffiths, written some two years after the incident I am describing.

"... community work itself has come to be associated with left wing political activism. I do not like [this] for two reasons.

"In the first place I do not like it because I believe it is based upon a delusion. The delusion consists of believing that community work is concerned with political action and that

were priests, ministers, religious, church and community workers at work in local churches and communities. That is what they wished to remain. They wanted to make their contributions through their vocational work.

So we focused on promoting change through the work that they did with people as ministers, priests, religious and church and community workers. Everyone was amazed at what emerged. They saw their ministries in a new light. The following extracts illustrate the points made.

One of the changes that they wished to see was "a deeper and wider mutual understanding between people divided by religious and political faction, resulting in less fear, more trust and more loving relationships". They said they could contribute towards achieving these changes by getting local groups of Christians to meet people of different denominations in different areas. First they would begin in their own communities with those whose differences are considerable but less than those between separated communities. This, they felt, would enable them to learn about the processes of crossing divides before tackling the bigger divisions between people and communities. They would build personal relationships through cultural activities before tackling the hard questions of sectarian divisions. They said that they needed to get as many people as possible engaged in the kind of exercise in which they were involved (those engaged in discussing the problem of failure in Chapter One said the same). They felt that it was important to get the following people to think in the way that they had done because they influenced large numbers of other

---

therefore through community work one can have an influence on politics. There is no evidence to support this belief: indeed there is much contradictory evidence. In Ulster where I worked for many years during the seventies I found myself working occasionally with community groups and organizations that were prepared to set aside conventional ideas of legality and morality in pursuit of their aim. Even then with all the considerable force that they could muster and all the recklessness they displayed they could not effectively play a political role. All that they could do at the political level was to interdict on occasion; all their best socially-useful work was undertaken at a sub-political level. Direct action may provide new services on a self help basis or affect the outcome of a particular decision which has to be made; but generally it can have no effect on decision-making systems and therefore has no political significance.

"Secondly I do not like this association because it would identify a strategy for effecting social change with a political ideology in a way which would not only prevent other political groups from embracing it but even encourage partisan opposition to it. The values of community development are plain to see and it may very well be that they might have appeal to more people of one political persuasion than another.

"But that is not a sufficient argument for making them the property of one political grouping rather than another. Moreover the attempt to do so, as we are witnessing today in the espousal of certain forms of voluntary action by the party in government, carries with it the grave danger of splitting voluntary action and those associated with its promotion into two rival camps. If that were to happen we would all find ourselves serving someone else's political purposes and rather than having an influence on politics we would instead lose our own credibility. As professionals seeking to promote community development that credibility rests upon our expertise and our integrity and not upon the political principles and affiliation which we may personally hold."[42]

people: clergy and lay leaders, extremists (and between them they had pastoral relationships with such people from all sides), teachers, youth and community workers, the media.

One of the things that they said would help them to do this was an analysis by Dr Henry Grant[43] of the social and religious interaction between the various faction groups which followed violent events. Another thing that would help was to follow the way in which their discussions had been structured: open and free exchanges about whether or not to discuss the implications of the "troubles for them" and the arrangements for doing so; establishing the objective of the discussion; considering an analysis of the socio-religious dynamics of the troubles (in this case the one by Dr Grant); identifying the changes that they felt could have far-reaching effects for good in Northern Ireland and the various things needed to make those changes; determining just what they could do towards making those changes through their work in the church and the community.

Others focused on what they could do to achieve the same changes through their pastoral work with people of all denominations who were bereaved, threatened, hurt and frightened by violent action, whatever their religious affiliations. Extended and deep pastoral counselling of individuals and groups provided opportunities to work through many of the deep questions relating to fear, bitterness, disillusionment, depression, hopelessness, desires for revenge, forgiveness, and Christian and other responses to tit-for-tat killings which would break the chain reactions of evil. In fact, they saw that by staying in role they could try to strengthen the moral and spiritual infrastructures, with all that this could mean for healing and peace.

These kinds of discussions influenced the work of the Jesuit Project described in Chapter Four which was done on one of the later courses in the series. It also greatly influenced the thinking of the Revd Fred Graham, a Church of Ireland priest who later wrote a dissertation about his attempts to promote better ecumenical relationships in a staunchly Protestant rural parish in Belfast.[44]

I have told this story because it illustrates quite vividly that there is much that can be done in relation to major contextual issues through working with people locally in church and community in all kinds of situations. Other things have to be done by politicians and people of other professions. That is understood. What we are concentrating on is the unique contribution that can be made through church and community work in urban, rural and suburban settings; and that is determined by attending to the interface between the situation and the critical contextual issues.

NOTES AND REFERENCES

1. Whitehead, A.N., T*he Aims of Education and Other Essays* (London: Benn, 1932, 6th impression 1966), p. 156 f.

2. I discuss this in Chapter 12. I plan to develop it further in a companion volume to this book, *An Invaluable Resource: Work Consultancy in Church and Community Work.*

3. Holland, Joe & Peter Henriot, *Social Analysis: Linking Faith and Justice* (Maryknoll. N.Y.: Orbis Books in collaboration with The Center of Concern, revised and enlarged edition 1983), p. 90; cf. p. 15 and 7.

4. I have learnt much about the theology and practice of waiting from Vanstone, W.H., *The Structure of Waiting* (London: Darton, Longman & Todd, 1982).

5. Fromm, Erich, *To Have or To Be* (London: Jonathan Cape, 1978) pp. 90ff. Cf. Lovell, George, *Human and Religious Factors in Church and Community Work* (London: Grail Publications, 1982) pp. 27f.

6. I owe this term to Morgan, Gareth, *Images of Organizations* (Sage Publications, 1986), p. 105 ff; cf. pp. 84 ff.

7. *Ibid.,* p. 106.

8. *Ibid.,* p. 106

9. Cf. Matthew 22:34–40 and Mark 10:19.

10. I discuss what I understand to be the distinctions between purposes and objectives in *Human and Religious Factors in Church and Community Work*, pp. 46 ff. Others use different terminologies to make the same distinctions, e.g. long- and short-term objectives; aim and objective.

11. Cf. Dewey, John, *Experience and Education* (London: Collier-Macmillan, 1968), Chapter 6, "The Meaning of Purpose", in which he shows the importance of the "participation of the learner in the formation of the purposes which direct his activities in the learning process" (p. 67). He also wrote:

> A genuine purpose always starts with an impulse. Obstruction of the immediate execution of an impulse converts it into a desire. Nevertheless neither impulse nor desire is itself a purpose. A purpose is an end-view. That is, it involves foresight of the consequences which will result from acting upon impulse. Foresight of consequences involves the operation of intelligence. (*Ibid.,* p. 67 f).

> The formation of purposes is, then, a rather complex intellectual operation. It involves (1) observation of surrounding conditions; (2) knowledge of what has happened in similar situations in the past, a knowledge obtained partly by recollection and partly from the information, advice, and warning of those who have had a wider experience; and (3) judgement which puts together what is observed and what is recalled to see what they signify. A purpose differs from an original impulse and desire through its translation into a plan and method of action based upon foresight of the consequences of acting under given observed conditions in a certain way. (*Ibid.,* p. 68 f).

12. Cf. Jaques, Elliott, *A General Theory of Bureaucracy* (London: Heinemann, 1976), p. 102.

13. See note 10 above.

14. The case study is described in Lovell, George & Catherine Widdicombe, *Churches and Communities: An Approach to Development in the Local Church* (Tunbridge Wells: Search Press, 1978 reprinted 1986), pp. 125–132.

15. Sanford, John A., *Ministry Burnout* (New York: Paulist Press, 1982) describes burnout as a person "devoured from within by fiery energy until, like a gutted house, nothing is left".

He says the problems of burnout and the exhausted ego are first cousins.

16. I have been aware of this attribute for some time but I am indebted to Prof. Charles Handy for his telling way of describing it. Unfortunately I cannot locate the reference.

17. Cf. Lovell, *Human and Religious Factors in Church and Community Work*, pp. 12 ff, and Lovell, *The Church and Community Development: An Introduction* (Grail Publications and Chester House Publications, 1972), Chapter 7.

18. Cf. McKelvey, Bill, *Organizational Systemics: Taxonomy, Evolution, Classification* (University of California Press, 1982), pp. 75–92, where he discusses autogenic and allogenic modes of organization, their environmental "coupling" and their "order".

19. Karl E. Weick has described the process through which we shape and structure our realities as a process of *enactment:* cf. Morgan, *Images of Organization*, p. 130. Morgan discusses this in a useful section entitled "Creating Organizational Reality" (pp. 128 ff). Weick examines the concept in a chapter in a book by Shaw, Barry M. & Gerald R. Salancik (eds) *New Directions in Organizational Behaviour* (Chicago: St Clair Press, 1977) entitled "Enactment Processes in Organizations". He describes ways in which people have a major role in creating the world towards which they subsequently respond and suggests that "the process of sensemaking in each case (that he gives) is better understood by examining what is in people's heads and imposed by them on a stream of events than by trying to describe what is 'out there'". Cf. also *Journal of Management Studies* 25: 4 (July 1988), "Enacted Sensemaking In Crisis Situations", for an exposition of the "enactment perspective".

20. "Group think" is a well-researched "collective pattern of defensive avoidance". The symptoms of this condition are: an illusion of invulnerability, rationalizing to discount warnings of error, unquestioned belief in a group's inherent morality, stereotyped views of rivals and enemies as evil, pressure against dissenters, self-censorship of deviants, a shared illusion of unanimity, self-appointed "mind guards". Cf. Jarvis, Irving L. & Leon Mann, *Decision Making: A Psychological Analysis of Conflict, Choice and Commitment* (Free Press, 1977) pp. 129 ff, and an article in the *Guardian* by Dr Frank Heller, Director of the Centre for Decision Making Studies, Tavistock Institute of Human Relations, entitled "The Danger of Group Think", *Guardian* 31 Jan. 1983. I agree with Gareth Morgan, *ibid.,* that "this kind of group think has been reproduced in thousands of decision-making situations in organizations of all kinds" (p. 202).

21. Morgan, Gareth, *ibid.*, (see note 6 above), shows how this can happen through "single-loop learning" and the importance of "double-loop learning" (pp. 87 ff).

22. There is a considerable amount of emphasis in community development about working with the "vertical" and "horizontal" patterns of community and the "local" and "non-local": cf. *Involvement in Community: A Christian Contribution. A Report by the Community Development Group, William Temple Foundation in collaboration with the Community Work Advisory Group, British Council of Churches* (William Temple Foundation, 1980), Chapter 3 *et al*, and Warren, Roland L. & Larry Lyon, *New Perspectives on the American Community* (The Dorsey Press, 1983), especially Section Three.

23. Green, Robin, *Only Connect: Worship and Liturgy From the Perspective of Pastoral Care* (London: Darton, Longman and Todd, 1987), p. 8.

24. Methodist Conference Agenda, 1986: "A Context for Policy Decisions", pp. 531–533.

25. See note 21 above and Lovell, George, *Reflective Practitioners in Church and Community Work* (1992), pp. 20 ff.

26. An excellent publication, *Evaluation of Community Work* (The London Council of Social Service, 1978), describes, illustrates and assesses the following seven "evaluation models": **Goal Model,** evaluating the outcome of work done in relation to pre-determined objectives; **System Model,** evaluating the effect of work upon human systems; **Impressionistic Enquiry**, recording impressions of what is happening; **Opinion Surveys**, researching

people's views on changes and developments; **Blue-Ribbon Committees/Testimonials**, named after blue ribbon committees in the U.S.A. which praise work programmes; **Textbook Precepts**, assessing work done in relation to theoretical standards set down in text books; and **Historical Approach**, evaluating through critically examining the twists and turns of the history of the work. This combines aspects of (a) and (b). I describe a system of evaluation based on directional analysis which I evolved and used in my Ph.D. Thesis: *An Action Research Project to Test the Applicability of the Non-Directive Concepts in a Church, Youth and Community Centre Setting* (Institute of Education, Faculty of Arts, University of London, 1973).

27. Young, Michael, *The Metronomic Society—Natural Rhythms and Human Timetables* (London: Thames & Hudson, 1988), helped me to a better understanding of the importance of working to human rhythms and what is involved in doing so.

28. This title is based on a description of a community sociologist as one who is his/her own "research instrument" by Bell, Colin & Howard Newby , *Community Studies: An Introduction to the Sociology of the Local Community* (London: George Allen & Unwin, 1971, fourth impression 1982), p. 62.

29. See Bell & Newby *(ibid.)* for a description of the use of participant observation methods in community studies.

30. Lovell, *Human and Religious Factors in Church and Community Work*, pp. 29 ff.

31. There are many books and articles and chapters in books on social research on participant observation. Ones I have found helpful are:

Spradley, James P., *Participant Observation* (New York: Holt, Rinehart and Winston, 1980)

Kane, Eileen, *Doing Your Own Research* (London: Marion Boyars, 1983)

An Avec Occasional Paper makes a comparative analysis of the advantages and disadvantages of survey and active and passive participant observation methods.

32. Argyle, Michael, *The Social Psychology of Work* (Harmondsworth: Penguin Books, 1972), p. 96.

33. *Ibid.,* p. 96.

34. *Ibid.,* p. 96.

35. The whole process was comprehensively documented. Reports were published in the *Methodist Recorder*. An article in *Epworth Review* described the process in some detail: "Relationships in Mission", by Leslie J. Griffiths (Volume 15, No. 2, May 1988, pp. 85–94).

36. Cf. Rogers, Maria & Ralph B. Spence, *Leadership and Authority in the Local Community: A report to the fourth International Congress on Mental Health by the Preparatory Commission on Autonomous Groups and Mental Health Autonomous Groups Bulletin* Vol. VII, No 4—Vol. VIII, No. 1 Summer–Autumn, 1952. This is the only publication known to me which takes seriously the controlling part played by networks and grapevines in the development of community. See p. 25 *et al.*

37. Warren, *op. cit.* p. 419.

38. Bell & Newby *Community Studies*, p. 25.

39. Bell & Newby, *op. cit.* p. 24 f.

40. A good example of collecting and assessing information received critically using these processes is given in Lovell & Widdicombe, *Churches and Communities: An approach to development in the local church*, pp. 96 ff.

41. Morgan—see note 19 above—gives a very useful way of examining the positive and negative feedback between inter-related contextual factors by drawing connecting "loops":

cf. pp. 247 ff.

42. Griffiths, Hywel, An Address given to Southern Region Conference 21st March, 1981 entitled, *Community Work In The 80s: Paid and Voluntary Action* (1981), p. 9 f.

43. Cf. Grant, Henry, S.J., an article in *Studies* (Summer 1983), pp. 145–155 entitled "Understanding The Northern Irish Troubles: A Preliminary to Action". This was based upon the lecture he gave to the Avec Course at Larne in May 1982.

44. Graham, Fred L., *Ecumenical Initiatives in a Rural Parish* (a dissertation for the Avec/ RIHE Diploma in Church and Community Development, 1988).

CHAPTER SIX

Designing

Designing is "a kind of making".[1] Designers juggle things until they get a conceptual picture of the creative interaction between parts of a system that will do what they want it to do. Designs model how things work or how designers think that they will work. Producing designs is an important part of the processes we are describing.

Deciding the word to use to describe this important activity was difficult. "Designing" is not a word in common use in church and community work. Of itself this is significant; it points to its neglect. It is widely used in engineering, building, the arts and the world of fashion. I could not think of a better one. Designing, so closely associated with making and inventing things in every aspect of human life, is a key activity in constructive development work. "Planning" is another possible word but I prefer to use this for making the organizational arrangements of just how, when and by whom designs are to be translated into action.

Consciously or unconsciously we design work programmes and projects to meet our understandings of how people and things actually do work, how we think that they should work and how we think things should be done. Consequently, underlying all human action is a design which reflects reality as we perceive it. Some designs work, others don't. Trying to make bad, inappropriate or impossible designs work is the source of many problems I encounter in church and community development work.[2] Such designs squander energy unproductively and cause scarce resources to be spent prolifically on repairing damage and salvaging projects rather than doing the job they were meant to do. Faulty designs bedevil (play the devil with) development work, workers and people. Workers and people become frustrated and disillusioned and experience conflict and pain. And sometimes they can blame themselves rather than the design. In some cases the effects of using bad designs make it impossible to do anything constructive along similar lines for some considerable time.

For the main part I find designs are implicit rather than explicit. Consequently, clergy and laity do not normally work to them nor at them. More often than not, the inner design is formed by planning the outer action—or through using traditional, inherited or standard designs for church and community work such as clubs, playgroups, neighbourhood schemes, church audits. Rarely do workers, in my experience, address themselves directly and purposefully to the *design* of their own programmes. Only a few of them have acquired the ability to do so. Once they are alerted to the importance of designing and given some tools with which to do it they work at it with verve, as can be seen from the work that the Jesuits did which is described in Chapter 4.

Designing, one of the most neglected aspects of all forms of church and community development work, is one of the most exciting but demanding activities, which pays high dividends. In this chapter I attempt to describe it and to give some clues about how to go about it. Then I invite you to consider the ideas about designing in relation to the worked examples in Part One.

I. DESIGNS

Preparing for creative action involves crossing the Rubicon between two complementary creative activities: analysis and design. To analyse is to take things apart in order to identify their inner nature and how they function. To design church and community work programmes is to conceptualize patterns of human behaviour, action and organization which will achieve desired ends in specific situations and contexts because they fit what is known from theology, theory, analysis and experience about working with people and God. Designs are, in fact, models that disclose the relationships and organizational dynamics that are not normally observable. Designs show how to put the "parts" together so that they work. A design, therefore, comprises a creative system of causal connections between people and organizations necessary to a programme of development work. The design in Figure 6:1 described in Chapter Four illustrates this definition—fortunately it is easier to illustrate the design process than to describe and define it.[3]

This diagram shows the pattern of working relationships that the Jesuit Team believed would achieve their purposes in Portadown. Such designs are to church and community workers what architects' drawings are to builders. They show what needs to be constructed but they do not indicate how to do so. Our illustration, for example, does not show how to establish the working relationships nor the order in which to do so—but it does show the relationships that are needed to make the project work. Working out how to build those relationships is part of what is involved in making the design operative in Portadown; that is, in taking it from the "drawing board" and embodying it in the workplace. Doing this involves planning, organizing and doing. At best these activities follow designing. Regrettably, because, as we have noted, designing is neglected, they are generally carried out without conscious reference to the design implicit in them. But no matter how carefully they are done they cannot be a substitute for designing and they are always more effective when the design is used explicitly. In fact, designing and planning and organizing are most likely to be done well when they are seen as discrete sequential activities.

Other examples of designs in this book are: the bishop's work contexts

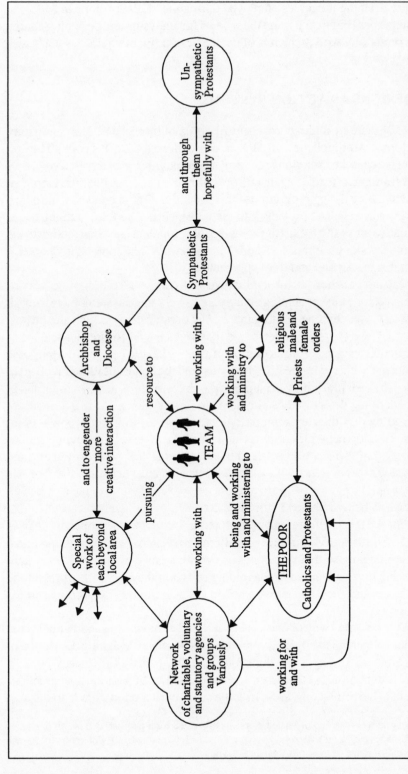

FIGURE 6:1. PATTERN OF WORKING RELATIONSHIPS: FULLY ASPIRED: PARTLY ACHIEVED

161

(Figure 3:1); the processes employed during the "Relationships In Mission" consultations (Figure 5:3); and the schema for analysing and designing church and community work, which is of itself a design (Figure 5:2).

II. DESIGNS AS ACTION-SYSTEMS

Basically there are three approaches to the promotion of church and community development through the use of the processes described in this book. The first is to make churches, religious and secular communities and Christian voluntary agencies more effective agents of overall human and spiritual development through their existing programmes and structures. The second is to introduce new programmes and projects into these agencies. The third is to introduce alternative ways and means of promoting development and contributing to the common good. Chapters 1, 2 and 3 illustrate the first approach; Chapter 4 illustrates the second and third approaches.

These approaches variously involve designing or re-designing action-systems[4] of one kind or another. If they are to work these systems have to mesh positively with churches, communities, and organizations, which are the host systems.* They comprise inter-related parts which work, or are meant to work, in particular ways according to the functions they have to perform, the purposes they have to achieve in specific situations, and the beliefs of those involved in them. They vary infinitely in nature, type, size, structure, and dynamic, and in the underlying design. Those involved in these systems can reject or accept ideas to modify their existing design and proposals to introduce new ones. Thus, development programmes and projects involve conceiving action-systems that will work in the human systems that will host them and alongside other systems with which they need to engage creatively. For this to happen it must be possible to introduce the action-system of the new design without its being rejected before it is accepted by and embodied in the host system. All this is illustrated by the project in Portadown described in Chapter 4. The Jesuits were introducing an alternative way of being and doing into a host community so that they could work with a range of Catholic, Protestant and secular organizations. By avoiding rejection they gave their project the time necessary for it to be embodied in the church, religious orders and the community.

Thinking in this way of one system entering or modifying another helps me to think more realistically and comprehensively when designing development programmes. It makes me think systemically. It makes me check for a fit between action and host systems. It reminds me that the host and not the action-system is the primary system. In some cases the action-system is to the host

---

*A system is "a group of related elements organized for a purpose".[5] It is "an organized whole made up of the interdependent elements that can be defined only with reference to each other and in terms of their positions in the whole".[6]

system what scaffolding is to a building and a starter motor to the engine. In other cases it is a new sub-system. Thinking in this way helps me to avoid designing programmes which are "linear task models"[7] that cut through host systems destructively[8].

III. ASPECTS OF DESIGNING

Analysis is commonly thought of as a science and designing as an art. My experience is that each is both an art and a science. One of the dangers of thinking of designing as an art is that it can imply that one's ability to design depends upon having artistic gifts. Certainly some people have more of a flair for designing church and community work development programmes and projects than others have. However, my experience over and again is that people who claim to have no natural gifts in this direction can be pleasantly surprised at what they can in fact do. Awareness of the nature of the activity and the simple devices I will describe can release in workers imaginative and creative design ability that they did not know they had. My aim in this section and the next is modest; it is to share ideas that have helped me and clergy, religious and laity working at all levels in the church and community to design programmes.

Designing church and community work programmes starts to become possible for me when I break it down into four discrete tasks.

1. Determining precisely what the design has to do, i.e. what it has to produce, the functions it has to perform and the ends to which it has to contribute and, equally important, what it has not to do (cf. the discussion about "noxiants").

2. Identifying the "givens" within which or in relation to which the design has to function effectively. I call these design criteria. They include things such as: beliefs about the ways in which one should/should not deal with people in general and in particular settings and circumstances, culture, purposes, human and physical resources, work rhythms of the participants, contracts, commitments, constraints of particular situations, local factors. Designs that will work have simply got to meet these criteria.

3. Thinking out designs (I discuss aids to doing this in the next section).

4. Testing out designs. One way to do this is by the designers themselves checking a design with the function (1 above) and the criteria (2 above), or by checking the design with people who know whether or not the design will work in the situation for which it is intended and whether or not it is a fit with the workers' frames of reference. Time after time I have seen such people suggest modifications that made

the difference between success and failure. Sometimes it is possible to test designs through pilot projects, but that is not always possible. The Portadown project is a case in point.

The sequence is not invariable. In the design of the Portadown project, for example, the best statement of purpose came when the design was complete; "givens" emerged as we proceeded with the design and we were testing out the design for viability as each part of the design emerged.

These processes are directed towards designing programmes and projects for specific situations. They have to fit given circumstances—suitably adapted, they may well fit other situations, of course. All situational designs, however, have to fit the grand design of the Kingdom of God and meet the criteria derived from our understanding of it. What we are about, therefore, is situational and theological designing. Consequently, the study of the workplace and its context needs to be undertaken along with the study of the Kingdom.

IV. AIDS

This section continues the discussion started in the previous one about the *how* of designing by attempting to answer a clutch of questions. How do you find the causal connections in human affairs which enable people to live and work together ever more effectively and efficiently? How do you design programmes and projects which positively affect being, culture and spirituality? How do you find ways of going about things that mesh into given realities and engender purposeful progress? Here I share quite simple things that have helped me and others to do these things.

1. Forming Patterns

All human situations are complex. Finding how things could go together creatively is not easy. When I am trying to do a jigsaw puzzle I put as many of the pieces as possible on a tray so that I can start to see which pieces fit together. This helps me to find "straight edges" which frame the picture puzzle, to collect pieces that seem to go together and to start to work on parts of the jigsaw.

A similar procedure helps me to design development work programmes. I set out on a piece of paper notes of the "things" that could be part of the design. Reflecting on what I have found myself doing intuitively for many years, I discern a recurring pattern in the way in which I do this. Purposes, beliefs, and design criteria I tend to put around the edges because they constitute the principal frame of reference. In the centre and towards the left I tend to put the development tasks—in the centre because of the need to focus on doing them and on the left because that gives room to plot the process towards the purposes which I invariably put top-right and away from the things to be avoided in the bottom-right. Alongside this I note the available human and physical resources, the events (meetings, services), the groups, the structures, the procedures which could possibly become part of the design. This process is not as orderly as it would seem from this description—it never comes out in the same way twice. Sometimes there is much on the paper, other times a few words or symbols. The objectives of this part of the exercise are twofold: to bring all these things into consciousness and to lay them out so that they can be seen, looked and stared at, and mulled over; and to ensure that critical and troublesome things are not overlooked. It is amazing how often doing this brings other highly relevant information and factors into consciousness and into play which just had not occurred to people during the analysis.

Now people can start designing by concentrating on all that is on the sheet until possibilities start to arise and connections are made by discovering how events, resources and people could possibly contribute towards achieving purposes; by discerning causal sequences and creative structures.

This is a simple device involving setting out the parts as a prelude for looking for patterns—but who but an absolute master would think of playing chess without the pieces on a board visible to sight? I have never known it fail to help people to get involved in designing.

Sometimes the general outline of a grand design stands out and it is so clearly right that it only remains to fill in the detail. When this happens I find it advisable to check it against any other possible alternatives that can be conceived. When no design comes immediately to mind I try to think and get others to think of as many ideas as possible without reference to their merit, feasibility or viability. Frequently people who previously said that they were stuck and had no ideas before the things were put on paper find to their surprise that they do have ideas. They start to put pieces together until a coherent design is produced and framed with reference points. When no design emerges I try one or more of the following devices.

Reflecting on the things that could form parts of the design. This can be done, for instance, by concentrating on the information until it "speaks to you". That involves waiting in patience upon the situation. Patterns often emerge as we simply gaze at things, concentrate on this and that, pursue thoughts that emerge, browse, focus in and out on this and that. (I actually look at it from another perspective and squint at it.)

Consciously searching for a design by: working out who and what are essential to the design; searching out the connections that will enable them to work together to achieve the desired results; and finding ways of portraying objectively and succinctly the emergent design so that others can consider it critically.

Brainstorming. The approach here is almost the opposite to reflecting. It is a way of eliciting creative thinking through generating an atmosphere in which people share whatever thoughts occur to them as they occur, without reflecting upon their merit. To encourage people to think aloud, to engage in "free-association", the atmosphere must be non-critical and non-judgmental.[9] One thought triggers off another.

Brainstorming is normally associated with groups, but it can be done by individuals. I do it often. One of the ways in which I do it is by simply putting things on a piece of paper as they occur as quickly as I can to keep up the momentum, to allow one thought to spark off another and to stifle relective thinking until I cannot think of any other ideas. Another way that I do it is by tracing out the free association of my thoughts by putting them on paper with connecting lines. When I come to the end of a train of thought I start again with the next idea. Eventually there is a pattern of my thinking on paper. Tony Buzan calls these "brain patterns".[10] This of course can be done in, by and for a group. Once the ideas and thoughts are out we/I can work on them. Some will be discarded, whilst others may well combine to form a design.

Lateral thinking. Edward de Bono coined this phrase. Lateral thinking is "sideways thinking", whereas the most common way of thinking is "straight-ahead thinking", or what de Bono calls *vertical thinking*. At best these are complementary modes of thinking.[11] One of the things that I got from de Bono's writings was the way I could obtain new insights by turning my attention from a problem that was defying solution by logical forward thinking (through, for example, using the problem-solving approach described in Chapter 2) to the first thing that caught my eye when I turned away from it.

An example comes to mind. Early one morning I was travelling up to London with a colleague with whom I was conducting a course. As we travelled there were two topics of conversation, the nature of lateral thinking and a deep concern we had that members of the course had shied off a topic that we thought was the key to a cluster of problems. Before we got off the train I suggested we think about the first thing that struck us in order to illustrate and test the lateral thinking method. What struck us was that in a moment of time the empty platform was flooded by commuters who were moving steadily through the narrow ticket collector's gate. Considering this we fastened on the flow problems that railway organizers must face. After doing this for some time we said almost in the same breath. "Our problem with the course is that we have not got the thinking flow right". An adjustment in the sequence was all that was needed; it corrected the design of the course.

Lateral thinking is a way in which things normally dissociated are brought into proximity. This can just happen: an apple falls and Newton grasps the theory of gravity; Jeremiah stared with a glassy gaze at a cauldron on a fire fanned by the wind from the north and knew in a moment that disaster would flare up from the north.[12] Such incidents are variously said to happen by chance or by providence. However that may be, they just happen; they cannot be foreseen. Lateral thinking is a way of "contriving" comparable experiences.

166

Comparing and contrasting the actual, the preferred (or the ideal) scenarios. Dr Gerard Egan[13] has evolved a method of designing "action strategies" by describing and comparing "current" and a range of "preferred scenarios". Questions that help to define the preferred scenarios are: What would the problem look like if solved? What would the opportunity look like if developed? What do you want things to look like? Once described, these scenarios can be contrasted and compared with a view to discerning what action could help to change the actual into the ideal and the project design that would facilitate it.

Viewing the actual and the preferred from different perspectives. Once the current and preferred scenarios are established, there are at least three perspectives from which to view them in the search for clues as to how to design programmes of action that move from the actual to the ideal. The first looks at both of them from some position objective to both; the second looks at the ideal from the actual; the third looks at the actual from the ideal.[14] Workers deeply involved in situations generally adopt the second perspective and find it difficult to move to the first or the third. People outside the situation adopt the first or third perspective and have to discipline themselves to gain something approximate to the second. Working on the third perspective is less common than working on the other two. It is the reverse of thinking and working our way forwards from what is to what we want. It is like imagining the way up a hill from the top rather than from the bottom. The interaction of perspectives can be generated by deliberately adopting each perspective in turn or by members of a group forming sub-groups, each taking one perspective and then sharing what emerges. Ideas for designs can come from these processes.

Identifying "constraints" and finding ways of releasing them. Designs frequently concentrate upon using and reinforcing the positive drives and the growth points and develop programmes that bypass the constraints. The Revd David Wasdell[15] suggests we should work on the constraints:

> Research into patterns of organization development, carried out repeatedly since before the Second World War, and confirmed in institution after institution, indicates that long-term development of an organization towards a given objective is rarely achieved simply by reinforcing the positive drives. Time and again such a strategy starts off well but at another level of the organization's behaviour, it triggers off further negative constraints and inhibits the performance of its task. These new constraints then mount until they overwhelm the new initiatives. At that point, whatever the energy put into the strategy, no apparent results are forthcoming. The organization becomes highly stressed, tends to withdraw its positive initiatives and moves into decline, retreating further away from the goals towards which it was trying to move. Christian congregations have proved to be no exception to this general rule.

Long-term church development requires the identification of those elements in the church's life which are acting as blocks, constraints, or inhibitors, of the church's achievement of the particular goal in question. Once those constraints have been identified, then strategic planning must focus on releasing the constraints, removing the inhibitions, overcoming the blockages, so freeing the church to move naturally under the power of its already active drives towards the goal it seeks to achieve.

Finding ways and means of overcoming and releasing constraints is one of the most important aspects of designing development work programmes and projects.

2. Visual Aids

Visual aids—charts, diagrams, maps, models, plans—have formed an important part of what I have said about designing. Sadly much designing and planning in church and community development work is done in people's heads and through talking things through. On many occasions I have sat through two or three hours of a planning meeting and no one has put a note on a piece of paper except myself: such a meeting comprises a group of "talking heads". I have been struggling to give coherent shape to what has been said on my pad. More often than not the people are neither trained nor used to designing and planning. Such groups have neither private notes nor common reference points readily provided by words, diagrams, charts on a board or a piece of newsprint. Most people simply cannot design sound development programmes whilst they remain "talking heads". In fact, I cannot see how it is possible to design without resorting to the use of diagrams. Amongst other things, using the diagrams draws upon the right hemisphere of the brain (the non-verbal) and complements the use of the left hemisphere (the verbal). (There is a section in Chapter 7 on the use of diagrams in analysis and design.) I find that the most useful diagrams simply come without words as I take up a pen to draw them.

Some people can design and plan in their heads and through talking but even then, as the following quotation shows, it is advisable to write them down:

While it is perfectly possible to develop a whole plan in one's head, it is better to write it down so that everyone can understand and agree what is to be done. This will avoid confusion later on, and it helps to ensure that an inexperienced manager thinks through the project and works out what needs to be done and who will do it.

Furthermore a written plan goes far beyond a brief description of the project . . . and will allow responsible sponsors and others to help identify pitfalls or opportunities for improvement.[16]

3. Separate Designing from Planning and Programming

Separating designing from planning and programming enables people to concentrate on designing freely and imaginatively. They are different kinds of activities, which, if attempted together, can confuse each other. When we turn from designing to putting designs to work we are involved in making arrangements of one kind or another with individuals and groups, organizing meetings and planning events. Doing these things test out the design and its viability and may well lead to adjustments to it.

V. COMPARING THEORY WITH PRACTICE

Reviewing Part One in the light of the ideas and suggestions in this chapter about designing is one way of exploring just how designs can emerge. You might consider, for instance, how, in Chapter 4, the project designs evolved, and the contributions made by the methods you have just read about. Another thing you might do is to model the design of the action plans emerging from the study of the case and problem in Chapters 1 and 2. Yet another thing to do is to examine the way in which the bishop made profound changes in the design of his theological project. (cf. Chapter 3.) To illustrate these changes I have modelled the original and the revised designs in Figures 6:2 and 6:3. The original design was one through which the bishop tried to get others to adopt the doctrine of justification by grace through faith. The revised design was one by which he intended to get people to share and explore their theological orientations. The original design is a linear change model aimed at development through the theological conversion of others to a particular doctrine. The revised design is very different: it is a systemic process aimed at all-round theological development through engendering mutual theological acceptance (a key element in "justification"), understanding and critical interaction between people. The original design evangelizes to a given theological position; the revised design evangelizes to a given pluralistic theological process. The original is "single-loop learning" (i.e. acting in relation to a set of norms); the revised is "double-loop learning" (i.e. taking a double look at the norms of all concerned).

Both designs could be divisive: in relation to the original design, some people would object to the theological content and to the implicit theology of the approach and method with its propensity towards theological uniformity and exclusivism; in relation to the revised design, some would object to the theology of the approach, which is overtly inclusive, pluralistic and collaborative. Initiators in both cases contribute their own theological ideas as well as facilitate the processes—even if these are different ones requiring different skills and commitments to different theological stances, positions and processes.

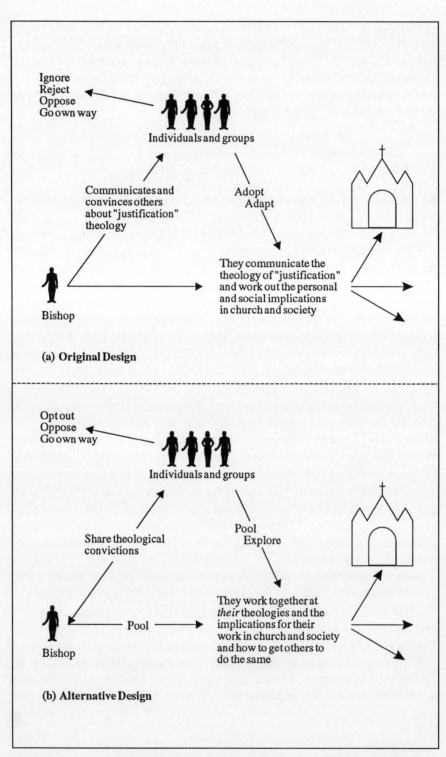

Ignore
Reject
Oppose
Go own way

Individuals and groups

Communicates and
convinces others
about "justification"
theology

Adopt
Adapt

Bishop

They communicate the
theology of "justification"
and work out the personal
and social implications
in church and society

(a) Original Design

Opt out
Oppose
Go own way

Individuals and groups

Share theological
convictions

Pool
Explore

Bishop

Pool

They work together at
their theologies and the
implications for their
work in church and society
and how to get others to
do the same

(b) Alternative Design

FIGURE 6:2. DESIGNS OF THEOLOGICAL PROJECTS IN CHAPTER 3

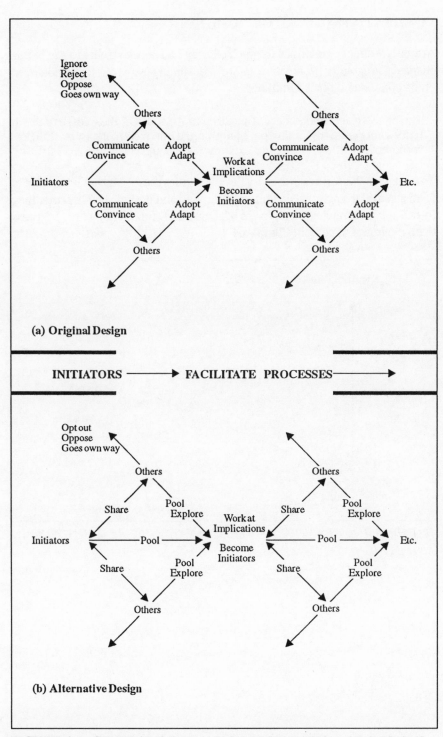

FIGURE 6:3. GENERAL SCHEMATIC PRESENTATION OF DESIGNS IN CHAPTER 3

VI. CREATIVE NATURE OF DESIGNING

Arthur Koestler summarizes so much of what I have been trying to say in this chapter. He captures the creative nature of designing in this quotation taken out of his context and placed in mine:

> The creative act is not an act of creation in the sense of the Old Testament. It does not create something out of nothing; it uncovers, selects, re-shuffles, combines, synthesizes already existing facts, ideas, faculties, skills.[17]

To engage in this kind of creativity three activities must be brought together to form a causal triangle: analysing, synthesizing and designing. Together they form a powerful nucleus in all forms of church and community work. I express them diagrammatically in Figure 6:4.

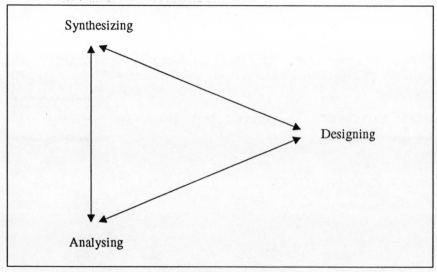

FIGURE 6:4. A CREATIVE NUCLEUS: ANALYSING, SYNTHESIZING AND DESIGNING

NOTES AND REFERENCES

1. Schon, Donald A., *Educating The Reflective Practitioner: Towards a New Design for Teaching and Learning in The Professions* (San Francisco & Oxford: Jossey-Bass Publishers, 1987), p. 41.

2. My experience is similar to that of secular agencies, according to a report prepared for the Department of the Environment by URBED (Urban and Economic Development) Ltd.: *Managing Urban Change: A Report on the Management Needs of Urban Programme Project Managers* (HMSO, 1988). "In both local authority and voluntary projects, problems often arise from the initial design .... One conclusion we drew from these case studies was that many of the problems encountered later on could be traced back to inadequate initial planning.... Thus good planning at the start of a project is extremely important." Planning here is near to what I mean by designing.

3. Other designs and models are given in: Lovell, George, *The Church and Community Development: An Introduction* (Avec Publication, 1972, 1992 reprint), pp. 8–13, 34, 42–55. Lovell, George & Catherine Widdicombe, *Churches and Communities: an approach to development in the local church* (Search Press, 1978), p. 25. Lovell, George, *Diagrammatic Modelling: An aid to Theological Reflection in Church and Community Development Work* (Avec Publication, 1980), p. 10. Lovell, George, *Human and Religious Factors in Church and Community Work* (Grail Publication, 1982), pp. 13, 25, 44, 51. See also Downes, Thomas, *The Parish as Learning Community* (Mahwah, N.J.: Paulist Press, 1979), Chapter 1 and p. 97.

4. I owe this term to Allen Pincus and Anne Minahan: cf. Chapter 5, "A Model for Social Work Practice" in *Integrating Social Work Methods* National Trust SS Library 31 (London: Allen & Unwin, 1977), Specht & Vickery (eds), p. 83.

5. Bullock, Alan & Oliver Stallybrass, *The Fontana Dictionary of Modern Thought* (London: Fontana/Collins, 1977), p. 621.

6. Palazzoli, Mara Selvina *et al, The Hidden Games of Organizations* (New York: Pantheon, 1986) following Ferdinand de Saussure, p. 175.

7. Pincus & Minahan, *op. cit.* p. 87.

8. David N. Thomas's book *The Making of Community Work* (London: Allen & Unwin, 1983) has some useful sections on community as a social system (pp. 46, 115, 296, 298–9 & 300–1).

9. Cf. *The Fontana Dictionary of Modern Thought* on "brainstorming".

10. *Use Your Head* (BBC, 1974), pp. 87 ff. It is also a way of making a record of a meeting. Cf. Widdicombe, Catherine, *Group Meetings That Work: A practical guide for working with different kinds of groups* (Slough: St Paul Publications, 1994), p. 50.

11. Cf. *The Use of Lateral Thinking* (Harmondsworth: Penguin, 1967), p. 139. I have found Arthur Koestler's ideas about "thinking aside" and bisociative mechanisms very helpful: cf. *The Act of Creation* (London: Hutchinson, 1964).

12. Jeremiah 1:13f.

13. I owe this reference to discussions with Sister Majella O'Keefe about a seminar paper which she produced for the Avec/RIHE Diploma in Church and Community Development, October 1987: *Ways and Means of Analysing and Designing Programmes of Work With People.* For further information about the work of Gerard Egan see "Overview of a Practical Model of Organizational Change". (A new book is about to be published on this.)

14. Again I owe the idea of this perspective from discussions with Sister Majella O'Keefe (*op. cit.*). She was drawing upon the work of Gaston Berger, *The Methodology of Prospective Programming.*

15. *Mission Audit* (published by the General Synod for Mission and Unity of the Church of England, 1984): cf. pp. 38 f.

16. See the URBED Report quoted in note 2 above.

17. Koestler, *The Act of Creation*, p. 120.

CHAPTER SEVEN

Basic Equipment

So far in this book I have demonstrated the skills, abilities and equipment required to analyse and design development work through describing how some people did it and examining the processes by which they did it. This is the counterpart in the written word to watching people do something and being told why they are doing it in that particular way. Actually the written word allows us to "watch" what is done in slow motion and to stop and examine any stage at will. This approach is significantly different from that of listing generic skills that people need to have in order to analyse and design on their own and in groups, communities and organizations.[1]

I have chosen this approach quite deliberately because it shows how, in analysing and designing, the personal and interpersonal processes, the tasks pursued, the skills and the abilities and equipment deployed are all of a piece. It illustrates how these things are embodied in reality and thus, to put it negatively, it avoids the separation of the parts. It is possible, of course, to list from what I have written the things people need in order to do this work. You might find it helpful to do so and to note those things you have acquired and those which you need to develop. There are things that can be drawn out which equip people to engage in every aspect of analysis and design. In this chapter I discuss the use of words, diagrams, questions and hypotheses or hunches.

My experience is that I and those with whom I work are most creative when we work at things through the spoken and written word and through depicting things in diagrams. These three activities—talking, writing things down and constructing diagrams—draw upon a wide range of our faculties through the left and right hemispheres of our brains and they "speak" to each other. A distinguished economist and Nobel Prize winner, Sir John Hicks, testifies to the same kind of experience. He is reported to have said that he always explains his propositions in words, in diagrams and in mathematics and that he only publishes when he can do all three.[2]

The combination of words, diagrams and formulae challenges the common belief "that 'thinking' is synonymous with verbal thinking".[3] "Often", says Woodworth, "we have to get away from speech in order to think clearly".[4] And Koestler claims that the "distrust of words is a trait often found among those who create with their eyes" and he provides evidence that many scientists "distrust conceptual thought" and rely on "visual imagery".[5] All this illustrates different ways in which people think. The combined use in group work of these methods enables people who think in different ways to make their contributions to better effect and it allows individuals to draw upon the different ways in which they think.

I am aware that by restricting myself to my own experience and concentrating on these four things that I have found helpful I am missing out other ways that help people to think, analyse and design. Omitting them is not to dismiss them; it is simply to acknowledge that I have not used, researched and tested them sufficiently to write about their use in the processes of analysis and design that I am examining.

Now to the four pieces of basic equipment.

I. WORDS: SPOKEN AND WRITTEN[6]

Church and community development is "talking work" (in contradistinction to manual or craft work)[7] aimed at getting people thinking, working and growing together and giving a voice and say to all participants. It is putting words and language to work for human and spiritual development.

Words are the tools of thought and communication. They can be instruments of analysis, design, planning and carrying out work programmes with people. "Our ability to reflect on our experience", says David Smail, "is only as good as the linguistic tools available to us to do so".[8] Qualitative verbal interaction of a unique kind is the key to the corporate application of the processes of analysis and design that we are considering. This interaction is open and free whilst being focused, disciplined, structured and purposeful. It aims to give a voice and say to all participants and to take all contributions seriously. (I am amazed at the effects of a worker's taking seriously the first verbal contribution by a member of a newly formed group. Repeatedly I sense surprise, if not shock, and a quietness as the group takes on a quite different attitude and ethos modelled on the worker's response.)

To promote this kind of interaction workers have to work as diligently with the words of others as with their own; they have to help people to find words to express themselves adequately; they have to help people to move from arguing, debating and using rhetoric to thinking things through together using all their resources and insights; they have to help people when words are being used in anger to hurt, to confront the issues constructively and to begin to care for each other; they have to act as translators and to find words to cross chasms of misunderstanding and disagreement as they help groups to find a *lingua franca*. (A large ecumenical team of well-educated professional people to whom I acted as consultant eventually came to the conclusion that to overcome the acute difficulties they were facing they needed a "more adequate working vocabulary".)

To do all this, people and workers have to engage in open unrehearsed verbal exchanges—apart, that is, from prepared opening pieces which are of great importance—in situations that can be supercharged with emotion, positively

176

and negatively. People and workers need considerable skills to work collectively with words in these ways, especially when they are working with people differing considerably in their verbal facility. They also need certain commitments, which we will consider later.

For me, a preacher, to become involved in this kind of talking work involved a conversion as shaking, painful and liberating as any I have experienced. It was *from* habitually using verbal facilities for my purposes and often, to my shame, unfairly against those of others *to* a commitment to use them for others, to put them, such as they were, at the service of others and their well-being and development. This means, for instance, making sure that all suggestions, whatever you might think of them, are equally well articulated so that the quality of the description is not confused with the quality of the idea. When this is done, people are more likely to select ideas on their merits; the better idea is not lost to another simply because it was badly described. This conversion took place in the late 1960s and I have been working out its implications ever since. (There are, of course, occasions when it is right to use verbal facilities against others.)

I am convinced that the quality and effectiveness of the work done in the church and in the community is directly proportional to the quality of the verbal exchanges that suffuse it. The adoption of the non-directive approach is an inevitable consequence of this conclusion. But I am not under any illusion about the difficulties of promoting this kind of talking work and adopting a non-directive approach. For one thing, in all walks of life, words and talking are widely used to sell, persuade, cajole, manipulate, threaten, impress, etc. Then again, those with the greatest facility with words in positions of authority may not have the deepest insights or the best ideas but they often have the will and the power to dominate and quash others: more perceptive, less articulate people can be marginalized by less perceptive, more articulate and powerful ones.

Sadly, words can also be weapons that undermine collaborative action, task groups and community. Opportunities to talk things out together have been so misused that meetings are often dismissed as talking shops, i.e. places where there is a free flow of words without commitment and action. This has to be avoided. It is the death of church and community development, just as talking to good effect is its life-blood. Meetings need to be talking workshops in which people use words and other means of communication constructively in the ways illustrated in Part One. The main point that I wish to make here is that for the Church (and other organizations) to become involved in promoting the kind of free-flowing open verbal exchanges described above, laity, ministers, priests and religious simply have to learn, as I had to, a mode of talking work so different from the one to which they are most accustomed that it is tantamount to acquiring another language, with its own vocabulary, grammar and syntax. What facility I have with this language I learnt first through experiential education[9] and then through group and community work.

For the main part, in most churches in the liturgical context one or two people preach to and speak for congregations whose verbal responses are strictly limited to those prescribed. This is the antithesis of the talking work we are considering. I am not suggesting, as I might have done some years ago, that this liturgical mode should be replaced by that necessary when people are analysing and designing church and community work together. Traditional services of worship are vitally important to me[10]—so much so that I find that discussion during services can detract from their value substantially. (Discussion afterwards is quite a different matter.) Nor am I arguing against debating and lecturing, they have their place. Worship, debating, lecturing and other forms of talking work can stimulate inner dialogues that promote human and spiritual development.[11] What I am arguing is that workers and organizations aiming to promote holistic development need to be taking the skills that I describe seriously and that such development is most likely to occur when the different ways of using words are used and experienced appropriately in concert, so that, for example, workers worship together and worshippers work together.

The verbal ability to preach does not necessarily mean the ability to lecture or work with people in groups. Preachers and lecturers share their thinking through projecting it; whilst workers promote shared thinking. Sermons are preached in situations designed for one person's thinking to be made overt whilst that of the congregation remains covert; community work is designed to make as much of each person's thinking as possible overt with due respect for privacy. Preachers and lecturers deal in set pieces, community workers work with many set pieces and those that are composed on the spot. Preaching is, amongst other things, declaring what needs to be done, how it should be done, challenging people to do it and leaving the doing to those who may. Church and community work helps people to decide for themselves what needs to be done *and* to talk out what they are going to do.

There are many ways of acquiring the ability to engage in non-directive talking work by reading about it, experiencing it and doing it. Fortuitously, I have found that writing up this kind of talking work has been a way of learning in depth about how to do it (and not to do it!) and it has greatly enhanced the talking and group work. During the 1960s, when we were first using this mode of talking work, the late Dorothy Household and I developed a way of writing about it which we called "recording".[12] A record is a written structured account of a meeting between two or more people giving an orderly presentation of:

— the overt purposes, objectives, and tasks of a discussion;

— any relevant information about the way in which it was conducted;

— any decisions made or conclusions arrived at by the members;

— any of the underlying considerations, arguments, reasons and feelings which led the members to their decisions and conclusions;

— any information about the apparent group processes and the overt interaction of the members necessary for an understanding of whatever happened during the discussion;

— the worker's reflections and implications for future discussions.

In the first instance we started to write these records to avoid groups going over the same ground *ad nauseam*. Then we realized that they performed many functions and so I have used the method extensively in different ways ever since. What we found was that:

- records, by portraying the life and work of a group, help it to get to know itself and to build up its identity, to see how it is functioning and malfunctioning and provide common reference points and discussion building blocks;

- records provide opportunities for workers and people to learn about themselves, each other, their beliefs and their environment, through the linguistic exercises necessarily involved in achieving their purposes, solving their problems and meeting their needs—therefore they are educational and developmental tools;

- records stimulate people to express themselves more precisely and therefore to learn how to use language more critically and creatively;

- records enable people to realize they have a contribution to make;

- records aid efficiency, communication and self-evaluation;

- records are self-training and research tools.

Therefore recording and records greatly enhance the quality and effectiveness of talking work and, by causing everyone to think and reflect in greater depth than they would otherwise do, they help everyone—not only workers—to be better equipped to engage in this kind of talking work. And they enable those who are better at writing than speaking to make significant contributions.

II. DIAGRAMS

Diagrams play an important part in the work I do. They are a natural part of the way in which I communicate. Examples are to be found in this book but they are much tidier than working diagrams. People I meet find the diagrams I draw very helpful but few have used them previously in their church and community work. A large percentage soon start to draw their own diagrams and show considerable skill in doing so. All they needed to start them off was an experience of them. A small percentage say that they follow diagrams when used by others but that they do not add meaning to their thinking and that they would never construct them or use them. A very small percentage tolerate them but do not like them. But for the majority they open up new and exciting worlds of thought and are tools for thinking.

Diagrams are line drawings showing the parts of things or how they work. They select, simplify and exaggerate aspects of reality seen to be significant for the purposes in hand and play down or ignore those that are not. Koestler compares them to cartoons:

Every drawing on the blackboard—whether it is meant to represent the wiring diagram of a radio set or the circulation of the blood, the structure of a molecule or the weather over the Atlantic—is based on the same method as the cartoonist's: selective emphasis on the relevant factors and omission of the rest. A map bears the same relation to a landscape as a character-sketch to a face; every chart, diagram, or model, every schematic or symbolic representation of physical or mental processes, is an unemotional caricature of reality.[13]

Some diagrams are what Ramsey calls "picturing" or scale models—a drawing of a building indicating how it is used or a map of an area showing where organizations and churches are located are examples of this kind of diagram. Other diagrams are what Ramsey calls "disclosure" models. They reveal something of the inner structure and essential shape of things; they disclose the connections between variables and processes of cause and effect; they show how things do or could fit together.[14] Both kinds of diagrams are useful but it is the latter that are the creative tools of analysis and design in church and community development work. (Examples of disclosure diagrams are Figures 2:2, 3:2, 4:1&2, 5:2, 6:2&3, 8:1.) Other diagrams show the different stages, optimal phasing and timing of a series of inter-related tasks. Such diagrams are commonly referred to as "critical paths" or "flow charts". (Examples are Figures 2:3, 5:3; Displays 5:1 and 11:1.)

Just how and why, then, are diagrams useful? They help us to talk about things we find difficult or impossible to describe. Discussing theological models, Ramsey says that they can "enable us to make sense of discourse whose logical structure is so perplexing as to inhibit literacy"; they can "enable us to talk of what eludes us"; and they enable us to "map large-scale interpretations of phenomena".[15] This applies to all kinds of diagrams. Moreover, once constructed, they are invaluable aids to discussion. People can identify unmistakably things to which they are referring by pointing to them and using a minimum number of words. Making points through verbal exchanges requires more time and more concentrated attention is required to follow precisely what is being said. The consequent economy in making points combined with the vividness with which they are made and the ease and clarity with which they are grasped, generates a dynamic in the exchanges between people which stimulates and facilitates creative thinking. Ideas flow freely. Diagrams objectify the discussion—there is a tangible output which people

180

have produced together. This keeps the momentum going not least because it tends to reduce defensiveness and people's being possessive about "their" ideas.

An important aspect of diagrams is that they represent positions that things occupy in the scheme of things and the relationships between them. This can bring descriptions of things and lists of points to life. (Cf. "The Diagrammatic Overview of The Book" in the "Purpose and Structure of The Book".) Above all, diagrams add non-verbal dimensions to our comprehension of things and our discourse about them. Thus they enhance participation in analysing and designing by enabling us to use the side of our brain that thinks in pictures rather than words—and that helps those who do their best thinking in this way to make their contributions. Finally, many people find diagrams easy to remember. It follows that diagrams are useful for conceptualizing, analysing and explaining things and for designing projects and programmes.

There are, however, disadvantages, limitations and dangers in using them. They are approximate; they represent some things but not others; they are not comprehensive statements of reality. Thus it is dangerous to read too much into them. They are most useful in highlighting key characteristics about complexly related entities; they are least useful in presenting subtle nuances. In fact, they can mask the need for accurate verbal descriptions of nuances that diagrams simply cannot convey. Diagrams that are really helpful are not always easy to construct, whilst ones that dysfunctionally misrepresent things come all too easily. Whilst some diagrams communicate widely, others do so only when people see them built up and the effectiveness of others is restricted to those involved in their construction—they simply do not travel!

As I have already said, by and large people readily use all types of diagrams that are provided. Most people are not as adept at producing disclosure diagrams as they are at producing the other forms. Consequently they are inclined to overwork and misuse the other types of diagrams and even to use them as though they were disclosure models.

How, then, do you draw diagrams? As far as analysis and design are concerned, the diagrams that I construct and use emerge from my interaction with people and the situations in which they are engaged.* They come from "reading" the situations. There are examples of this in Chapter Four. Professor Gareth Morgan, in an outstanding book about understanding organizations, says:

> . . . the trick is to learn how to engage in a kind of conversation with the situation one is trying to understand. Rather than impose a viewpoint on a situation, one should allow the situation to reveal how it can be understood from other vantage points. In a way we can say that one should always be

---

*Some diagrams that result from studying the theory, theology and practice of a wide range of experience model underlying processes and become analytical tools. Figure 5:2 is an example.

sensitive to the fact that a situation 'has its own opinion' . . . as one develops the art of reading situations, critical analysis and evaluation become a way of thinking. One quickly learns to recognize important cues and to uncover crucial insights.[16]

Diagrams emerge from that kind of "conversation"—not always, but more often than not. To be more specific than this with certainty is not possible because I cannot discern all the inner conscious and unconscious processes and the part played by the left and right hemispheres of my brain. (I understand that the left is verbal, analytical, digital, abstract, rational, linear, temporal, and logical, and uses signs; whilst the right is non-verbal, synthetic, spatial, analogic, non-rational, holistic, non-temporal, intuitive and uses symbols.[17]) I glimpse three different and, I suspect, inter-related ways in which diagrams come to me.

The first is a conscious process. I listen and look for the principal features, reference points and entities in a situation and what people are saying about them. I do this with great attention and concentration. I focus on them in turn and lock them in my consciousness. Possibly I write them haphazardly on a piece of paper. (They could be key people or groups, events, issues, etc.) Then—but it is in parallel not in sequence because one is thinking about all the things at the same time—I look for connections, patterns of interactions, discontinuities, factions, etc. At this stage my questions will be directed towards clarifying any ideas or hunches about these things. In short, I am building up in my mind, and possibly jotting down on paper, a picture of the system or sub-system, the parts and their structure.

Now it is necessary to find some way of putting the emerging mental picture into diagrammatic form to facilitate further and deeper discussion. (At all stages it is essential to be tentative so that other insights emerge freely and become part of the emerging conceptual picture. Insights and hunches need to be tested and corrected.) More often than not this process has started on my jotting pad. I then attempt to set out the entities, their inter-relationship and the patterns of interaction and some representation of the key processes that constitute positive and negative aspects of the inner dynamic of the system(s) in diagrammatic form. (This helps us to see how clearly related this activity is to designing and why working diagrams are so important to designing.) In a summary form, therefore, the conceptualizing stages associated with diagrams are:.

— listening and looking; and trying to look at things from different angles to see if other perspectives throw new light upon things;

— abstracting from the generalities what appear to be key factors;

— searching for connections between the key factors (how they fit or do not fit together, the interaction between them etc.);

— searching for ways to portray objectively and succinctly and clearly whatever I have "seen" or found so that I and others can consider critically whatever it is.

This involves:

— observing

— extracting/isolating

— interpreting

— relating

— conceptualizing

— representing.

The second way in which diagrams come to me is a combination of conscious and subliminal processes. I read meditatively and critically what people write, I listen intently to what they say, and I look at them as they are saying it. Through this process verbal and non-verbal communications are picked up which inform and shape diagrams; partly as described above and partly in hidden ways. I know this through experiences where I have identified the effect of non-verbal communications. For example, I was once working with a group of people from the same area. They were talking about several churches. I drew one or two map-diagrams placing the churches. After some time they said that I obviously knew the area. I did not, and I asked them what led them to think that I did. They said it was because I had put all the churches in the right relationship to each other geographically. The complexities ruled out chance. Pondering this, I realized that I had picked up non-verbal signals they had made by the movement of their eyes and heads to indicate the direction in which one church after another was located. I read these signals without "knowing" I had done so. I was reminded of what Jonathan Miller said on a TV programme about the importance of doctors attending to the non-verbal communications of patients when diagnosing. He maintains that they provide vital clues. For example, stabbing pains are indicated by stabbing the fingers to show where this takes place, direction and frequency.[18]

The third way in which I produce diagrams is, I believe, through the activity of the right side or hemisphere of my brain. My evidence for saying so is this. Time and again when working with individuals and groups I start to draw diagrams without any conscious mental picture of what I am going to draw. As I start, I generally say what is now my party piece to cover my anxiety about the outcome: "I do not know whether I can do this, but may I try to draw a diagram?"—and I start without giving anyone the chance to say no! More often than not a useful diagram emerges, generally of the disclosure genre. As soon as I start to draw the diagram I begin to explain it, presumably the activity of the left side of my brain. I have seen others do the same. At various times

I have urged people who have said that they have a feeling about a situation but no clear idea "to draw without thinking". More often than not they produce a diagram that illuminates things—sometimes it is their first diagram.

These are three ways of constructing diagrams inductively. Concentrated attention must be given to verbal and non-verbal communications. Some of this can be constructed into diagrams through the predominant use of the left side of the brain; some through the right side of the brain. Take courage into both hands and just start to draw without thinking in words. Once the diagrams are out, they lend themselves to analysis.

Some diagrams communicate their message immediately and unmistakably without much effort on the reader's part. But, as we have seen, other diagrams speak only to those who study them carefully, and doing that calls for application. For me this is most difficult when a diagram is a complex of lines and arrows connecting several "boxes" or circles and when either there is too much or too little verbal explanation. One wonders where to start, just what the arrows mean and what is the distinction between full and dotted lines, etc., etc. These difficulties arise when people have to read a diagram they have not seen constructed, and since most published diagrams are the final product, the stages in their construction are rarely given. Questions that help to read diagrams are:

—   what are the principal entities?

—   why are they arranged as they are?

—   what is the diagram saying about the relationship between the entities?

—   what is the diagram as a whole saying to me?

—   what do I think about it?

In fact, these and similar questions help to recapitulate stages in the construction of a completed diagram.

Building up diagrams in dialogue can be exciting and productive. The process is alive, vital and dynamic, but it can be disappointing when they are presented to others in their final state to find that they are dead and uninspiring, they have lost their dynamic and excitement. Examples of diagrams built up in a consultancy session are given in Figure 3:1.

Now look at the diagrams in this book!

III. QUESTIONS

Analysing and designing church and community work involves pursuing appropriate questions related to human affairs in specific situations and contexts. Questions are basic tools; using them is part of the craft of this work; questioning is a core process of analysis and design. What this means in practice is illustrated in Chapter One, Working on a Problem. Those with questioning minds—workers and people—take to this quite naturally. But there are many workers and people in church and community work who need to analyse but who do not have questioning minds. Some of them actually feel uncomfortable in analysing problems, cases and situations because they feel it is being judgmental, hypercritical and uncharitable and therefore unchristian. Frequently people will opt out of diagnosing a case by springing to the defence of the worker. Before they can continue they have to be assured that it is necessary to diagnose rigorously to "prescribe" acccurately. Practice and experience apart, two things have helped me and all kinds of other people to use and develop their ability to question: an understanding of different kinds of questions and sequences of basic questions.

1. Different Kinds of Questions

Unloaded questions (e.g. "What do you aim to achieve through this project?") are more likely to promote direct, open, honest exchanges than loaded questions ("Do you agree that the aim of this project should be . . . ?") which focus attention on the thinking of the questioner rather than that of the one being questioned and upon the implications of the invitation to agree or collude and on what kind of an answer to make. Unloaded questions facilitate qualitative exchanges between people and enable people to think and to think together. Loaded questions are manipulative devices which can lead to deviousness and insincere relationships.

Karl Tomm,[19] writing about systemic family therapy, has usefully distinguished four types of questions.

1. "Lineal" questions, which have an "investigative intent".
E.g. Who did what? Where? When? Why?

2. "Circular" questions, which have an "exploratory" intent.
Circular and "circularity" I find somewhat confusing terms, but the questioning activity it points to is important. I understand by this method the questioner "behaves like an explorer" on the assumption "that everything is somehow connected to everything else". Questions are formulated to bring out the "patterns that connect" persons, objects, actions, perceptions, ideas, feelings, events, beliefs, contexts, and so on in systems.[20] Tomm illustrates this form of questioning in this way:

> Thus, a more systemic therapist may begin the interview . . . : "How is it that we find ourselves together today?" (I called because I am worried about my husband's depression), "Who else worries?" (The kids), "Who do you think worries the most?" (She does), "Who do you imagine worries the least?" (I guess I do), "What does she do when she worries?" (She complains a lot . . . mainly about money and bills), "What do you do when she shows you that

she is worrying?" (I don't bother her . . . just keep to myself), "Who sees your wife's worrying the most?" (The kids, they talk about it a lot), "Do your kids agree?" (Yes), "What does your father usually do when you and your mother talk?" (He usually goes to bed), "And when your father goes to bed, what does your mother do?" (She just gets more worried), and so on.[21]

This kind of questioning, which teases out the different ways in which different people are acting, reacting and relating, greatly helps me to get a much more comprehensive understanding of all kinds of groups, communities, churches and organizations and prevents me from getting fixed on what is happening to one individual in a group or one group in a church. It helps me to see things not from one but many perspectives.

3. "Strategic" questions, which have a corrective intent.
E.g. Why is it, do you think, that you do not try harder to get people to talk in committees?

4. "Reflexive" questions, which have a "facilitative" intent.
E.g. What do you think the committee would do if you told them just what you think? What do you think you would feel like if they did that? What do you think you would do? These kinds of questions cause people to reflect upon situations, actions, new options, beliefs etc. They can help people to "new perspectives, new directions and new options" and "to generate new connections and new solutions on their own". However, care must be exercised, because opening up a multiplicity of new possibilities can be confusing when purposes are not clear.

Ian MacKay[22] gives another classification; the main categories are:

— **open questions;**
   "Please tell me about . . .?" "What do you think about . . . .?"

— **probe questions;**
   "How do you mean?" "What would you do if . . .?"

— **closed questions;**
   These are questions to establish facts: "How long did you work there?"

— **link questions;**
   To effect the transition from one form of questioning to another. "You said you were interested in . . . what particularly interests you?" "Why?"

— **counter-productive questions;**
   These questions are leading, trick, multiple, marathon, ambiguous, rhetorical and discriminatory.

MacKay considers these and subsidiary questions in relation to purpose, question form and illustrations.

186

2. Sequences of Questions

Sequences of questions I call "facilitating structures". The problem-tackling sequence given in Chapter One and the case study method in Chapter Two are such structures and there are sequences in the examples given above, whilst the method of working on situations and projects in Chapters Three and Four are facilitating structures made up of a sequence of tasks and questions. These facilitating structures have wide use but they do not fit all the work I do by any means. Sometimes they can be adapted; at other times new questions and sequences of questions and tasks have to be worked out. Sequences which I devised for people engaged in committee work illustrate this.

Preparing for Meetings

Why and What?

Why am I bringing this matter to the committee?

What do I want them to do or to decide?

Am I clear enough about the "why" and the "what" and the choices to be made?

Being Realistic

Can this committee deal with the subject in the time?

How can I save their time?

Homework

Have I got enough information?

Have I done all the work I can/must do beforehand?

Timing

Is this the best time to raise the subject?

Decision-Making in Meetings

What must be decided?

When must it be decided?

Who must decide?

Gather and share all relevant information

List choices

Choice 1 pros and cons

Choice 2 pros and cons, etc.

What is our decision?

Who is going to do what?

This all-too-brief introduction shows just how versatile a development tool the humble question really is and how interesting and absorbing using it can be.[23]

IV. HYPOTHESES

Increasingly I am finding hypotheses very useful in the analysis and design of church and community work.

A hypothesis is a provisional supposition which accounts for the available information and which serves as a starting point and as a guide for further exploration. Hypotheses are hunches, ideas or theories which need to be stated clearly and adopted tentatively until they are disproved or proved.[24] Such an attitude towards them is as critical as their content because their value is lost when they are stated as hypotheses and treated as established theories or explanations. What matters is that they are useful in analysis and design.

What I am finding particularly useful are systemic hypotheses, an idea I got from a particular approach to family therapy and organizational behaviour.[25] Such hypotheses relate to human systems and the functional, structural and affective relationships between their parts. Consequently they are more about systemic and multiple causation than linear causation.* I have not found this easy to grasp and apply but my efforts to do so have given me a much more comprehensive perspective on situations and paid high dividends. The hypothesis I formulated in relation to the Bishop's work in Chapter 3 is one attempt that I made.

Dr Gillian Stamp's analysis of the place and function of Deaneries in the Church of England illustrates the nature of systemic hypotheses.[27] Her hypotheses are:

- The deanery has emerged as an attempted resolution of unresolved tensions in the theology and the policy of Church of England.

- The espousal of inappropriate images is adding confusion to the attempts to unravel and restore appropriate internal and external relationships.

- Inside the church there is a gap between the parish and the diocese. This is echoed by a gap in ministry between the domestic and the regional.

- Whether the deanery is a device or an entity, the single term is being stretched to cover, at least, two distinctly different institutional forms.

- The function of hierarchy is not subordination but supplementation.

Examples almost at random of the kind of hypotheses that I have established and used in studying work situation with principal workers are:

---

*Edwin H. Friedman differentiates between these kinds of causation through the diagrams in Figure 7:a opposite.[26]

188

The movement from strong central control to shared control and openness in the diocese has disturbed its stability and made it volatile: it is essential to identify just what needs to be done to generate the homeostasis (or equilibrium) the system now needs.

Remedial action needs to be taken immediately in relation to the uneasy relationship between the informal, professional and apostolic aspects of the life of this religious congregation.

The diocesan system is not working as well as it might do because key figures are not able to work to both the parochial and diocesan sub-systems; they focus on one or the other but not on both.

I seem to formulate these by very much the same processes by which I construct diagrams and designs through an analytical dialogue with what I know of the workers and their situations. The great value of formulating these hypotheses is that they engender a perspective that attends to how the parts are working, or not working together for good, and thus they help to identify the action required to make a system work better.

Words, diagrams, questions and hypotheses are all tools that can be used for or against the best interests of people and workers. As I have presented them they equip people to promote human and spiritual development because they are shaped to be the executive instruments of action that is essentially non-directive. For them to be deployed consistently for these ends the ability to use them must be compounded with the commitments described in Chapters 8 and 10 and the appropriate personal and social skills described in this book.

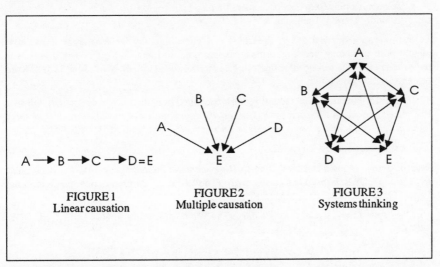

FIGURE 1
Linear causation

FIGURE 2
Multiple causation

FIGURE 3
Systems thinking

FIGURE 7:1. THREE FORMS OF CAUSATION

In figure 1: A causes B; B causes C; C causes D; D causes E. Figure 2 is also linear thinking. Figure 3 is different: A, B,C and D come together as interdependent forces to cause E through the complex interaction between them.

NOTES AND REFERENCES

1. Many textbooks on community work and community development describe the skills required. See, for example, Batten, T.R. & M., *The Non-Directive Approach in Group and Community Work* (Avec Publication, 1988); Thomas, D.N., *The Making of Community Work* (London: Allen & Unwin, 1983); The William Temple Foundation Occasional Paper, *Involvement in Community: A Christian Contribution* (William Temple Foundation, 1980).

2. I owe this information to Walter Eltis's contribution to an article on "The Experts' Expert: Market Forces" in the *Observer Magazine*, 12 March 1989. Ian T. Ramsey, *Models & Mystery* (London: OUP, 1964), says Lord Kelvin said "If I can make a mechanical model, I can understand it" (p. 2).

3. Cf. Koestler, Arthur, *The Act of Creation* (London: Hutchinson, 1964), p. 173. I find his chapter on "Thinking Aside" and particularly the sections on "The Word and The Vision" and "The Snares of Language" most illuminating in relation to the subject-matter of this chapter.

4. I owe this quotation to Koestler, *ibid.*, p. 173.

5. Koestler, *ibid.*, p. 171.

6. I wrote this section before reading David Deek's excellent chapter "Basic Resources: Words" in his book *Pastoral Theology: An Enquiry* (London: Epworth Press, 1987), pp. 9 ff.

7. The phrase "talking work" I owe to Argyle, Michael, *The Social Psychology of Work* (Harmondsworth: Penguin, 1972), p. 129 ff.

8. Smail, David, *Illusion and Reality: The Meaning of Anxiety* (London & Melbourne: Dent, 1984), p. 64.

9. For an exposition of experiential education see Dewey, John, *Experience and Education* (London: Macmillan, 1983 reprinted 1968); Hubery, Douglas *The Experiential Approach to Christian Education* (National Sunday School Union, 1960); Goldman, Ronald *Readiness for Religion: A Basis for Developmental Religious Education* (London: Routledge & Kegan Paul, 1965) *et al.*

10. Cf. Green, Robin, *Only Connect: Worship and Liturgy from the Perspective of Pastoral Care* (London: Darton, Longman & Todd, 1987).

11. An extraordinary article on "Preaching & Counselling" by Dr W. Berger shows how ideally both preaching and counselling can promote an inner dialogue. The article was published in the Dutch *Journal voor Pastorale Psychologie* (Vol. IV No. 2, June 1972). Avec has an English translation.

12. Further information about recording can be obtained from Avec. See also my unpublished PhD thesis *An action research project to test the applicability of the non-directive concept in a church, youth and community centre setting* pp. 80–86, 126ff, 151, 202, 607ff.

13. Koestler, Arthur, *op. cit.* p. 72.

14. I discussed models and modelling in *Diagrammatic Modelling: An Aid to Theological Reflection in Church and Community Work* (The William Temple Foundation Occasional Paper Number 4, 1980). See pp. 15 ff in particular.

15. Cf. Ramsey, Ian, *Models and Mystery* (The Whidden Lecture for 1963) (Oxford: OUP, 1964), p. 14, 15: cf. pp. 5, 13, 48, 53.

16. Morgan, Gareth, *Images of Organization* (Sage Publications, 1986), p. 337.

17. Dr Han-Ruedi Weber gives an extremely helpful description of the respective functions of the left or right hemispheres of the brain in an article entitled "Thinking in Images". I am drawing upon a summary of the article by Margaret Dewey in the series *Thinking Mission*, No. 39, (Summer 1983), issued by The United Society for the Propogation of the Gospel, 15 Tufton Street, London SW1 3QR. The article first appeared in the July 1982 *Ecumenical*

Review under the title "Interpreting Biblical Images". For further discussion of this phenomena see: *The Intelligent Eye* by R.L. Gregory (London: Weidenfeld and Nicolson, 1979); *Drawing on the Right Side of the Brain: How to unlock your hidden artistic talent* by Betty Edwards (London: Fontana/Collins, 1979); *The Right Brain: A new understanding of the unconscious mind and its creative powers* by Thomas R. Blakeslee (London: Macmillan Press, 1980); *Writing the Natural Way* by Gabriele Lusser Rico (Los Angeles: J.P. Tarcher, 1983).

18. There are some interesting ideas about "visual access cues" by Bandler, Richard & Grinder, John in *Frogs Into Princes: Neuro Linguistic Programme,* edited by Steve Andreas (formerly John O. Stevens) (NLP, 1979), pp. 25–27.

19. I am drawing upon three unpublished articles by Karl Tomm: *Interventive Interviewing: Part I. Strategizing as a fourth guideline for the therapist; Interventive Interviewing: Part II. Reflexive questioning as a means to enable self healing; Interventive Interviewing: Part III. Intending to ask lineal, circular, strategic and reflexive questions,* but chiefly upon Part III.

20. There is an exposition of "circularity" in *Family Process,* Vol. 19 Number 1, (March 1980) "Hypothesizing—Circularity—Neutrality: Three Guidelines for the Conductor of the Session", by Mara Palazzoli, M.D., Luigi Boscolo, M.D., Gianfranco Cecchin, M.D., and Giuliana Prata, M.D.

21. Karl Tomm, *op. cit.* Part III, p. 8.

22. MacKay, Ian, *A Guide to Asking Questions* (British Association for Commercial & Industrial Education, 16 Park Crescent, London W1N 4AP).

23. There are some interesting illustrations of the use of questions and discussions about them in Day, Robin *Grand Inquisitor: Memoirs by Sir Robin Day* (London: Weidenfeld and Nicolson, 1989): see particularly pp. 45 ff, 50 ff, 56 ff, 106 ff, 114 ff, 173 ff, 180 ff, 198 f, 238, 244 ff, 248 ff.

24. I am told that, strictly speaking, hypotheses can be disproved but not proved.

25. The development and use of systemic hypotheses is well illustrated in *Family Process,* Vol. 19 Number 1 (March 1980), in an article entitled "Hypothesizing—Circularity—Neutrality: Three Guidelines for the Conductor of the Session", by Mara Selvini Palazzoli, Luigi Boscolo, Gianfrancho Cecchin and Giuliana Prata, p. 5; an article by Mara Selvini Palazzoli and others already quoted; and in *The Hidden Games of Organizations* (New York: Pantheon Books, 1986), by Mara Selvini Palazzoli and Luigi Anolli, Paola di Blasio, Lucia Giossi, Innocenzo Pisano, Carolo Ricci, Marica Sacchi and Valeria Ugazio. This book contains some very interesting case studies. For the background to the development of these ideas by the "Milan Group" see: *Weekend Observer,* 27 March 1988, for an article on Mara Palazzoli entitled "Family Circles", p. 35 ff; *Journal of Family Therapy* 5:165–177 (1983), "The Emergence of a Comprehensive Systems Approach" by Mara Selvini Palazzoli; *Journal of Family Therapy* 6:299-307 (1984), "Behind the Scenes of the Organization: some guidelines for the expert in human relations", also by Palazzoli.

26. Friedman, Edwin H., *Generation to Generation: Family Process in Church and Synagogue* (New York & London: The Guilford Press, 1985), p. 15 ff.

27. Stamp, Gillian, *Is Your Deanery Really Necessary?* (A Brunel Institute of Organisational and Social Studies, BIOSS, Paper, 1986): cf. also *Crucible* (October–December 1985) an article by Professor Stamp entitled "Does the Deanery Make a Difference?".

CHAPTER EIGHT

Using the Process

The processes of analysis and design described in this book are most likely to promote the holistic development of people and their environment when they are used to help workers:

— to think through things themselves;
— to determine how to help other people with whom they work to do the same.

These twin objectives are pursued in all the worked examples in Part One and suffuse the detailed discussion of the methodology. Achieving the first helps workers to be more effective agents of reflective action for the common good; achieving the second helps to create churches, organizations and communities that are more effective agents of reflective action for the common good. Creating such communities is important because reflective practitioners need reflective communities just as reflective communities need reflective practitioners. They go together. It is difficult for either to survive without the other. Communities of reflective agents are multipliers, they beget learning communities of reflective agents which foster human and spiritual growth and development. But being a reflective practitioner in community and generating reflective communities are difficult jobs. The processes I have described seem like a counsel of perfection when contrasted with the realities of the messy ways in which we think through things individually and collectively. The family case study graphically illustrates aspects of these realities with which we are all too familiar. The question we need to address is what—other than the things we have already described—will help us to use the analytical and design processes in working situations?

I. WORKING PRIVATELY AND PUBLICLY

First, let us look at some of the relevant features of the settings and relationships within and through which we have to reflect and promote reflection. Some things we have to think through and work out privately. Other things we have to do publicly in groups, committees, councils, chapters, and various other kinds of meetings. That which we do privately can be done either on our own or with colleagues, co-workers, consultants and friends—some of whom we work with publicly as well. Private work domains are closed systems, the boundaries of which are under the control of the participants and maintained through confidentiality. Public work domains are open systems. I represent these things diagrammatically in Figure 8:1.[1]

We are focusing on workers or practitioners so they are at the centre of all this. They are pivotal figures who embody within themselves their experiences of the domains that intersect and interact within them. The circular arrow around the central figure indicates that all the time, in private and in public, thoughts, ideas and feelings are pulsating through the worker's heart and mind. Some people refer to this as the "inner dialogue" or "self-talk". I prefer to call it "interior personal work" because we have to work at it in order to make our best contributions.

Sometimes this personal work is very rewarding and exciting. Things come together within us and make creative links between ourselves, our circumstances and those with whom we are working. At other times we simply cannot think straight. Feelings we cannot discipline and control prevent rational thought. This happens in the private and the public domains, when we are working on our own as well as when we are working with others. The family communion case study described the experiences most of us have from time to time when we just cannot work out within us how to respond to the circumstances in which we find ourselves. Acting out of the inner confusion that this causes can be damaging. Much of this personal work, in private and in public, is, in fact, stewing over interpersonal relationships, experiences, and problems.

Diagrams of a similar kind can be drawn for every participant in any collective activity. Connecting up one or two of these diagrams quickly reveals the complexity of the interaction in collective thinking activities!

The diagram indicates the complexity of the systems within which we work things out but it does not do justice to them. They are dynamic, and classification tends to obscure this. The neatly ordered settings and patterns of thinking interact and interpenetrate. A telephone call suddenly breaks into the middle of our private work, drags us into the public arena and puts us on the spot possibly in relation to the very thing we were trying to sort out. Then again, what happened in the discussion with one group interacts positively or negatively with that in another (cf. the case study on children at communion).

Workers have to move between private and public and that involves crossing various physical, environmental, psychological and spiritual boundaries. They have also got to move from one way of thinking about things to another. At best there is a creative flow in the movement; at worst it undermines morale. At times, for instance, I find difficulty in settling down to work on my own on complex human issues in the solitary isolation of my study after a week with a group. I feel bereft of the richness of the interaction of the group and the assurance, confidence and mutual reinforcement that comes from joint decision-making. Faced with the difficulties of working alone, the advantages of being in a group loom large and I yearn to be back in that setting! On the other hand,

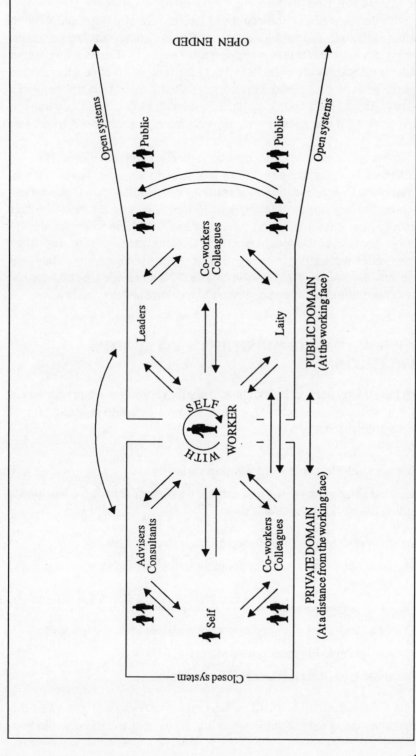

FIGURE 8:1. PRIVATE AND PUBLIC WORK DOMAINS

195

faced with an impasse in a group about a critical decision I can yearn for private work where I am "free" to think and decide on my own!

In both domains discussion can take place in formal groups and through informal exchanges and through what is said on the grapevines and networks. Rigorous thinking in formal groups equips people to discuss things more rigorously informally. And the formal thinking is most effective when it takes seriously what is being said informally. What happens on the networks seriously affects, for good or ill, developmental work carried out through formal groups. It can either enable or undermine projects and workers and leaders.

Churches and neighbourhood organizations become communities of reflective practitioners when as many people as possible are thinking things through, separately and together, in the various settings and relationships, in private and in public, and when their thinking jells to give a purposeful thrust to their endeavours towards the common good. I value the thinking processes already described because, as they can be used in all the settings and relationships, they make significant contributions towards creating such communities. They help all concerned to live, work and worship together. They provide a methodological common denominator. They create a unitive culture and spirituality.

II. GENERATING COMMUNITIES OF REFLECTIVE
PRACTITIONERS

Much has already been said about how to use these processes in private and in public. What follows helps us to use them to generate communities of reflective practitioners.

1. Taking Each Person's Contribution seriously

In the kind of communal work situations we are considering, participants, including the workers, can think about:

(a) their own experiences, thoughts, ideas, feelings, etc.;

(b) what others think and feel about their (the participant's) thoughts and feelings;

(c) other people's experiences, thoughts, ideas, feelings, etc.;

(d) what they think about other people's experiences, thoughts, etc.;

(e) the systemic interaction between (a) to (d);

(f) the shared ideas that emerge as "our" thinking.

All the work described in Part One was effective because it generated this comprehensive pattern of thinking. Commonly, but mistakenly, the non-directive approach is associated exclusively with getting people individually and collectively to think about their own thoughts. Without in any way detracting from the importance of doing this, some developments will take place only when people think seriously about the ideas of others including those of their workers. The non-directive approach and the analytical processes described in this book make vital contributions towards promoting and facilitating the different aspects of thinking noted above. Promoting and engaging in this multi-faceted thinking involves workers, colleagues, co-workers and laity variously acting towards each other as consultants and consultors. (I develop this idea in Chapter Twelve.) Continual exchange of these roles contributes to the formation of learning communities by building up open networks of egalitarian and interchangeable working relationships. In turn this makes for well-equipped, cohesive and flexible communities of reflective practitioners.

2. Workers intervening, engaging, withdrawing, waiting and returning

Helping other people, individuals and groups, to think through aspects of their work involves continual cycles of action: intervening, engaging, withdrawing, waiting, returning, intervening . . . and so on.

Directive and non-directive action are two forms of **intervention and engagement**.[2] Both are necessary. They are equally direct and forthright. Directive action must be responsible, loving and caring—not arrogant, autocratic and dictatorial; non-directive action must be warm, compassionate and close—not clinically cold and distant. Neither directive nor non-directive action is *ipso facto* right or wrong: doing too much *for* or *with* people can inhibit development, as can doing too little *for* or *with* people. Both approaches are necessary because, if we are to live and develop, some things must be done *for us*, some things must be left for us to do *for ourselves* and *with others* and some things we will only be able to do if someone works *with us*, alongside us.

Choices have to be made continually between approaches in relation to reference points and circumstances.[3] Changes and development in people and circumstances make previous choices of approach inappropriate, dysfunctional or disastrous. For example, what it was appropriate for an adult to do *for* a child of five may be highly inappropriate for a child of twelve. Requests for a fixed formula for choice of approach must be resisted. Questions that help me are:

What must I do *for* these people at this time and in this situation?

What must I do alongside them, *with them*?

What must we do *together*?

What must I leave them to do *for themselves* and *with each other*?

How can I get into the appropriate mode of interaction—by, for example,

197

simply adopting what I consider to be an appropriate mode or by negotiating?

How must I withdraw so that my waiting and returning promote processes of development?

The questions are universally relevant; the answers, and therefore the action to be taken and the leads to be given, vary enormously from one situation to another and as people grow.

Withdrawal is a critical part of helping others to think. People often indicate the need for withdrawal by saying things like: "I need to think about that". "I must let that go through my mind". "I want to sleep on it". "I need time to mull that over". What people are saying through these statements is: "I cannot think any further with you or in your presence". Workers who do not respect or anticipate these requests inhibit further thought and block processes of development. Judging, sensing and negotiating the moment of withdrawal—either through physically leaving or dropping the subject—is an art to be cultivated.

A friend of mine, ex-public school and Oxbridge, was a member of a small team of people with similar backgrounds servicing working-class tenants' associations scattered over a large metropolitan area. To their consternation, after a very busy and productive initial period they found that they were simply not being used by the tenants. Eventually the chairman of the associations told them why they were not now being used. "You come. You are very helpful. But you do not know when we want you to go so that we can talk in our own way about what you've said. And we don't know how to tell you to go without being rude. If you were one of us we would know just what to say." An understanding was reached that when tenants had "finished" with the worker they would say so without ceremony, "That's all we need you for, John". This changed the whole pattern of relationships. The team was inundated with work.

Much of the skill is so to withdraw that people and workers feel free to approach each other as and when they feel the need to do so. This can be facilitated through establishing a mutual understanding about "withdrawing" and "re-entry" when establishing working relationships. (I have wasted a lot of nervous energy fretting over whether or not to approach people who have not got in touch when they said they would!)

So far the process has been discussed in terms of the action of a worker in relation to other people. When people of their own volition start to approach each other in these ways, the momentum of the development process is greatly enhanced. Seeing people become "workers" to each other and to the worker is humbling and exciting.

The engagement we have been thinking about is analysing and designing work programmes and projects and studying cases and problems. But it could be thinking through all kinds of human situations. Waiting, or what I like to call work-waiting, is the period when workers have to let others get on with their work freely, in their own way and in their own time. It is hard for workers to do this and to resist the temptation to interfere when they have nurtured the work, invested a lot of effort in it, taken it to their hearts and when they are anxious about its success and how things are going. However this may be, effectiveness depends upon waiting in patience and returning at the right moment.

Strangely, one of the things that helps me to recall the importance of waiting, and of enduring it, is a scene that comes into my mind of a master craftsman, a plasterer, waiting for the plaster or cement to get to a particular point in setting before smoothing or polishing it or adding another layer. Nothing, just nothing, would make him take premature action. My amateurish efforts in this and other similar things are frequently marred because I simply do not wait for the materials to do their own work—in my impatient indiscipline I add more plaster prematurely! When working with people the waiting time is variously circumvented. Workers return to "put things right" or to check on what is happening. Sometimes they act upon the questionable assumption that "it is easier and quicker to do it yourself than to wait for them". Others try to take short cuts by resorting to directive and autocratic action. Time is saved in the short term at the cost of development in the long term. People need *their* time to do *their* work. Workers simply must wait upon people. The work we did with the bishop and Father Patrick Doyle shows the value of their working with a group, withdrawing to do their private and personal work, and returning to share their most recent ideas.

W.H. Vanstone, in his quite remarkable book *The Stature of Waiting*, has greatly helped me to understand the theological and practical significance of waiting through his exposition of Jesus' "waiting" ministry after the betrayal.[4] Dr Gillian Stamp has produced two very useful models which help me to understand and negotiate the "withdrawal" and "waiting" in managerial working relationships. The first is what she describes as the "tripod of work" formed by three activities, "tasking, trusting and tending", in contradistinction to "handing over, mistrusting and controlling".[5] The second is a "triad of trust" which exists when the worker *trusts* his/her own judgement, the organization *trusts* the worker's judgement and when workers are *entrusted* with the purposes of the organization.[6] I have been helped to see just how to withdraw through delegating by a step-by-step process outlined by Andrew Forrest.[7]

Returning starts a new round of the cycle.

3. Commitment of Workers to Private Work

It is essential that workers commit themselves to private work, to short- and long-term preparation. The quality and effectiveness of all public work depends upon it. Hard private thinking is required of workers if they are to use the processes described in this book publicly to good effect and make their unique contribution to the thinking processes—they have, for instance, a perspective on the church/organization as a whole and information about it which no one else has. Getting this in a form which others in the organization can handle can take quite a bit of private work.

Over many centuries much effort has gone into helping ministers and priests to get the balance right between preparation and practice in relation to preaching and conducting worship, and between studying and visiting. Less effort has gone into getting the balance right between preparing to work with people and working with them. More effort has gone into the what and how of working face-to-face with people than into preparing to do so.

Several reasons can be advanced for this neglect. Preparing to work with people is notoriously difficult, especially done on one's own. Amongst other things it involves grappling with questions such as: precisely what is happening between the people in this situation, and how can I conceptualize and analyse it? How should I introduce this idea or that, to whom, when and in what order? Should I be doing this or that *for* or *with* them or should I leave them to do it by and for themselves? How can I help them to think through these things profitably in the very limited time and energy they have available at the end of a busy day in the middle of a demanding week? Getting people to think for themselves—especially about things they need to think about but do not want to—is more demanding than thinking about things for them.

Some priests with whom I worked steadfastly resisted private work because they said, "thinking things through privately on our own can move us on too fast and break down feelings of 'us' and 'ours' created by joint work between clergy and laity".[8] They wanted to do everything with the laity. They argued that in order to be non-directive and to avoid subtle manipulation it is necessary to start together with the people where they are. I am entirely sympathetic to the aim but my own experience has been that initiating non-directive work programmes requires careful planning if people and workers are to have the necessary freedom to engage with each other and do the things that they need and want to do. Preparation facilitates the use of non-directive group work skills and it also helps in another way. Having clarified my own purposes and ideas and gathered relevant information, I find that I give myself much more freely to others in the tasks of helping them to do their thinking. In short, using the processes myself on what I have to do is creative preparation for using them with others.

Another reason for the neglect of private work, especially study and research, is that it is the public work towards which workers' aims, thoughts, ideas and preparation point.[9] It calls them in demanding ways and quickly seduces them from private work possibly because it is public work to which they are predisposed. All this is reflected in the common practice of workers' entering time into their diaries for public work but not for the private work necessary to prepare for it and to follow it through.

Private work is all too easily squeezed out.

4. Commitment to thinking Things through time and again with Different Groups

Developing communities of reflective practitioners involves thinking things through time and again with individuals and groups as well as thinking things through in private. Both commitments are required. Sometimes it involves thinking things out from first principles with group after group and then getting all concerned to think about what has emerged. At other times it involves a worker or group thinking their way through something and then submitting their thinking for critical scrutiny to other people. This may have to be done in stages. Group one thinks about the initial ideas. Group two thinks about the ideas and the suggestions of group one and so on. Doing this is quite different from getting people to accept or adopt *in toto* the thinking of the first group. When it is not possible for everyone to think things out from first principles they can think about provisional plans in relation to their reference points and make profound observations. People can appraise things they could not design or build.

Biddle and Biddle[10] worked out a useful developmental process which involved starting with a basic nucleus of people who worked on some ideas for development and gradually formed a larger nucleus by working through their ideas with successive groups of people.

Using the same structures, processes, approaches and methods at each stage gives shape to the process. A key to the success of this sequential thinking is designing a critical path that enables one group to build upon and develop the thinking that has gone on before. We saw how this process went wrong in the family case study (Chapter One). The critical path has to be "managed"; generally speaking, this is a worker's job.

By the very nature of churches, organizations and religious orders, things are thought through in many different ways, relationships and formal and informal settings before conclusions are reached. Consequently discussions do not have a smooth run through a neat, discrete series of predetermined stages. They are stop-start, bitty, and discontinuous as one group or meeting after another has a go at thinking things through from this angle and that. In contrast to these actualities, the sequences I have set out in an orderly way in this book could appear to be a counsel of perfection. That may be, but for me it is a useful foil which helps me to put purposeful order and shape into discussions or series of discussions in different settings and relationships. It is also like a map; it helps me to see where a particular discussion fits into all that has to be done to think through something profoundly and comprehensively.

5. Acquiring the Ability to work in Private as well as in Public

Earlier I indicated some of the differences between the private and the public working environments. Examining the similarities and differences in more detail would be fascinating and illuminating. But here I must restrict myself to some of the things that contribute to working effectively in each domain, to being able to bridge the divide between them and to being able to move from one to the other. Abilities needing to be cultivated are listed in the chart below.

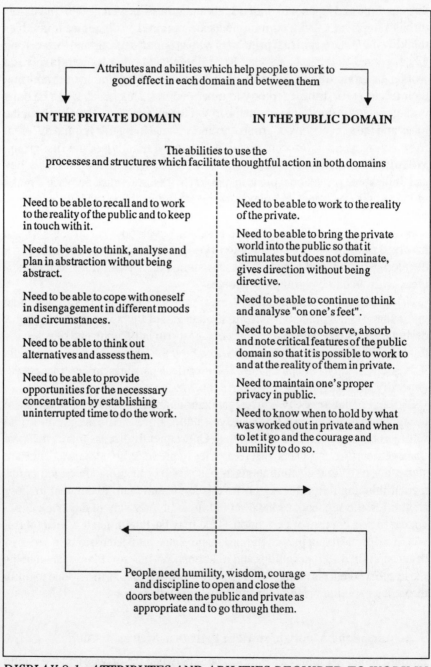

Attributes and abilities which help people to work to good effect in each domain and between them

IN THE PRIVATE DOMAIN

IN THE PUBLIC DOMAIN

The abilities to use the processes and structures which facilitate thoughtful action in both domains

Need to be able to recall and to work to the reality of the public and to keep in touch with it.

Need to be able to think, analyse and plan in abstraction without being abstract.

Need to be able to cope with oneself in disengagement in different moods and circumstances.

Need to be able to think out alternatives and assess them.

Need to be able to provide opportunities for the necesssary concentration by establishing uninterrupted time to do the work.

Need to be able to work to the reality of the private.

Need to be able to bring the private world into the public so that it stimulates but does not dominate, gives direction without being directive.

Need to be able to continue to think and analyse "on one's feet".

Need to be able to observe, absorb and note critical features of the public domain so that it is possible to work to and at the reality of them in private.

Need to maintain one's proper privacy in public.

Need to know when to hold by what was worked out in private and when to let it go and the courage and humility to do so.

People need humility, wisdom, courage and discipline to open and close the doors between the public and private as appropriate and to go through them.

DISPLAY 8:1. ATTRIBUTES AND ABILITIES REQUIRED TO WORK IN PRIVATE AND PUBLIC DOMAINS

6. Managing the Transition from the Personal and Private to the Public

Teilhard de Chardin said that "the passage from the individual to the collective is the critical problem of human energy".[11] I venture to add that the reverse journey is a critical problem too. Making these journeys involves opening doors between the private and public, the personal and interpersonal and going through them, and that requires humility, wisdom, courage, discipline and various props and aids. It also calls for judgement in deciding what is apposite to each domain and in maintaining socio-religious systems that are appropriately open/closed, public/private, closed/open and private/public. In any relationship it is essential to provide for togetherness and privacy; they are the hallmarks of good community.

The "passage from the individual to the collective" involves crossing many boundaries as we move from the private to the public and from one group to another. Some of these boundaries are physical, others are psychological, cultural and environmental. They relate to belonging and to the ways in which people do things. Being conscious of these boundaries helps me to prepare to cross them.[12]

The aim is to get a creative interaction, positive meshing and engagement, between the private and public and between the personal and interpersonal work; between thinking things out within yourself, "self-talk", and talking things out with others. Many things can impede such processes. Talking before and without thinking is one of them. Another is the withholding of thoughts until they have matured and been tested. A very highly intelligent member of a group with which I worked created a bad dynamic because of his long silences. People became progressively more anxious to know what he was thinking. Eventually he told us that he thought everything through several times before he shared his thinking because he was prepared to do so only when he felt that his thinking could not be faulted. His approach meant that he had opted out of what the other members of the group were doing, thinking things through together aloud. He was pursuing, in parallel, and not in sequence, a separate line of thought and contributing conclusions. That of course can be most productive, provided that it does not prevent the others from doing *their* thinking and break down the relationships between people. Getting the balance right between thinking aloud and thinking your own thoughts is a matter of judgement, timing, skill, confidence and of your willingness to give yourself to others and to be vulnerable.

For Christians this process is even more complicated when they are trying to discern the will and mind of God in relation to the matters under consideration.

7. Using the Process in all Settings and Relationships

Using suitable adaptations of the processes illustrated and described in Parts One and Two in all the settings and relationships has many advantages. It

203

— helps to objectify things, to handle affective content, to be realistic and to work at things systematically;

— provides a common format for community thinking;

— helps to handle the private in public and vice versa;

— helps people to think about their own and each other's ideas;

— legitimizes private, personal and shared public thinking;

— helps the transfer and the cross-reference of thinking from one setting, working relationship and domain to another.

III. TOWARDS ACQUIRING THE ABILITY TO USE THE PROCESS IN COMMUNITY

Whichever way you look at it, pursuing these processes is hard work. Reading about them can be intimidating. It all seems so complicated. Most people can and do willingly co-operate in the use of these processes when someone else is acting as worker/consultant. They do so gladly even though it can be demanding when they feel they are getting somewhere. Most of us continue to need someone to help us to think through things. Nevertheless, a desirable development is that people acquire the ability to use the processes themselves and gain the comparative analytical autonomy that goes with it. Some people take to the approach quite naturally and are soon using it themselves: frequently the process gives shape and order to that to which they already aspire. Other people have to make significant changes in their style of working in order to adopt this approach. Personal and private changes have to be accompanied by public and corporate changes in working relationships and methods. To attempt to make these changes with confidence people need to be assured that the processes are theologically sound, that they do not compromise their beliefs about such things as inspiration, and being "open to the leading of the Spirit". These questions are discussed later in the book when we have considered the underlying theory and theology of the approach (see Chapters 9 and 10). Here we confine ourselves to one or two suggestions about how to acquire the necessary skills. Again, I list them for economy in presentation. It is possible to acquire the abilities through:

• learning about processes and getting the feel of them, by observing, experiencing and evaluating other people using them in courses and work consultancy sessions;

• working as an apprentice or colleague with someone experienced in using them;

• adopting a piece-meal approach to acquiring the skills; (To learn and to improve one's performance of any complex sequence of operations it is necessary to concentrate on parts of it, and especially those parts with which we find most difficulty: it might be analysing or designing or deciding; or it might be a common element such as asking questions or recording observations with greater accuracy. Then it is necessary to build the skills together. This is the way in which I have acquired what ability I have.)

- studying worked examples (as we do in Part One) and doing case-study exercises; (I learnt a lot by analysing cases very much as I learnt about mathematics by doing exercises.[13])

- using basic formulations of the process such as the approach to problem-solving and case studies; (These two methods lend themselves to unobtrusive use. They pave the way to using more complicated structures and to designing your own.)

- working things out on paper as well as in your head and through the spoken word; (As I have said, I have learnt an enormous amount about these procedures by writing up records of what happened in programmes of work and analysing them at my leisure.)

- working with colleagues as co-workers to implement these ideas and to help each other towards improved performance through mutual support and criticism;

- corporate management of the process.

These learning methods are a combination of studying the processes themselves; of exploring their application to the private and public domains through worked examples and doing exercises; of direct experience of the processes without having primary responsibility for them; of trying them out in the private and in the public domains in partnership with others and on your own and evaluating progress. The learning is by study, experience, practice, trial and error, analysis and osmosis. At first progress may be slow and use of the methods ponderous if not gauche. They are assimilated through reflective practice. Gradually it becomes second nature to work at things in this way.

NOTES AND REFERENCES

1. This diagram is a revision of one I put in *Human and Religious Factors in Church and Community Work* (A Grail Publication, 1982), p. 44.

2. For an exposition of the approaches see Batten, T.R. & M., *The Non-Directive Approach* (Avec Publication, 1988), and Lovell, George, *The Church and Community Development— An Introduction* (Grail Publications/Chester House Publications, 1972).

3. The Battens, *op. cit.*, have a useful chapter on "Factors Affecting Choice".

4. I got many of the ideas about "waiting" from Canon W.H. Vanstone's book, *The Stature of Waiting* (London: Darton, Longman and Todd, 1982). Also, I got the idea of "work-waiting" from Vanstone's use of "social-waiting", i.e. the time spent on waiting upon the arrangements and convenience of others (cf. p. 46).

5. A Brunel Institute of Organization and Social Studies (BIOSS) Occasional Paper, *The Tripod of Work*, February 1987.

6. *Well-being & Stress at Work* by Gillian Stamp. BIOSS Occasional Paper, September 1988, p. 2.

7. *Delegation: Notes for Managers 19* (The Industrial Society, 1971, reprinted 1976). See particularly p. 12.

8. Cf. Lovell, George, *Human and Religious Factors in Church and Community Work.* pp. 44 ff.

9. Thomas, David, *The Making of Community Work* (London: Allen & Unwin, 1983), throws light on the nature of the change to be made by church and community workers by comments he makes about community workers:

> Mosley came to the opinion that "people working in the field of community development place little value upon formal evaluative research, and show in their writing little awareness of the thought habits which its practice encourages" (1971). These thought habits are easy to recognise but difficult to define. There is a certain quality that one finds in the thinking of good researchers and statisticians. It is a cautious, analytic style, a little clinical but certainly rigorous, and an ability to ask questions that startle previously held assumptions. It is a questioning, objective, take-nothing-for-granted approach. Community workers, on the other hand, are enthusiastic, committed, passionate, partisan and subjective when it comes to their own work and that of community groups. And so they should be. (p. 266.)

10. Biddle, William W. & Loureide Biddle, *The Community Development Process: The Rediscovery of Local Initiative* (New York: Holt, Rinehart & Winston, 1965). There is brief reference to the process in their book *Encouraging Community Development: A Training Guide For Local Workers* (1968).

11. I owe this quotation to David Thomas, *The Making of Community Work*, p. 289.

12. The introduction to the following book gives a most revealing account of the kind of boundaries that people working with communities have to cross: Henderson, Paul, David Jones and David Thomas (eds.), *The Boundaries of Change in Community Work*, National Institute of Social Services Library No. 37 (London: Allen & Unwin, 1980).

13. The following books give worked/unworked examples and case studies of the processes described in this book.

   Batten, T.R., with the collaboration of Madge Batten, *The Human Factor in Community Work* (London: OUP, 1965).

   Batten, T.R. with the collaboration of Madge Batten, *The Human Factor in Youth Work* (London: OUP, 1970). Out of print but available from some libraries.

Lovell, George & Catherine Widdicombe, *Churches and Communities: An Approach to Development in the Local Church* (Tunbridge Wells: Search Press, 1978).

Lovell, George, *An Action Research Project to Test the Applicability of the Non-Directive Concept in a Church, Youth and Community Centre Setting* (thesis submitted for the Degree of Doctor of Philosophy in the Institute of Education, Faculty of Arts, University of London, 1973). Unpublished.

Part Three

A Commentary on the Approach

In the first two parts of this book I have illustrated and annotated ways in which people themselves can study at appropriate points work in which they are engaged and make better-informed decisions about what to do next and how to do it. The processes of analysis and design encompass past and present experience and future action: what has been done and what has now to be done. They are essentially activities in the workplace, not the laboratory, even when workers withdraw temporarily to do them—they are *in vivo*.

CHAPTER NINE

The Nature of the Activity

One of the intrinsic difficulties of communicating the process we are considering is that no one word or phrase known to me does justice to its many facets. Over-emphasis of any one of these—including the non-directive approach—misrepresents it. So what I have attempted in this chapter is a kind of "diamond cutting exercise". In the first part I have "cut" as many facets of the nature of the approach as I can think of, as reflected by the core process and the various parts played by those who use it. Then I have examined some of the facets more fully.

I. MULTI-FACETED

The nature of the core process (from experience through critical and imaginative thoughts to creative action) is fascinatingly complex; discovering some of its facets has been one of the exciting privileges of living and working with it. I can best summarise it in the following way.

In its application it is —

- a human and spiritual activity;
- focused and centred on workers and their work, however mundane it is;
- proactive, and stimulates and facilitates others to be proactive;
- outwardly directed to wider socio-religious contexts and issues;
- interventionist, provocative and perturbing but respects the autonomy and privacy of others;
- structured and systematic—not to impose order and shape but to enable others to order and shape their working world as they need to;
- logical, affective and intuitive, giving equal attention to thoughts, feelings and hunches;
- specific but systemic and holistic, concentrating on people, situations and issues;
- practical because it is theoretical and theological;
- collaborative and generates mutual accountability;

- both a private and a public activity;
- reflection-in-action, and, when used rigorously, a form of action-research;
- hard but rewarding work!

In its effects it—

- uses and promotes theological understanding;
- engenders interdependency, which properly respects independence and dependence;
- distributes power;
- empowers people;
- mandates equal opportunities to participate;
- promotes creative consensus by revealing and working constructively at differences, factions and conflicts;
- promotes self-induced and inter-related human and spiritual development in secular and religious contexts;
- is educational without being didactic—it leads to perceptive ways of "knowing" about the human and the divine;[1]
- helps build socio-religious learning communities that can live and work for human well-being and the glory of God;
- equips people to work for development with each other and to be co-workers with Christ in the Church and in the world;
- is ecumenical, bringing together in common endeavour all kinds of people;
- makes contributions to all stages of human and spiritual development;
- is deeply satisfying!

In its intention, orientation and approach it—

- starts with people where they are, accepting them and their situations as they are;
- stands by people without attempting to take their place;[2]
- works to the rhythms of people;
- stimulates people to do all they can for the common good;
- is both inductive and deductive;
- is an act of faith in the abilities and willingness of others to pursue their own well-being and development and to work for the common good;

214

- is non-directive—religiously so in relation to the decisions people need to make for themselves;

- is complementary and integral to that which is done *for* us by God and other people;

- is inclusive rather than exclusive;

- contributes to all aspects of the ministry and mission of the Church;

- makes unique and essential contributions to the work economy of the kingdom of God.

It can be embodied in people (individuals and collectives) and their work through their—

- love of people and God;

- inner commitments, human graces and technical skills.

Unfortunately there is no word or phrase that points to the richly endowed nature of this approach. What a travesty it is, for want of a better word, to have to call it "non-directive"!

II. ORIENTED TO WORKERS AND THEIR WORK

The processes we are discussing are about ways in which people themselves separately and together can put their beliefs into effective practice and achieve their purposes for development in church and society. They are about people as *workers* (lay, religious and ordained) and about *their* work (with people rather than things); about the private and public work, that *workers* have to do within and beyond themselves to change things for the better within and beyond themselves. (Consequently workers and their situations are themselves their own "base workshops".) These processes promote a flow of task-centred behaviour from the creative core[3] of workers which empowers people to develop themselves and their environment. Figure 9:1 highlights the parts, the purposeful thrust and the principal axis of these processes.

The work we are considering "begins with a feeling of something lacking, something desired ... something to be created, something to be brought into being ... in the environment ... in the self".[4] Those engaged in it are committed to their vision of what could be, and highly motivated to bring what is into line with it. For those of us who are Christians such feelings will owe much to Jesus and what he taught. Moreover, we will see the work to be God's as well as ours and ourselves in a working partnership with the Divine, co-workers with Christ and God and our efforts as complementary to the "work of Christ";[5] i.e., to those things Jesus did for us through his death and resurrection which we

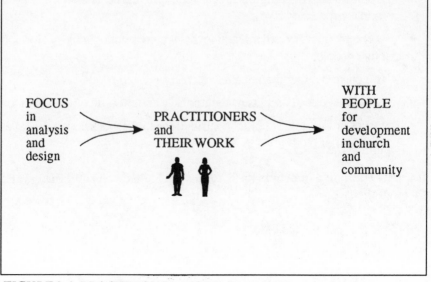

FIGURE 9:1. PRACTITIONER-WORK ORIENTED APPROACH

cannot do for ourselves. Therefore the work is purposeful and, as we saw earlier, set in ideological and theological frameworks and the human and spiritual values associated with them. Thus faith and human subjectivity help to define the work to be done and the way that it should be done. So the work, like the processes to be promoted, is deeply rooted in people and in their experience and understanding of things as they are and of God and God's Kingdom. Amongst other things, this means that the whole person is in action. Professor Elliott Jaques expresses this well:

> Work is an activity of the whole person. It is that behaviour which constitutes the primary plane of reality in which the individual relates his subjective world to the external world, transforming each in the process of creating some socially manifest output. It is a realization in the external work of a subjective project. It is the behaviour through which the individual experiences the reality of his core identity.[6]

Work of this kind is vocational. It is about the inner and outer worlds of workers and those with whom they work and the intimate and complex relationships between them and their environment—aspects of the indivisible reality of all church and community work.[7] It involves four kinds of work:

- the work of the mind;
- the work of the heart/soul;
- the work of the hand, i.e., the active engagement with situations;
- the work of the feet to put us in touch with co-workers.[8]

216

This kind of work is, in fact, vocational. As such, it has special powers over us; it affects us in one way or another quite dramatically because our hearts and souls are in it and because it is an outward visible expression of our most intimate and precious beliefs and purposes. These effects are complex. When, for example, the work is going well it can affect us positively or negatively: it can make us feel satisfied, humbled, thankful or it can make us feel self-satisfied, conceited and complacent. Similarly when it is going badly it can call forth reserves of creative energy we did not know we possessed or it can cause us to give up and feel a failure. In short vocational work is charged with all kinds of alternating positive and negative psycho-spiritual pulses whether it is going well or badly. Working creatively at these pulses is an important part of church and community development work.

However, the interaction between us and our work is more complex than this because the effects of our work upon us reverberate through complex socio-religious systems to which we belong; and throughout those same systems pulse the feelings others have about their work and ours. They variously harmonize, conflict, assure, confuse and confound. I illustrate this by constructing Figure 9:2, which shows how the work, when it is going well and when it going badly, can have both positive and negative effects upon the various relationships between workers and their relatives, friends, co-workers, church and God.

Adversity, for instance, can bring them all together or set them at variance as when workers or their relationships with others are being adversely affected by the work. In some instances relatives and friends can blame God and the church for difficulties their loved ones are experiencing in their work or for taking them away from them: in their anguish, and possibly loss of faith, they can argue that in the end it is God's work and calling and that of the Church—*they* called them and *they* got them into this mess.

Clearly, practitioners are most effective when the whole vocational system is functioning well. Any one of the sub-systems can prevent it from doing so. Work analysis and consultancy concentrate on making the practitioner-work sub-system as effective as it can be. That involves attending to the complex technology of church and community work *and* relating the work sub-system to the other sub-systems. This contribution is much needed, as are psychological and spiritual counselling. Sadly, however, all too often such counselling has been offered to practitioners who were psychologically and spiritually distressed because they were not able to do their work as well as they needed to do for their own well-being. What they actually required was the kind of help described in this book. Getting the work sub-system right makes significant contributions to the overall effectiveness and harmony of a practitioner's vocational system.

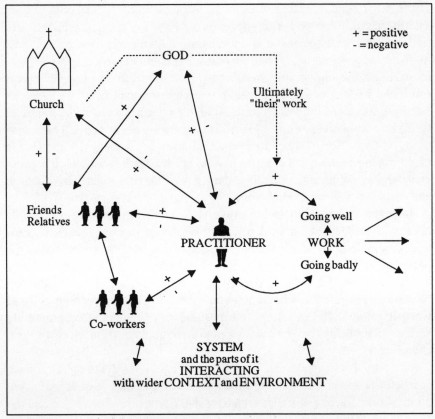

FIGURE 9:2. A PRACTITIONER'S VOCATIONAL CONTEXT

III. ROOTED LOCALLY, ORIENTED OUTWARDS

It follows from what has been said that the processes of analysis and design we are discussing are firmly rooted in people in specific churches, communities, and organizations, and in their purposes and beliefs. But they are not parochial. Whilst remaining rooted, they move outwards from the immediate actualities of people and their situations to the wider communities of which they are a part and to their socio-religious contexts. This is different from those processes that get people to approach their church and community work via sociological analyses of their overall context. Both approaches move outwards and inwards and engender interaction between the local and its context. However, the dominant thrust of one is outwards from the specific, and the other is inwards to the specific. Both must negotiate the interface between specific situations and their contexts, but in different directions. I make this point simply to clarify the nature of the processes I am describing. It is beyond the scope of this book to explore the differences further—though it is important to do so especially for pre-service training of those who work with people in church and community.

218

IV. REFLECTION-IN-ACTION[9]

One aspect of the nature of the processes is variously described as "reflection-in-action", "action-reflection" and experiential learning. And, when used rigorously on programmes with an innovative element, it can be described as action-research.[10] In Part One we saw the results of using the processes of analysis and design on specific pieces of work. Other things can accrue from the continuous use of the process over a period of time on problems, cases, work programmes, projects and the various activities undertaken by people in church and community. The work can be continuously assessed for what can be learnt from it, and whatever is learnt can be ploughed back to inform future decisions and action. This enables workers and people to build up their own body of knowledge about the work and how *they* can do it best, plus their own codes of good practice and the theory upon which they base them. Learning from experience in this way means that the process is inductive (working from the particular to the general). Applying what has been learnt to other situations means that it is also deductive (working from the general to the particular).[11] Sometimes the inductive method of drawing things out of specific experiences is equated with the non-directive approach and the deductive method with the directive approach. This is confusing. Induction involves attending to the situations in question. What is learnt can be used in a directive or non-directive manner.

This book as a whole exemplifies the nature and use of the reflection-in-action and the action-research method and the inductive and deductive methods. The chapters on tackling the problem of a sense of failure, on the family communion case study and on the study of the bishop's situation conclude with reflections on the use of the method. In the first two of these chapters I discuss the practice theory of working on problems and cases. Chapter 5 establishes a generic process by reflecting upon the outcome of the use of the methods described in Part One in an extensive and extended action-research programme of in-service training and consultancy work over a period of twenty years and more.

V. DEVELOPMENTAL, CONCENTRATING ON CHANGE FROM WITHIN

Identifying common elements in the outcome of the very different work study experiences described in Part One helps us to consider the developmental nature of the processes we are considering. The following significant changes had occurred in the workers and the resources available to them:

- they had a more profound understanding of themselves as workers (their beliefs, purposes, etc.) and of their working situation, therefore they were much more in command of themselves as workers and of their work (not necessarily of the work of others nor of the working situation as a whole);

- they had seen the importance of getting others to engage separately and together in the kind of processes of analysis and design in which they had been engaged; (This emerges most strikingly in the discussions about the problem of failure where the group said, "We must get this kind of discussion going amongst the people with whom we work!" and when the bishop saw the need to focus on other people's theological orientation to ministry as well as on his own.)

- they had inward experiences of developmental processes;

- they worked out development plans and designs which fitted them as workers and their situations;

- they gained some knowledge and profitable experiences of the use of analytical tools which they could continue to use and make available to those with whom they worked;

- they had more confidence;

- they had acquired new energy and enthusiasm.

In short, they had developed as workers and were better equipped within themselves to promote their own human and spiritual development and that of others—provided, that is, that they were committed to offering to others the kind of help that had been offered to them.

These and similar kinds of change occur when the workers themselves freely and willingly make those contributions from within themselves which they alone can make. Without this contribution the human and spiritual developments we want to see simply do not happen, no matter how much others do things to and for the workers and people. The thrust of our effort is persistently and consistently directed towards inducing development action from within individuals, groups communities, organizations and churches; i.e., the nature of the approach is that it concentrates on getting people to make their own contributions to their development and that of others. Such development is "a process by which people gain greater control over themselves, their environment and their future in order to realize the full potential of life that God has made possible".[12] It empowers people and enables them to change their environment. It gives them a better subjective purchase on their lives, work and circumstances. It facilitates egalitarian working relationships and power-sharing. It creates a work culture and spirituality which of itself is a medium of development. (I discuss these claims in Chapter 12.)

The processes are designed to promote these kinds of development. The very nature of them is that those who use them become actively involved in applying them to themselves and to the work in which they are engaged. When people become engaged in the processes the processes are at work in them inducing inward changes—and the more freely and willingly they give of themselves to the activity, the more creative the outcome. At the same time the processes safeguard against enablers and consultants doing those things for people that they simply have to do for themselves.

Clearly this contribution is only one part of that which is required for our temporal and eternal well-being, but it is an indispensable part at all stages of human and spiritual development, much neglected when undue attention is focused on what God and other people do for us—and must do for us. Relating this contribution to wide-ranging discussions about development as a concept, stages and processes of development in organizations and communities, theories of underdevelopment and the diverse approaches to promoting development is a task that desperately needs to be done, but one that is quite beyond the scope of this book.

To illustrate the nature of the processes, we have concentrated on the changes for the better that they can induce in workers. This could be described as reflexive development. As we have seen, the use of these approaches on the stuff of church and community life promotes the inter-related development of:

— Christians and non-Christians;

— the human and the spiritual, the physical, the intellectual and the moral;

— people and their environment;

— church and community;

— groups and organizations.[13]

VI. EDUCATIONAL

Two disciplines have contributed much to the evolution of community development: education and social work.[14] The processes of work analysis and design described in this book have evolved from pursuing the educational tradition in church and community work. Education is associated with essentially healthy and normal people who need to change, acquire more knowledge and understanding and become more competent if they are to be and to do what is required of them.[15] The people are seen as co-workers in making things better: not as clients as they are in social work; the changes are developmental, not remedial. The ethos, orientation and approach is educational and, because of the centrality of the non-directive approach, it involves people's learning together and from one another: collaborative learning, not some teaching others. This is so whether one is working with people who are "educated" or "uneducated", affluent or deprived; and the richest learning experiences occur when people who differ significantly in education, ideology, power, wealth and experience actually learn together and from each other. It is amazing what emerges from the study of a case such as the one about family communion in such a group of people. Time and again I have found that some of the most profound insights come from those with least power and education but a "wealth" of experience of living in comparatively powerless relationships. Learning together in order to work together for the common good[16] takes the patronage out of church and community work.

Many kinds of learning occur as people—paid and unpaid, those with and those without formal training and clergy, religious and laity—become reflective practitioners[17] through studying their work in the way described in this book in order to promote the common good. They learn about themselves as workers and about the people, situations, organizations, and churches with whom they work. They learn how to make their best contributions to their own human and spiritual development and that of others. They learn about other cultures and different ways of thinking and talking about things. Some of the learning is directly associated with acquiring knowledge and skills to do something that those involved really want to do, and some of it is incidental to that but highly valued.

VII. NON-DIRECTIVE

Facilitating other people to think for themselves about their own and other people's ideas is to be non-directive. This book demonstrates just what this means in specific situations and draws out the generic implications for general practice. Had I written the book a few years ago, discussion of this approach would have been a major section of it, probably appearing earlier. Reflecting on this, I realize that I have expounded the approach by showing what it looks like when it is written deep into the people who use it and into processes and methods they employ. Explicit references to the non-directive approach do appear here and there to elucidate the main thrust of the exposition, but I am struck by how little needs to be said about it directly when describing it in action. That is entirely in line with my experience when working with people. Once it becomes an integral part of us it is unobtrusive even though it radically affects our being and our doing. That is the nature of the approach, engaging with people purposefully, energetically and proactively without dominating them.

This illuminates an aspect of my experience. When people begin to adopt the approach they are inclined to say "we must take non-directive action" or to ask "how do we take non-directive action" or whether they should be directive or non-directive. This I find disturbing because it is singularly unhelpful. It can lead to being doctrinaire about the non-directive approach and failing to make creative connections with reality, which is what the approach is all about. It is much better to ask "What needs to be done to help the people in this situation in relation to our purposes and theirs?" (I return to this in Chapter 12.) Tackling such a question is more likely to get at the appropriate action, which will be an admixture of non-directive and directive action.[18]

VIII. BUT WHAT OF DEPENDENCY?

A major thrust in the approach we are considering is away from dependency and towards interdependency and independency. Vanstone highlights possible dangers of this approach, with its emphasis upon the action that people can and must take for their own well-being and development and that of others.

> The emphasis in agencies of social care is now on "enablement" rather than "help"; and the change of terminology is significant even when no change is involved in the procedure and practice of the agency.... The presupposition behind the new terminology is, of course, that what a person does for himself, as his own achievement, is of higher worth than that which is done to or for him by the help of others: that the practice of independence is, in itself, of greater worth or dignity than the condition of dependence.[19]
>
> Public opinion accords the highest worth and respect to those individual and corporate enterprises which are intended to maintain and enlarge the areas of human independence, to increase the possibilities of personal achievement, to provide greater scope for private initiative, to "enable" people into self-reliance and self-sufficiency. But perhaps these enterprises are no more than gallant or despairing gestures, no more effective than sand thrown against the wind or Mrs Partington's broom wielded against the advancing ocean. Perhaps the transition of the individual into a condition of ever more marked dependence or receptivity or passion is, for the foreseeable future, irreversible.
>
> It is not necessarily the case that man (*sic*) is most fully human when he is achiever rather than receiver, active rather than passive, subject rather than object of what is happening.[20]

He illustrates this by telling how the help given to an "almost totally dependent" person on a housing estate generated a sense of community and the "enrichment" and "blessing" which a helpless child has been to a whole family.[21]

This is a timely challenge from Vanstone. It evokes several responses in me. In varying ways and to a greater or lesser extent we are permanently dependent upon each other and God. Dependency is as much a part of interdependency as independence. Vanstone's illustrations are about different kinds of dependency: that of the child is a necessary part of development; the other of an undesirable disability. People can be enriched or debilitated by helping to meet the needs. That says more about the way others respond than about the state of dependency. Whilst I reject any suggestion that we play down the emphasis on enabling, I think that it is vitally important that the way we do enable does not marginalize those who are dependent. Working *with* rather than *for* people enhances their autonomy, dignity, and self-respect and prevents them from being objects of care *however dependent or independent they might be*. Therefore the processes I have described are as relevant to us in our dependent states as they are to us in our independent or interdependent states— whether they are primarily physical or moral or spiritual. These different dependent states are often confused and wrongly correlated. Dependency need not necessarily be a passive state.

When we are dependent we have to work quite hard at our inner and outer responses if we are to retain our dignity and privacy, to relate creatively to those upon whom we are dependent, to prevent them, for example, from patronizing us and to get them to provide what *we* need and want rather than what *they* think we need and want. Doing all this and building up reciprocal respect, love and care in dependency relationships is a demanding task. It promotes the development of "dependent" and "independent" parties to the caring relationship. But it is very difficult. Anyone who has been dependent upon others—those for instance who administer social and medical services, family and friends—knows just how difficult it can be. "Providers" and "carers" have a propensity to take over, patronize, overpower, "push people around", make people supplicate and trade on their gratitude. Consequently, dependent and independent parties have much to do in order to avoid the dangers and realise the potential of caring relationships. The processes I have described, and especially the case study and problem-solving methods, could be used by dependent and independent alike.

Bruce Reed has made an important contribution to the discussion about dependent needs and meeting them. He says that he and his colleagues have "coined the term 'extra-dependence', where 'extra-' means 'outside', to refer to conditions in which the individual may be inferred to regard himself (*sic*) as dependent upon a person or object other than himself for confirmation, protection and sustenance. Correspondingly, we use the term 'intra-dependence', in place of 'independence' to refer to conditions in which the individual may be inferred to regard his confirmation, protection and sustenance as in his own hands."[22] "Religion", he says, "provides a focus for behaviour in the extra-dependent mode of the oscillation process"[23] between these modes of dependency. All of us, he argues, have needs for controlled regression to extra-dependence and a return to intra-dependence. (Regression is Reed's word, not mine. I do not like it because it suggests the movement is undesirable.) Worship can and should facilitate this, he argues. I think that this gives important insights into the functions of religion and worship. It also provides theological insights into the processes I have described. Over and again, when these processes are used in task groups and consultancy sessions, creative oscillation occurs between extra- and intra-dependence.

IX. *IN VIVO*

By their very nature, these processes have to be applied to living human situations in relation to many things which are of enormous importance to people in church and in community. They have to be used with the animate to animate. To do this with rigour and loving care calls for sensitivity which comes from the realization that you are on holy ground when you are studying with people vocational work for human and spiritual well-being. Vocational analysis can be painful. What is important is to remember that the process is used *in vivo*, i.e., in the living body, not under laboratory conditions, in working situations and in consultancy and training sessions.

NOTES AND REFERENCES

1. Cf. Watts, Fraser & Mark Williams, *The Psychology of Religious Knowing* (Cambridge: CUP, 1988) and especially "the middle way", p. 153.

2. *Avec Occasional Papers Number 3* (1992), p. 2.

3. See Chapter 5, Stage 5, "Drawing Up Development Agendas".

4. Jaques, Elliott, *A General Theory of Bureaucracy* (London and Exeter, NH: Heinemann Educational, 1976, reprinted 1981), p. 101. Later he says: "The experience of the future is an experience in the present of a lack, of something missing, of something to be desired; but especially of something to be worked for. It is a conception in the present of something not yet realized but which might be realized by activity involving the exercise of judgement and discretion; that is, activity involving psychic effort" (p. 121 f).

5. A phrase used to indicate all that Christ did to secure our salvation and redemption and that of the world.

6. Jaques; *op. cit.*, p. 112: cf. pp. 113 f.

7. In this section I have drawn up some of the ideas shared by Charles Elliott in *Comfortable Compassion: Poverty Power and the Church* (London: Hodder and Stoughton, 1987). He argues that tackling problems of poverty and suffering involves "a two-fold process, a dialectical relationship between the outward, material world and the inner spiritual world" (p. 119).

8. Charles Elliott says these are the four main elements of the inward and outward journeys. *op. cit.*, p. 182 f.

9. I owe this term to Schon, Donald A., *Educating The Reflective Practitioner* (San Francisco: Jossey-Bass Publishers, 1987): cf. Part Two, pp. 41 ff.

10. Cf. Lovell, George, *Human and Religious Factors in Church and Community Work* (A Grail Publication, 1982), pp. 52 ff for a brief statement about action-research. "Innovative element" is one of three factors Michael Bayley identifies which all action research programmes should include, the other two being that researchers should be involved in the development of the aims and strategies which comprise the innovative element and that there should be a continuous process of interaction between workers and researchers. Cf. *Dinnington Papers: Neighbourhood Services Project: Paper No. 1, Origins, Strategy and Proposed Evaluation*, (March 1981) p. 33.

11. There is a very useful induction-deduction model by A.W. Ghent which is quoted by McKelvey, Bill in *Organizational Systematics: Taxonomy, Evolution, Classification* (University of California Press, 1982), p. 19.

12. Sider, Ronald, *Evangelicals and Development: Towards a Theology of Social Change,* Contemporary Issues in Social Ethics Volume 2 (Exeter: The Paternoster Press, 1981), p. 19.

13. Cf. Lovell, George, *Human and Religious Factors in Church and Community Work*, pp. 12 ff. Lovell, George , *The Church and Community Development: An Introduction* (An Avec Publication, 1972, reprinted 1992), Chapters 7 and 8.

14. Brokensha, David & Peter Hodge, *Community Development: An Interpretation* (Chandler Publishing Co., 1969), trace out the educational and social roots of community development. They say that "the contribution of education is especially clear in the historical forerunners of community development of the former United Kingdom dependent territories" (p. 25). Thomas, David, *The Making of Community Work* (London: Allen & Unwin, 1983) describes the conflict during the period 1966–68 between those who were involved in preparing the widely influential Calouste Gulbenkian Foundation Report *Community Work and Social Change: The Report of a Study Group on Training* (London: Longman, 1968) about the educational and social work emphases in community development. Thomas gives an open

and honest analysis of the conflict which T.R. Batten, one of the principal participants, considers to be fair and accurate. The social work emphasis prevailed. (Cf. pp 25–36).

15. Here I am indebted to an article by Armstrong, R. and Davies, C.T.: "The Educational Element in Community Work in Britain", which appeared in the *Community Development Journal* Volume 10:3 (October 1975): cf. p. 155 f.

16. John Atherton suggests that "the common good", an image from the Anglican Holy Communion service, along with the Body of Christ, provides "an *inspiration* for vision and involvement and guide lines for *informing* the content of vision and involvement". Cf. *Faith in The Nation: A Christian Vision for Great Britain* (London: SPCK, 1988), pp. 31 ff and 44.

17. Cf. reference 9.

18. See Batten, T.R. & M., *The Non-Directive Approach* (An Avec Publication, 1988) and Lovell, George, *The Church and Community Development: An Introduction* (Grail Publications/Chester House Publications, 1972 revised 1980).

19. Vanstone, W.H., *The Stature of Waiting* (London: Darton, Longman & Todd, 1982), pp. 44 f.

20. *Op. cit.*, p. 50.

21. *Op. cit.*, p. 55 ff.

22. Reed, Bruce, *The Dynamics of Religion: Process and Movement in Christian Churches* (London: Darton, Longman & Todd, 1978), p. 32.

23. *Op. cit.*, p. 51.

CHAPTER TEN

Theology in the Approach

This chapter is about the theology in the approach to work analysis and design described in this book. As the approach and processes are central to church and community development, it is a partial commentary on the theology of that discipline. But it is not a theology of church and community development: that would have to cover other vital questions such as its contribution to the development of church and society and its place in the mission of the church.

Biblically speaking, the justifications for dedicated involvement in the processes are manifold. They help us to fulfil Christ's command, "Love the Lord your God with all your heart, with all your soul, with all your strength and with all your mind; and your neighbour as yourself".[1] They help us to show ourself "worthy of God's approval as a worker with no cause for shame".[2] They assist us to work out our own "salvation in fear and trembling; for it is God who works in you, inspiring both the will and the deed, for his own chosen purpose".[3] They help to equip us to share in "God's work",[4] which Jesus said is ongoing: "My Father continues to work, and I must work too".[5] They help us to be co-workers ("fellow-workers" in the New Testament)[6] with "Jesus, a prophet mighty in work and word".[7] And his work aims "to reconcile all things to himself, making peace through the shedding of his blood on the cross—all things whether on earth or in heaven".[8]

What, then, is the theology in this thinking work which is oriented towards human and spiritual development beyond and within the church? I explore this by considering theological

— objectives

— commitments

— content

— activities

— competencies.

I. THEOLOGICAL OBJECTIVES

In Chapter Five we saw that the beliefs of those engaged in thinking through their work are important reference points at all stages of the process. Making the best use of the processes involves those engaged in them pursuing several theological (or ideological) objectives. They are:

(a) to develop those attributes in ourselves and in others by which we and they are
- in touch with our own beliefs and able to examine them critically;
- able to understand and empathize with the beliefs of others;
- able to discuss beliefs with those with different beliefs;
- able to modify and change our beliefs as we see the need to do so;
- able, separately and together, to put our beliefs into practice.

(b) to use our beliefs habitually as primary reference points in analysing, designing, planning, programming, carrying out and evaluating our work and dealing creatively with positive and negative theological feed-back, and to get others to do the same;

(c) to deepen our understanding and experience of being co-workers with Jesus;

(d) to reflect theologically on our work and experience and to promote this practice among others;

(e) to enhance our ability, and that of others, to work for human and spiritual development with people whose beliefs differ significantly from ours and to explore those differences with them.

Making progress towards these objectives has far-reaching effects. Amongst other things it would:

- help individuals and groups to be theologically firm and flexible rather than theologically shapeless or rigid;
- enhance the quality of work and the satisfaction that people have in doing it, with all that that can mean for worship;
- promote theological growth and conversion(s) of individuals, churches groups and communities and enable people to keep up theologically with their experience;
- introduce theology and biblical principles into social and community work in a natural and wholesome manner and make explicit that which is intrinsic to it;
- enable individuals and collectives to communicate their beliefs more clearly and convincingly through the "body language" of action programmes;

— help to infuse contemporary pluralism with new life and theological vigour through enabling people with different beliefs to work and dialogue more purposefully and with integrity to their convictions (I pursue this further in Chapter Twelve);

— make clear that theology is as much about the way you work at and use your beliefs as it is about what you believe and why you believe it;

— encourage more people to "use" their beliefs in their work and then to theologize about the outcome.

II. COMMITMENTS

Commitment is the bonding of ourselves, from deep within ourselves, to people, principles, God through giving, pledging, covenanting, dedicating, fastening ourselves to them. It is the result of beliefs, convictions, purposes and our insights. It is an expression of the mind, heart and will. It is an inner transaction with something beyond us which forges connections of enormous importance to us. It is a dynamic movement of the human spirit by which we become involved at deeper levels in human and divine endeavours. The nature, quality, strength and durability of our commitment determine the practical, moral and spiritual value of our engagement with people for development. There is no substitute at all for commitment. The absence of it will show through any form of professionalism or battery of skills or technology. Yet its importance in development work is frequently overshadowed by our preoccupation with ways and means of doing things. There is a tendency to assume it and to allow it to be implicit rather than explicit. To compensate for this, a group of us studying the theology of church and community development felt it important to make our commitments quite explicit and to examine them and their implications.[9] Kenneth B. Wilson, writing from a secular perspective, thinks that they are so important that they should be a subject for research:

> The issue of commitment is central to community development and is clearly subject to research. The various types and levels of commitment which result in community development need to be identified and their causes and consequences assessed. One important line of research would be to identify and map the interplay of self-seeking and community-service motives underlying the various types of structural orientation. . . . Such research might be geared towards clarifying the distinction and the relationship between power and leadership in community action. Commitments of the individual, as these are manifested behaviourally within a situational context, provide an important link between theories of personal and social organization.[10]

Commitments are written deep into my exposition of work study. We need to make them quite explicit because they reveal critical aspects of the theology in the approach and processes. In summary form they can be expressed as follows:

- The commitment to work primarily *with* all people for self-induced change rather than to provide services *for* them.

- The commitments to get people to work *with* and *for* each other for the common good, including those who differ from each other significantly.

- The commitment to collaborate rather than compete and to mandate equal opportunities to participate.

- The commitment to active purposeful involvement in church and community rather than to a spectator or commentator role.[11]

- The commitment to work with churches, communities and organizations as systems, not simply as collections of individuals or congregations.[12]

- The commitment to church and community *and* to the issues which emerge from it and impinge upon it.[13]

- The commitment to open processes of educational dialogue within which people freely articulate their needs in their own way through their own cultural norms.[14]

- The commitment to getting people thinking and thinking again.

- The commitment to power sharing and mutual accountability.[15]

- The commitment to promote those processes of change in others, ourselves and structures that facilitate human and spiritual betterment.

- The commitment to work at actual situations, no matter how small or large, and to do so in context.

- The commitment to work through and in the Church for overall betterment of people in church and society as a whole rather than any one part of it.[16]

(m) The commitment to work at theory and theology situationally and academically.

(n) The commitment to assimilate and to live out as a way of life the principles, concepts and approaches inherent in this approach to working with people.[17]

Convictions of various kinds underly these commitments. Amongst them are: attention to minute particulars promotes profound and far-reaching human and spiritual development; people have rich resources for development which are most effective when they are freely and willingly deployed; that by birth and divine endowment people have rights to freedom and power;[18] that these commitments are congruent with the ministry and mission of the church; that the rigorous use of intelligence for the common good plays an important part in Christian life and work. *Convictions, commitments, skills and abilities when bonded together form a powerful nucleus in individuals, groups, organizations and churches.* Such nuclei strengthen the will, generate and release energy and promote determined and persistent application to developmental tasks— provided, that is, that they do not make people into "heavy ideologues".[19] The character and constitution of the nuclei, combined with the human and spiritual resources available, determine the job that people can tackle in terms of complexity, difficulty and duration.

Such nuclei are created, strengthened and weakened in a thousand different ways, some of them quite unpredictable. This is especially true of convictions and commitments. (For instance, I first came to understand what commitment really meant when, as an engineer, I was a member of a multi-disciplinary team researching problems of escape from aircraft in emergencies. Medical doctors in the team were so committed to the research that they risked their lives to get information that could only be obtained by their acting as guinea-pigs and using their medical knowledge to observe what happened to their bodies in simulated crash and escape conditions.) One way in which these nuclei are formed and built up is through the use of the work-study processes we are considering and especially through their use in groups led by people committed to them. It also happens in consultancy sessions.

Three things help to explain this. Pursuing the processes involves working at the practical, technical, theoretical and theological issues in vocational work which variously contribute to the building-up of the elements of the nuclei— skills, convictions and commitments. Secondly, the action taken by workers and consultants comes from their nuclei. Third, the use of the processes generates a particular spirituality, which I discuss in Chapter 12. Thus the elements of the nuclei are communicated at various levels of consciousness through experiencing the process. When the analytical process helps people with issues of concern to them, they associate not only with the outcome but with the nuclei that made it possible. Attending to the development and maintenance of these nuclei involves using theology as well as the social and behavioural sciences.

III. THEOLOGICAL CONTENT

Doing theology is working on our own experience in the light of our own beliefs and those of others *and* working on our own beliefs in the light of our experience and the beliefs and experiences of others.[20] All those who use the processess described in this book to study their own work with people and that of others will engage in this kind of theological activity whatever they themselves believe or do not believe: doing theology is, in fact, an inescapable part of the processes as it is of doing church and community development work. Amongst other things this involves:

1. theological engagement with a wide range of subject-matter;

2. working with human and divine relationships;

3. the interaction between similar and dissimilar belief-action systems which promotes creative interplay between doing the work and doing theology.

1. Subject Matter

The wide range of subject-matter about which church and community workers have to think theologically as they pursue these processes includes: the Bible and the theological traditions of the churches and organizations with which they are working; the nature of the church, society and their organizations; critical contemporary contextual issues; the ministry and mission of the church; human well-being and the common good; development and the competencies required to promote it, the attributes, roles and functions of ministers, priests, religious and laity in church and society and the approaches and methods they adopt; church and community development processes and the non-directive approach and their places in Christian ministry and mission and the work of the Church; specific work situations; the beliefs of the workers and their colleagues.

Differentiating the subject-matter helps us to see the theological tasks inherent in pursuing the analytical processes. One task is to think theologically about each aspect of the subject-matter. Another is to think theologically about relationships between one aspect of the subject-matter and another, e.g. the spiritual ethos of a religious group, the ways in which they traditionally work with people, and the processes described in this book. Particular attention needs to focus on any dissonance because this can lead to creative change and to putting aspects of the subject-matter together in coherent patterns of theological thought. (It helps me to think of this as making "theological mosaics".) Such patterns are however, soon disturbed in a minor, if not major, way by further thought and experience. That is inevitable in any programme of human and spiritual development. This approach means that the theological activity suffuses and transcends the processes and prevents it from being an optional extra.

2. Human and Divine Relationships

Processes of analysis and design, like community development, to which they are central, are about working with God and with people. Consequently, in one way or another and at one level or another, they are concerned, not only with people's beliefs, but with their religious experiences and their spiritual relationships with each other and God—or about their absence.

234

Some people believe in God without claiming to have a relationship with him. For others the personal experience of, and personal relationship with, God are the quintessence of life and religion. Researches have shown that large numbers of people not associated with religious organizations have various kinds of mystical or extra-sensory experiences which have profound effects upon them but which they do not normally share.[21] Christians variously experience living relationships with God, Jesus and the Holy Spirit through prayer, worship and everyday events. God calls them, Jesus is with them, (Emmanuel), the Holy Spirit leads and guides them. They feel that they work for God; they are co-workers with Christ.

Thus, within and beyond the human relationships that are the normative stuff of community work, there are human–divine relationships and mystical experiences which must be the stuff of church and community development work. These relationships exercise spiritual authority in the lives of those who experience them and frequently determine vocational choices and apostolates. When they are in good repair they engender commitment to human well being and they enthuse and energize people. Whether in good repair or not, their influence, like that of unknown reference groups, can be profound and quite beyond logical deduction. But, whilst mystical experiences and spiritual relationships are clearly important in development work, they do not get the attention they deserve because they cause problems for development workers. For one thing, they are even more difficult to understand and analyse than human relationships—and they are difficult enough. There is widespread embarrassment in talking about them and many people are sceptical about them. It is all too easy to neglect them, as, I am sorry to say, I have done at times. It is so much easier to talk about beliefs than about "spiritual relationships".

One of the models that helps me to take all this into account is a trihedral of relationships, a triangular pyramid. The points represent self, others, the physical environment and God. The lines represent the relationships. To my mind's eye it looks something like Figure 10:1.

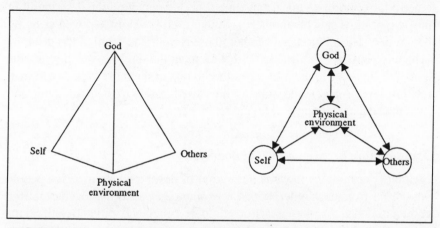

FIGURE 10:1. A TRIHEDRAL OF RELATIONSHIPS

235

People would model these relationships differently. They might, for instance, invert Figure 10:1 or lay it on its side to show God as the ground of all being and to avoid hierarchical inferences. Some people might substitute an ideology for God. However this might be, for me this trihedral of relationships underlies all human affairs, even though it is impossible to define with accuracy all the lines—they are easily blurred by the way in which human and divine relationships infuse each other. Aspects of it may be covered and confused by institutions, churches, communities, groups or individuals, or by the way disciplines variously focus on individuals (counselling, case work, psychotherapy), on collectives (sociology, anthropology), on God (theology), or on the physical environment (physical scientists, technicians, artisans).

Then again, the shape is constantly changing because the relationships are inter-related. Change one and the others are changed. Indeed Jesus teaches us that restoring our relationship with God involves first mending our relationships with others.[22] Working with people in church and community variously involves working with them individually and collectively on each and all the relationships, sometimes focusing on one and sometimes on another of them, systematically and haphazardly as circumstances require.

Whichever aspect we are concentrating upon, we will make our best contributions when we work consciously to the whole, whatever our own beliefs might be: easier said than done. The processes are designed to help us do just that by assisting us to work with people on their needs and the issues that interest them in and from the area of human experience marked out by self, others and the physical environment and through beliefs to as much of their mystical experiences and spiritual relationships as people need and can work on; no less and no more.

What I am trying to do through working to this trihedral of relationships is to emulate the ministry of Christ. Essentially, as I see it, through his life, death and resurrection Jesus is *giving* people to each other, to God and to the world which he loves in satisfying, creative, loving relationships. An event at the crucifixion epitomizes this for me in an enacted parable. John describes it in this way: "Jesus saw his mother, with the disciple whom he loved standing beside her. He said to her, 'Mother, there is your son'; and to the disciple, 'There is your mother'; and from that moment the disciple took her into his home".[23] Jesus gave them to each other in one of the most sacred of human relationships, mother and son, as he gave himself to both of them and established a new triangle of loving relationships.

3. Interaction between Belief-Action Systems

Making contributions towards these kind of developments involves people who differ from each other, in one way or another, working together for the common good *and* exploring each other's ideas, beliefs and spiritual relationships and the deep things of existence. For me these two things—work and dialogue

—are symbiotic activities of Christian mission which facilitate each other. Quite quickly the use of the processes I have described reveals differences. One of the things that has helped me to get people engaged in work and dialogue is a simple conceptual device which can be used to demonstrate points of agreement and disagreement. It is presented in Figure 10:2.

This diagram helps individuals and groups to see where they stand in relation to others by setting out in parallel their respective beliefs, spirituality, purposes, objectives, approach, method and activities. It helps to see precisely where there is agreement and disagreement between the people, where their thought and action converges and diverges, where there is conflict and consensus.

Those who wish to make common cause with others can use it to assess whether there is a sufficiently strong basis of agreement and mutual acceptance to enable them to work together and to explore their differences as they do so. This helps people to take each other seriously. It can be done quite simply and directly: "It seems we have similar objectives but different beliefs and approaches. Have we a basis for a partnership and for discussing our differences if that proves to be necessary?" Any understanding (contract) that is established in this way provides a basis for *all* to engage in joint ventures openly and with integrity. It avoids the well-meaning but dangerous use of commonly accepted sayings which play down the differences simply to get into working relationships. One that comes to mind is: "We're all the same underneath and we worship the same God anyway". It also helps to challenge those who refuse to have anything to do with others on the false assumption that they are totally and unacceptably different: "They're different from us." One of the things I have had to work against in church circles is a very strong tendency to be suspicious and frightened of working on equal terms with people who do not confess their belief system in their language.

Whilst I was on sabbatical leave in 1986 at Tantur, an Ecumenical Institute for Theological Research situated in the West Bank between Jerusalem and Bethlehem, I heard a rabbi who was highly committed to his faith and to working for peace with the Palestinians say with great emotion: "I can pray with the people with whom I cannot work and I can work with the people with whom I cannot pray". I felt for him deeply. I have had the same experience. The processes I am describing have helped me to work and dialogue with people previously segregated by the barriers and boundaries of culture, class, belief and spirituality.

Holding together work and dialogue is vitally important in Christian action for development. Writing about relationships between Christians and people of other faiths, Kenneth Cracknell enunciates these "four principles of dialogue":

Dialogue begins when people meet each other.
Dialogue depends upon mutual understanding and mutual trust.
Dialogue makes it possible to share in service to the community.
Dialogue becomes the medium of authentic witness.[24]

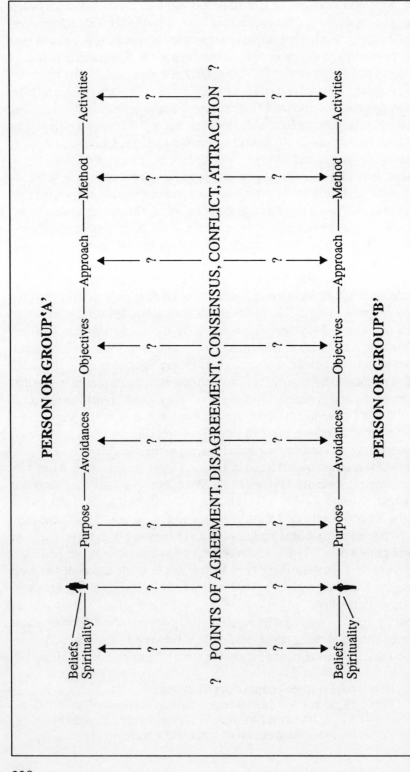

FIGURE 10:2. SOME POSSIBLE POINTS OF CONCORD AND DISSONANCE

I would add that dialogue is a means of human and spiritual development. Working together in churches, religious organizations and communities provides opportunities to extend and deepen it in every possible way.

IV. THEOLOGICAL ACTIVITIES

To use the analytical processes in church and community work people have to engage in several different but complementary theological activities. They have to clarify and articulate the beliefs upon which they intend to act in general and in particular situations; to apply them to the work in hand; to handle theological feedback; to analyse and reflect on the experience; and to assimilate any theological implications for them and for their work. (These activities could be variously described as different forms of theology: applied, empirical, existential, experiential, process, dialectical, pastoral and practical.)

Rarely is the process as orderly as this sequence. It is an integral part of a work programme, not a process adjacent to and at a distance from it. Consequently beliefs and events, two powerful dynamic forces, interact complexly: beliefs and commitments kick-start work programmes and provide a continuing thrust; events generate feedback which either confirms theological presuppositions or it challenges them and stimulates analysis, reflection and the review of beliefs and possibly their revision.

All these aspects of the theological activity are going on as the work continues: theological activities, work and spiritual relationships overlap and intersect. This is complicated, especially if the theological basis of programmes to which workers are committed is challenged—and even worse if they begin to doubt it. The case study in Chapter Two illustrates this. Beliefs that the teachers and minister shared about children and communion and their plans to put them into effect started off a sequence of events that led to theological conflict. The plans were abandoned because no way was found of handling the theological feedback, but the work with the children and the communion services had to continue whilst the theological analysis and reflection went on. Another example is the theological dissonance I experienced through practising the non-directive approach and engaging in community development work. Elsewhere I have described this and my search for theological help to cope with it.[25] Diagrammatically I represent the theological activities in Figure 10:3. I follow it with notes on each of the principal phases.

1. Articulating Beliefs

Bruce Rahtjen,[26] a biblical theologian who became an experiential theologian, helpfully differentiates between:

public theology, which is what we say we believe, our public self;

239

240

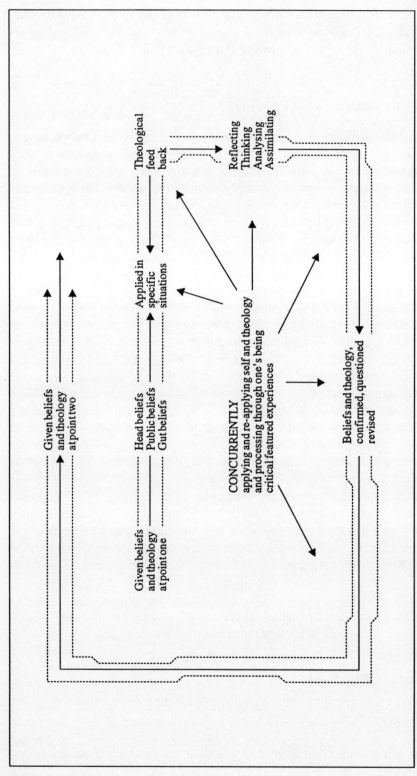

FIGURE 10:3. SOME THEOLOGICAL ACTIVITIES

head theology, which is what we believe we believe: our thinking self;

visceral theology, which is what we show we believe through our life-style, value systems and commitments: our feeling self.

Head theology is that with which we are consciously in touch whereas there may be aspects of our visceral theology (our gut beliefs) of which we are not conscious. We bring these three theological selves to any work in which we are engaged. I have represented this by three undulating lines to represent the way in which our head, public and visceral theologies are sometimes close together and sometimes apart. They rarely entirely coincide. Rahtjen and his colleagues organized sensitivity group workshops to help the feeling, thinking and public theological selves to interact more creatively. I have worked for this end through different means.

One of the things I have done is to get people to write about their beliefs, i.e., the beliefs, principles, concepts, assumptions, ideas and purposes which have been fundamental to their life and work. Some responded by giving an account of their public theology and a minority by referring to the theological statements of their church or organization. But by far the greatest majority described, but not without difficulty, aspects of their head and visceral theology. Strangely the requirement that the statement be brief helped them to do this. Another thing that I have found more recently has helped people, is to ask them before they attempt to express their beliefs to reflect on their working life and ministry up to the present and to describe people, concepts, events which are landmarks in their working life, journey, or story. (See Appendix I.)

Discussions that are thoroughly non-directive are another thing that I have found helps people to go deeper into their head and visceral theologies. Examples of the way in which people have expressed their beliefs are given in Chapters Three and Four. Working at things in the ways described helps to integrate the public, head and visceral theologies. It was these processes that helped the bishop to look at just what was involved in pursuing his beliefs about justification by faith with the clergy and church workers.

2. Application and Feedback

Many advantages accrue in church and community development work from people being in touch with their beliefs in the ways described in the previous section. It promotes their theological development, equips them for theological dialogue and helps them to embody their beliefs in action programmes through:

— helping them to understand and accept their belief and unbelief and their theological commitment and lack of it;

— making their beliefs more readily available for use in reflection and analysis and for review and revision.

In short, the argument is that theological creativity can be stimulated by theological clarity about belief and disbelief and spiritual relationships.

What we said earlier in Chapter Five about handling feedback in general also applies to handling theological feedback in particular.

3. Reflection and Analysis

A distinction we have already mentioned needs to be noted here. Applying our theology to work situations and analysing things theologically are in the active mood whereas reflecting on things theologically is in the attentive or receptive mood. In this mood it is possible to listen for what things might "say" to us or what God might say to us through them. Alternating between these two modes of activity helps us to get to the theological heart of things. The approaches and methods described in this book help us to do so but as Michael Taylor has written,

> There is no process of reflection which can, if followed step by step, lead us inevitably to the answers to our questions, as if having correctly programmed the theological computer we have only to wait for it to produce the required results. Rather, the process of reflection nourishes our minds and provides them with a far richer store of new material out of which we have to make a judgement and take a decision. It provides food for action and not just for thought, but it will never decide for us what action to take.[27]

But they do help us to confirm or revise our beliefs and to bring into a more creative unison our theology and our spiritual relationships.

V. THEOLOGICAL COMPETENCIES ENGENDERED

Theologically speaking, I value this approach to the analysis and design of church and community work and the processes which facilitate it for several reasons. It enables people to maintain a creative tension between action and belief, work and theology: their separation is anathema. It helps people towards a better personal and mutual understanding of their spiritual selves. It enables people who differ significantly in belief and theology to work together for the common good with integrity. Working together engenders relationships, mutual understanding, trust and common experiences of success, failure and difficulty. These things enable people to talk together about the deeper things of life and faith and to explore their different beliefs, theology and spiritual experiences and to apply what they learn in the work they do for the common good. And as the application of beliefs is accompanied by theological reflection, it helps people to revise their beliefs. This is truly developmental. It properly complements that which God does for us in Christ and through others. For me, therefore, it occupies an important place in the ministry and mission of the Church and the work of the kingdom of God.

NOTES AND REFERENCES

1. Luke 11:27f NEB.

2. 2 Timothy 2:15 REB.

3. Philippians 2:12 REB.

4. 2 Corinthians 6:1 REB.

5. John 5:17 REB.

6. Romans 16:3 REB.

7. Luke 24:19. A literal translation of *en ergo kai logo.*

8. Colossians 1:20 REB.

9. The members of the group were: Revd Tony Addy, Revd Dr John Atherton, Revd Alan Gawith, Revd Dr George Lovell, Revd Prof. David Jenkins, Revd Harry Salmon, Fr Austin Smith, and Mr Richard Tetlow. The report was: *Involvement in Community: A Christian Contribution* (The William Temple Foundation, 1980). In the report some of these commitments were expressed first negatively and then positively. I have reversed that order (cf. pp. 25 ff).

10. Warren, Roland & Larry Lyon (eds), *New Perspectives on the American City* (The Dorsey Press, 1983), p. 6.

11. *Involvement in Community* (see note 9 above): cf. p. 25.

12. Cf. op. cit., p. 26.

13. Cf. op. cit., p. 27.

14. Cf. op. cit., p. 26.

15. Cf. op. cit., pp. 72 ff, 52 and 54.

16. Cf. op. cit., p. 26 f.

17. Cf. op. cit., Chapter Five

18. Cf. *Human Rights: A Study for the International Year for Human Rights* (London: Heinemann Educational, 1967).

19. Thomas, David, *The Making of Community Work* (London: Allen & Unwin, 1983), p. 138.

20. I have taken this from some notes I wrote some years ago in an Avec Handout *Some Notes on Experiential Theology.* I cannot remember whether I quoted or composed them! My apologies to the author if I quoted them.

21. This has been demonstrated by the Religious Experience Research Unit set up by Sir Alister Hardy at Manchester College, Oxford.

22. Cf. Matthew 5:23.

23. John 19:26 f NEB.

24. Cracknell, Kenneth, *Towards A New Relationship: Christians and People of Other Faiths* (London: Epworth Press, 1986), pp. 113 ff.

25. Lovell, George, *Diagrammatic Modelling: An Aid to Theological Reflection in Church and Community Development Work* (An Avec Publication). See particularly pp. 2 ff, and 28 ff.

26. Rahtjen, Bruce D. with Bryce Kramer and Ken Mitchell, *A Workbook In Experiential Theology* (A Publication of Associates in Experiential Theology Inc., 1977).

27. Taylor, Michael H., *Learning To Care: Christian Reflection on Pastoral Practice* (a volume in the New Library of Pastoral Care, edited by Derek Blows, (London: SPCK, 1983), p. 102.

243

Part Four

Application

CHAPTER ELEVEN

Persuaded but Daunted?

For many people to be persuaded of the value of the thinking processes described in this book is to be daunted, sometimes overwhelmed, by the thought of using them themselves in their work. Over and again I have seen these feelings gradually come over groups of people and depress them. This happens most often when people have experienced the value of the processes over a period of time through courses or consultancy sessions and they are reflecting on the implications for themselves of these experiences. And it happens even when we have discussed how to use the processes step by step as we have gone along—as, in fact, we have in this book—and people have felt confident at each stage that they themselves could use this method or that. Reflecting on the process as a whole when no aspect has been mastered is much more intimidating. Consequently, as you might be doing just that at this stage of the book, this is the time to look at four frequently recurring strands in the experience of being disturbed and daunted by the thought of using these methods rigorously:

— negative feelings about past practices;

— feeling inadequate to the intellectual challenges of thinking about work with people for human and spiritual development;

— the difficulties of finding the time and energy to acquire and use these processes in the working situation;

— the fear of losing control through getting people thinking for themselves, i.e. through adopting a non-directive approach.

I. NEGATIVE FEELINGS ABOUT PAST PRACTICES

Convictions about the need for change in our ways of working can make us feel badly about our past and present practices, which can now appear to be misguided, ineffectual or wrong. Time without number I have heard and voiced the plaintive cries, "If I had only known that ten (twenty, thirty or forty) years ago." "I should have been taught this in College." "Oh, the opportunities that I have missed and the time I have wasted." All too easily attention can be diverted from the challenge of the present through preoccupation with our remorse about the past. These feelings have to be overcome if we are to release

the energies, and to secure the freedom that we need to make our best response to the challenge of change and the problems associated with it. A
thought that helps me to do this is that, whatever the merits and de-merits of our
previous ways of working and our culpability in using them, the most important
thing is that they have brought us to this moment of insight, opportunity and
challenge. That is *the* way that *we* came. This is the point from which *we* must
start. We might have come by another route, but we did not. (I have to struggle
with myself to gain this orientation to the past and the present. I have to work
hard to overcome my negative feelings about my past performance and missed
opportunities. I have a strong propensity to go on blaming myself and others
unhelpfully and at times masochistically.) Therefore, the vital questions are,
"Where do I (we) go from here?" "Should I make changes in the way in which
I work and if so what changes and how should I make them?" All too easily
we can avoid the issues by dallying with questions such as, "Did I get here by
the best possible route?"

Focusing on the here and now and the future in this way enables us to use
rather than misuse our past experience of working with people and the insights
into ourselves as workers. Evaluated experience and insights provide invaluable
information by which we ourselves can assess present ways of working and
any others that are on offer. Putting experience to such good use helps us to
feel much better about the painful past because it helps to redress it. Doing this
is, in fact, to use the reflective practices described in this book to tackle the
negative feelings that they have had a part in generating.

Perhaps this is the moment for you to pursue this matter further. If so, the
questions in Display 11:1 might help you to reflect on your ways of working
and to identify any changes you might want to make.

II. FEELING INADEQUATE TO THE INTELLECTUAL
   CHALLENGES

Some people feel they do not have not the intellect to think things through in
the ways suggested. This is painful, especially when they are convinced that
thinking things through thoroughly and in depth for themselves and with others
is of the essence of working with people in community for human and spiritual
development, and that is what they want to do—a painful conjunction of
thoughts, feelings and aspirations when all this is at the heart of your vocational
yearnings. I know about this through repeatedly not being able to get my mind
round some vital subject or to put my thoughts into creative order. This
continuing experience must be taken seriously to see if there are things which
will help us to handle it better and to think as effectively as we can. I restrict
myself to the things that I have found helpful.

First, it is necessary to acknowledge that our intellectual abilities can never

1. Note significant characteristics of the ways in which you:
      — think, feel and worry about your work in general;
      — work out what you are going to do and how you are going to do it (proactive thinking and planning);
      — work through things that go wrong (reactive thinking);
      — fail to keep thinking.

2. Note the characteristics that you consider useful and any ways in which they could be developed to improve your effectiveness.

3. Note any characteristics that you consider unhelpful.

4. Reflecting on this book with its emphasis on reflection-in-action and any other approaches or methods which you have read about or experienced, note the ones you wish to acquire or develop.

5. What would be the overall effects, positive and negative, of
      — making any changes noted in 2, 3 and 4?
      — not making them?

6. What problems would you have to overcome
      — to make the changes?
      — if you did not make them?
   And how could you overcome them?

7. What do your responses to 1–6 say to you?

8. What would contribute to a realistic work/worker development programme for you?

DISPLAY 11:1. TAKING STOCK

master the complexity of the human and spiritual subject-matter with which we are grappling. The latter is always more than a match for the former. Therefore we are not intellectually deficient because we cannot master it. Getting our minds around human events and situations is difficult and at times quite impossible because they are so complex and the theories that purport to interpret them are often confusing and conflicting. Comprehensive understanding always eludes us. At times we simply cannot understand what is going on. Even in relation to the most ordinary human events we have to act in ignorance of vital information no matter how hard we think, and rely on such things as hunches, intuitions, guesses, probability. These limitations derive from our inability to think *and* from the nature and mystery of the human situation. Accepting this can help to get things into proportion, to realize our status before God and his creation, to marvel and respect the mystery with which we are working and of which we are a part and to give ourselves to using our minds to get the best understanding *we* can get of the situations in which we are working. Awareness of the limitations of our understanding helps to save us from the dangers of presumptive behaviour and arrogance.

Second, vital clues to understanding the things we are concerned about are in the people and their situation. Focusing on them and listening to them is a way to understanding. The non-directive approach is important here. Those who use it aim to help all kinds of people, separately and together, to think seriously, deeply, analytically, imaginatively and purposefully for themselves about the substance of work, life and faith and to act upon their conclusions. This involves paying very careful attention to the thinking of others. It takes practitioners into the inner places of individuals, groups, communities and organizations (religious and secular) where the human and divine are at work: places where there is a glorious confusion between processes of human growth and salvation and where the activities of God, self and others are fused. It enables them to do this with the respect God accords to us all. It takes their work and ministry to the very heart of human life. They could not be in a better position from which to reflect, nor could they have more relevant information, knowledge and insights upon which to reflect and act. Those who habitually take directive action are less likely to get into such privileged positions because they are inclined to overlay the thoughts of others with their own thinking and plans.

Using the non-directive approach means, therefore, that we are more likely to get to the heart of the matter and to be able to think realistically. It also means that we have more thoughts to think about.[1] Tools for thinking are needed. That is what we have provided in this book.

Third, concentrating only on the ability of individual workers to think things through misses an important dimension. Development depends upon people thinking things through together. The issue, therefore, is not whether *I* can get my mind around things but whether *we* can get our minds around things and whether *we* can help *each other* to do just that. Emphasis upon individual

250

competence can detract from the collective competence. Accepting this enhances our ability to think, generates mutuality and underpins our humility.

There are in fact two closely related themes in this book: enhancing the individual practitioner's ability for "reflection-in-action";[2] and the generation of reflective communities, organizations and churches in order that the members, separately and together, may become more effective agents of reflective action for the common good. Holding these together is a unique contribution of church and community development. Doing so is important because, as we have seen, reflective practitioners need reflective communities just as reflective communities need reflective practitioners. They go together. It is very difficult for either to survive without the other. My experience prompts an untested hypothesis, that those who fail to become habitual reflective practitioners are those who are unable to find or generate reflective groups, churches and communities. But, as we have said, communities of reflective agents are multipliers; they beget learning communities of reflective agents: they release the learning potential in church and community work which fosters human and spiritual growth and development.

Fourth, one of the problems is that thinking seriously about working with people for development in church and community takes us into so many disciplines, such as theology, the social and behavioural sciences and adult education. They all have significant contributions to make to church and community work. There is a temptation to think that to use these disciplines we have to master them. Most of us cannot master even one of them. I think of my excursions into other disciplines as foraging expeditions. I am looking for things which will help me in my work and I test their efficacy in relation to my own discipline and my experience of working with people in church and community for human and spiritual development. In fact, the processes I have described provide ways of finding out what works and what does not work—and how and why.

Fifth, it is helpful to clarify what we do not know; i.e. to define our areas of ignorance. This helps us to decide what action to take just as much as defining what we do know. It can lead us to seek more information by observation, research, survey or study. It helps us to know when to be tentative.

Sixth, it is necessary to give ourselves to the specifics of our situation and experience in relation to as much of the whole as we can grasp. Parts are within our grasp when the whole is not. The belief that all things cohere in Christ[3] releases me to give myself to the parts in the context of the Kingdom.

Finally, it is vital to keep on thinking; to remain a reflective practitioner, no matter how difficult it seems to be. I find that it always pays some dividends, and the more I get stuck the more I get out of it at the end. This helps me to struggle through the hard and painful aspects of thinking things through. This is one aspect of my experience where journeying is as important as arriving.

The temptation to opt out of thinking about our work must be avoided. Standard procedures and rubrics are useful. They help to find thinking space but they can never be a substitute for thinking. As we have noted earlier, given that time for this is limited, we need to select carefully how we use it.

In various ways these things help to overcome intellectual intimidation and the accompanying emotional frustration, to take up the challenge of thinking things through and to enjoy the excitement of doing so. But they have not helped me to eliminate the frustration nor to avoid the pain.

III. DIFFICULTIES OF FINDING TIME AND ENERGY

Workers already stretched are at a loss to know how to find the time, energy and support necessary to change their own ways of working and to promote changes in the work culture of their church or organization. Quite often they feel that the task is hopeless. It is, if they are thinking in terms of immediate wholesale change. Making radical changes in work practice is a long-term development task and needs to be approached as such.

As we have seen, the process can start with quite small but important changes such as asking unloaded rather than loaded questions or using the problem-solving approach to tackle difficulties. If this proves to be helpful, as it is likely to do, people will soon notice that things are being done differently and enquire about the changes. That is a good beginning to a programme of education for change. Another way to introduce change is for workers to discuss with those with whom they work this way of working and the desirability and feasibility of making changes. Doing this effectively involves workers' adopting the non-directive approach, which means that the processes are demonstrated as they are discussed. The discussions might also include a comparison of the advantages and disadvantages of previous ways of working, of those suggested here and of making changes. (Display 11:1 could help people to do this.)

Quite often, for instance, when people act without due thought they have to spend a lot of time racking their brains to find ways of overcoming problems that could have been avoided by forethought. Time and energy is absorbed in crisis management, whereas the approach in this book uses energy in a more purposeful, creative, satisfying and economic manner. Of course, there will always be problems, because we never do things perfectly and because of the unpredictability of human thought and behaviour. But more problems will be foreseen and avoided. Put starkly, the choice is between investing more time in thinking things through and less in sorting out messes. I am committed to thinking things through as thoroughly as circumstances permit because this leads to action that is most likely to be productive and satisfying: it builds up one's ability to work at things spontaneously; and it conserves time and energy to work at emergencies and problems caused by errors of judgement which are always with us and which could not have been foreseen.

From personal experience I know that it is possible to find time and energy, but not easy, especially in the initial stages. Generally speaking, we find time for what we really want to do. For seven years up to 1993 I led two-year part-time diploma courses in church and community development. All the participants had considerable experience in church and community work and had responsible jobs; some of them held senior positions in one or other of five denominations. They studied their work and wrote a dissertation about it. The aim was to discover how they could do their work better in the present and be more effective workers in the future. They found it difficult to make time to do the studies. By the end of the course, however, most of them had built in time for studying and researching their work as they did it: they had in fact overcome the "tyranny of the short-term".[4] They considered this hard-won change to be so important that they vowed to maintain it.

Readers who wish to change their ways of working might consider the alternative ways of doing so sketched out in the final section of Chapter Eight.

IV. FEAR OF LOSING CONTROL

People who benefit from using the approaches we have described frequently find themselves experiencing the following sequence of thoughts and feelings: a sense of greater control over themselves as workers and their work because they feel that they have got their minds round it; the desire to use the approaches to help others to do the same; the conviction that thinking things through for yourself and with others is essential to human and spiritual development; the realization that inevitably this will mean others gaining increasingly more control over things related to "your" work and life; fear of losing control; temptation to withdraw from acting non-directively towards those "under" your authority. Groups, organizations and churches as well as individuals experience this sequence.

The fear of losing control, with its rational and irrational elements, has to be taken seriously. It inhibits non-directive action and it nullifies attempts to take it. To gain the advantages of this approach, the fear of losing control has to be overcome and the dangers of doing so avoided. Understandably, clergy and laity of all denominations are most apprehensive of working on equal terms with people from whom they differ and those they have good reasons to believe will not be responsible. Working at the following has variously helped me to cope with these fears and to take calculated risks responsibly.

All that I say presupposes opportunities for face-to-face negotiations about sharing between people in positions of strength and weakness. It presupposes some willingness all round to share, even if it is reluctant willingness based upon questionable motives. I am not addressing the situations where those with power have no intention of giving it up and those without power are determined to gain it. What follows has some relevance to such power conflicts, as do the approaches and methods I have described, but power struggles raise issues beyond the scope of this book.

1. Facing the Fears

Facing the fears and examining their substance is a necessity. I find it helpful to write down or say aloud what are the worst things that can happen. This gets me away from dwelling on fearful feelings to working at avoiding or overcoming real dangers. That is, I am working on a vital part of the development agenda related to using the approaches beyond myself. Having done so I am more likely to be able to help others to deal with their fears of losing control. I am reminded of this biblical text:

> Fear, Fiend and Fate
> Are upon thee, Earth-dweller!
> Who runs from the voice of Fear,
> Falls down to the Fiend;
> Who clambers up from the Fiend,
> Is snared by Fate![5]

2. Recalling the Sheer Necessity of Everybody being in Control

Generally speaking, people make their best contributions to their own development and that of others when they feel in control of themselves and the part they are playing and when they feel they have a real say in the corporate control of anything in which they are engaged with others. For these conditions to exist—and it is of vital importance that they do in development programmes—individual control must respect collective control and vice versa. Both kinds of control must complement and reinforce each other; they must not compromise each other. This is tricky to obtain and demanding to maintain. The approaches and methods I have described facilitate this duality of control, never perfectly, often with difficulty, but generally creatively.

As we have noted, the analytical processes help workers to gain the maximum inner and personal control that it is possible for them to have in their circumstances over themselves as workers and their work. Putting their information and thoughts in order, analysing them and determining the implications gives them a thorough grasp of their own realities which frees, energizes and enthuses them. The more value they put on this experience the more they want it for others. They can help them to get it through introducing them to the same analytical processes. They can help groups to gain control through working *with* them, openly and on equal terms in the same analytical way. The outcome is dual work control, both personal and collective.

3. Giving up Control does not necessarily mean losing It

Transferring power and sharing control does not necessarily mean losing power and control. Corporate control of resources is much stronger than individual control. At best it is regulated by checks and balances.

4. Genuine Sharing of Control and Power

Sharing power and control is most likely to be effective when all parties feel comfortable with it, and, when arrangements to share genuinely represent stated intentions. Pseudo-sharing is counter-productive. People soon see it for what it is. Duplicity is counter-developmental. A common example illustrates this. To avoid the danger of losing control, many churches or organizations which enter into joint projects with others and "share" their premises and resources with them make sure that they retain the power to veto plans by, for example, having sufficient members on committees to outvote those with whom they are "sharing". This common surreptitious device can marginalize the minority, making them feel unequal participants and generating mistrust and faction. A much better way is to discuss mutual responsibility and accountability associated with shared control and, possibly, the circumstances under which those with ultimate responsibility will use their veto and the manner in which they will do so. Clear understandings based on freely negotiated contracts are bases for power-sharing most likely to lead to development. It is good practice to work on the basis that it is easier to give more than to take back what has been "given". Giving what can be given—and some responsibilities and authority cannot be shared—enables people to learn how to give and receive increasingly more.

5. Promoting Creative Forms of Participation and Sharing

Participating in communal life and shared tasks is not necessarily and always a good thing. Devastating experiences in families and in groups can injure people psychologically and spiritually, sometimes permanently. Aiming to get everyone participating (involved) equally in every aspect of a project is unrealistic and undesirable and can, for example, induce participatory processes which paralyse groups and render them ineffectual. Working to these realities is complicated by doctrinaire adherence to full egalitarian participation. Nonetheless, human and spiritual development depends upon people getting involved with each other. Some of the things which I find promote creative participation are:

- worthwhile tasks which are clearly understood and freely accepted with some enthusiasm by participants;

- agreed ways of going about tasks which enable people to get on with them to their satisfaction;

- participants having parts (i.e. roles and functions) about which they are clear and which they want to play;

- good working relationships;

- appropriate forms of participation.

These things interact to build up the quality of the participation. Engaging in worthwhile tasks can be frustrating when the way of going about things simply does not work—and the frustration is all the greater because the task is worthwhile. The introduction of procedures which do work—and that is what this book is about—breeds hope and generates enthusiastic participation. Here I want to comment in more detail on the last point.

Participation in human life is pluriform. Different modes of participation are more or less appropriate to people and their circumstances. No one form is always right. Establishing those that are appropriate from the repertoire of possibilities is part of the art of promoting development. I can best illustrate this by focusing on people—an individual or a group—who have the power to act in relation to some activity or other; for instance, organizing services of worship or leisure facilities. There are several things they can do. They can organize the facilities themselves or they can recruit others to do so on their behalf. Or they might discuss the need with others, consult them about the kind of services required and then decide and act. In all these cases they remain in control whilst providing opportunities for people to participate in different ways, ranging from using the services to negotiating the kind of services needed and wanted. On the other hand, the people with power might decide that they want to delegate, co-operate, collaborate, devolve or enter into partnership with others. In all these cases they share control and they and others participate on a different power basis and in different ways. These are but a few of the different modes of participation.[6] I represent them in Figure 11:1.

Basically there are, in fact, two forms of participation. The forms of participation above the centre point in Figure 11:1 allow people to *share in* the activities of the group with power on their terms. They might influence the way things are done but substantive power is not tranferred to them. The forms of participation below the centre point are quite different because power is *shared out*.[7] Getting people to *share in* what *we control* is very different from *sharing out* our power and control so that control and power are in the hands of others or an augmented "we". It is vital that we know in which of these forms of sharing and controlling we are engaged. Confusion, which bedevils developmental processes, occurs when one party thinks power is being shared out whereas in fact they are being invited to share in activities others control. After making these distinctions in a lecture someone said that he now saw why his attempts to consult a particular group failed and generated bad feelings. The group were acting as though the consultation were a negotiation. Clarity about the form of the participation proposed is vital. It helps people to decide whether or not they wish to engage in that form of participation: if they do, it helps them to participate to good effect; if not, it helps them to negotiate a form in which they are prepared to participate.

No one form of participation is always appropriate. I remember Dr Batten saying that he and Mrs Batten enjoyed dancing. Were the proprietors of the dance hall, he said, to press him to help organize the establishment, they would

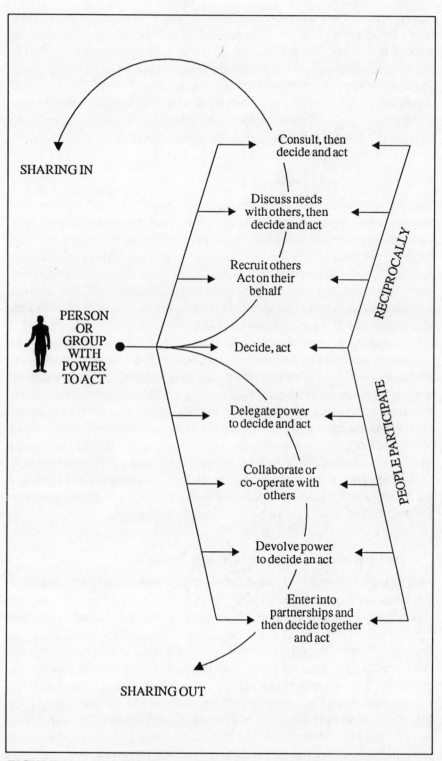

FIGURE 11:1. MODES OF PARTICIPATION: SHARING IN AND OUT

cease to attend. He wanted to dance, not to organize the event. He paid so that others could arrange for them to participate in this activity and no other. Appropriate forms of participation are determined by considering what is feasible and functional in the light of the needs and wants of all the participants, the form of sharing they can manage, and the developmental reference points.

Qualitative participation has many rewards: it facilitates purposeful creativity; it generates deep satisfaction and a sense of well-being; and it is an agent of all-round development in and through all the participants.

6. Sharing the Need to share

When people become committed to the non-directive approach they can feel that they must, as a matter of urgency, share or surrender in a much more vigorous way any power or control that they might have. The urgency can engender or exacerbate the fear of losing control. It can also drive people to act in contradiction to their new-found convictions about the non-directive approach when the felt need to share overpowers the fear of losing control. It is essential that this battle of feelings be resolved logically, not emotionally. To insist on power-sharing is to exercise a powerful form of control. It is to coerce people to have more power and control—and many people fear gaining control and power just as others fear losing them. It is, in fact, to be directive about non-directive working relationships. Means are at variance with beliefs and ends, and that transmits confusing and confounding signals. The urge to share must be controlled so that it does not lead to imposition. Sharing that is consonant with the non-directive approach starts with discussing with those implicated as openly and equally as possible the felt need to share and the associated emotions. Shared decisions to share or not to share are a sound basis on which to proceed. They help to hold in creative tension (or to resolve) feelings about the need to share and the fear of losing control. (There is further discussion about participation in Chapter 12 in relation to leadership.)

7. Prior Agreements about how to handle Problems

Prior agreement about how to handle problems can help to deal with them when they arrive and to reduce the fear of losing control. What I find helpful is mutual understanding about the importance of working our way through problems together and not giving up at the first difficulty; about ways and means of dealing with any difficulties that might arise; about the kind of difficulties we can foresee. This means that everyone is on early alert to work together on problems. Such an understanding makes it so much easier to raise problems because there is an easy opening: "When we decided to do this together we agreed that we would talk to each other about any difficulties rather than letting them slide. I am glad we did because there is something I need to discuss with you". People feel much more in control when there are agreed procedures and working relationships to deal with those things which can make them feel they are losing control. Of course, we have to do this in such a way that it does not create the problems—even as we are anticipating them we are hoping they will not materialize.

8. Accepting that Complete Control is neither Possible nor Desirable

There is no intention in what I have written to infer that the diligent use of these processes—or for that matter any others—could enable people to have *complete* control over themselves, their work and their circumstances. That is not possible and it is probably undesirable. Much that happens to us and those with whom we live and work is beyond our control.[8] Moreover, some of the main power points in society lie outside the local churches, communities and agencies.[9] We never have complete control over ourselves, and we have the most minimal and fragile control over others. This we must accept but we must not allow it to undermine our attempts to work together with others for as much individual and collective control as possible over those things that affect our well-being and salvation. The processes described in this book help us to do just that.

Hopefully you will see what daunted you as part of your development agenda and you will be encouraged to tackle it with enthusiasm.

NOTES AND REFERENCES

1. Lovell, George, *Reflective Practitioners in Church and Community Work:* the 1992 Avec Annual General Meeting Lecture (An Avec Occasional Paper, 1992), p. 3. First published as *Analysis and Design: Ways of Realising The Learning Potential in Church and Community Work.*

2. *Ibid.*, p. 2.

3. Cf. Colossians 1:13 ff.

4. *Involvement in Community: A Christian Contribution:* a report by the Community Development Group William Temple Foundation in collaboration with the Community Work Advisory Group British Council of Churches (1980), p. 40.

5. Isaiah 24:17–18, as translated by Frost, Brice Stanley, *Old Testament Apocalyptic* (London: Epworth Press, 1952), p. 149.

6. Cf. Richardson, Ann, *Participation* (London: Routledge & Kegan Paul, 1983). There is an interesting discussion of Sherry R. Arnstein's eight rungs on the ladder of citizen participation in Cahn, Edgar S. & B. A. Passett (eds), *Citizens' Participation: Effecting Community Participation* (London: Praeger, 1971). See also the cube of participation in Hallett, Christine, *Critical Issues In Participation* (Association of Community Workers Publication, 1987), p. 12.

7. The distinctions between sharing in and sharing out I owe to an excellent article by Mostyn Davies entitled "Sharing-in and Sharing-out" in *Theology* (?Spring 1977), pp. 91–94.

8. Sumner & Warren describe this kind of change as "crescive change", i.e. that which occurs independently of us. Cf. Warren, Roland L. , *The Community In America* (University Press of America, 3rd ed., 1978), p. 362.

9. Cf. *Involvement in Community: A Christian Contribution, op. cit.*, p. 38 f.

CHAPTER TWELVE

Contemporary Relevance

This book is an exposition of ways and means of analysing and designing core processes of church and community development work. They promote the inter-related development of church and community, Christians and non-Christians, people and their environment, and the human and the spiritual. In this chapter, in order to demonstrate just how relevant these processes are to our contemporary situation, I am going to discuss the following principal effects and consequences of acquiring and using them:

1. they build up a more highly skilled, job-satisfied work force in the Churches, religious orders and allied organizations in relation to every aspect and kind of church and community work;

2. they enable workers and people to get a better subjective purchase on their lives, work and circumstances;

3. they contribute to the de-privatization of religion;

4. they generate egalitarian working relationships and facilitate the sharing of power and responsibility;

5. they promote ever widening circles of co-operation and dialogue between people of different faiths and none;

6. they can be used to provide back-up work consultancy services for workers;

7. they provide research data that can be used to enhance and develop church and community work generally;

8. they create a work culture and spirituality which is a medium of development.

Before proceeding to demonstrate the "effects and consequences" I think it would be helpful to distinguish two inter-related ways of getting at what needs to be done to promote human and spiritual well-being and development.

One way is through undertaking large-scale studies of church and society to determine the overall implications and the different kinds of action to be taken by people in various positions. Another way is through people themselves studying the work situation in which they are involved and the impact of their environment to determine what action they can take. (Work situations can be anything from a neighbourhood care group or a local Church to an international organization.)

Primarily this book is about this second way. Each of the ways is most likely to be effective when it is adequately cross-referenced with the other, i.e. when local action studies are checked out against the implications of overall studies and when large-scale studies are informed by the insights that come from the perspective of those intimately involved with an aspect of the whole. There are several ways in which people studying their own situation can do this: through reading books such as the ones quoted in this Chapter; through discussions with people who have a wider view of things; through using consultants; through contrasting their reference points with those of others. Most of my effort has gone into studying specific work situations and helping others to do so. Alongside this I have given as much time as I could to examining overall studies in my own field. This has profoundly influenced my study of work situations. However, it must be said that there are difficulties in becoming familiar with overall studies when you are deeply engaged in working at your own situation. Time is one problem. Another is finding the objectivity, courage and energy to pursue the implications of overall studies that throw some doubt on what you are doing. (This is an aspect of handling our overall context discussed in the last part of Chapter 5.)

Much of what follows comes from considering my experience of the processes and procedures central to this book in the light of a select number of overall studies.

I. A MORE HIGHLY SKILLED AND JOB-SATISFIED WORKFORCE

It is evident from what has already been said that the effects on workers and their work of the use of these processes is beneficial: it improves the quality and quantity of work done and its effectiveness; it gives workers greater job satisfaction; it enhances their qualities as workers; it builds up within churches and organizations a more highly skilled workforce. The procedures have also helped people to enter into or to establish themselves more securely in what Professor Gillian Stamp describes as the "well-being work mode".[1] She says that "more tends to be written about the experience and consequences of stress than about well-being. A word that is very widely used to describe the state of well-being is 'flow'. People in flow feel alert, energetic, motivated, competent and creative ..."[2] People in stress, on the other hand, are "tired rather than alert, dull rather than creative, prone to poor judgements which deplete self-confidence and increase self-consciousness, ill at ease with the work as it progresses, constantly questioning self and others as the work proceeds".[3] Anything that helps people to enter or to stay in the well-being mode is obviously of importance in a situation where stress and "burn-out" are a matter of concern.[4]

The processes, therefore, help to build up a more highly skilled workforce and to enhance the job satisfaction of its members. It follows that all clergy, religious and laity, wherever they are working and whatever positions they hold, need to be able to use such processes and to help others to do so. It needs to be part of their basic equipment acquired through study, pre-service and in-service training, and evaluated experience. Gradually this is happening and people are working for the embodiment of these approaches into the working practices of churches, organizations and community programmes.

The processes are generic; they are as relevant to work with churches as they are with communities.* Indeed, as we have already seen, holistic development requires that they be used in churches, organizations and communities to promote the inter-related development of church and community, Christians and non-Christians, people and their environment and the human and the spiritual. Only then will these bodies use their full potential for the well-being and development of people.

An ever-increasing number of people are using these analytical approaches in their work. I have found them relevant to every form of church and community work; to clergy, deacons, deaconesses, religious and laity, and to women and men working at all levels. They are at the heart of church and community development. Various reports, papers and books show the importance of this newly emerging discipline. For instance, *Faith In The City: A Call for Action by Church and Nation*, The Report of the Archbishop of Canterbury's Commission on Urban Priority Areas,[5] emphasized the importance for such areas of community work and community development.

II. A SUBJECTIVE PURCHASE ON WORK AND LIFE THROUGH USING OUR INTUITIVE SENSITIVITY

This section draws heavily upon the work of Professor David Smail. From his wide experience as a clinical psychologist and as head of clinical psychology services in Nottingham he concludes that we are being seduced from our "intuitive sensitivity" and treating ourselves and others like objects rather than subjects, and that this has very bad effects upon our psychological health and our general social well-being.[6]

Intuitive sensitivity+ is the faculty which, he says, gives us access to "the

---

*Some of them are useful in counselling, in the private and personal domain and in business and industry. For instance the approaches to problems and cases are particularly helpful in thinking and sorting out knotty inter-personal relationships between members of families, friends, colleagues and bosses. Some of this is subsumed under church work but the wider application in business and industry is beyond the scope of this book.

+ Smail is self-conscious of the use of this term: "the very fact that I am driven to use such a clumsily unsatisfactory term as 'intuitive sensitivity' shows how impoverished is our conceptual apparatus for the understanding of this faculty".[7] Later he adds, "... perhaps in part because of the degree to which it has been spurned and ignored in our culture and consequently is as a faculty poorly understood and weakly developed from a conceptual standpoint, it is quite easily put in the service of self-deception. Even so, it is, in the last resort, all we have to go on".[8]

intricate and finely balanced subjective world in which we conduct our relationships with each other, register and react to the impressions we give and receive, administer and respond to offers of love or threats of annihilation".[9] Immediate knowledge of interpersonal truth is transmitted through intuitive sensitivity. This faculty is acquired through being an "embodied subject in a difficult and often cruel world";[10] it is learnt through "embodied transactions with the world".[11] It is through our embodied relationships with our circumstances that we gain a "subjective purchase" on our predicament.[12] All this is the case because "however sophisticated our ability to deceive ourselves, we actually *are* engaged *bodily* in a *real* world which cannot be wished (or talked) away".[13]

One of the main reasons that Smail gives for this situation is that there is much in contemporary society that leads people to believe that reality is to be found in the objective, and illusion in the subjective. This causes us to lose the "freedom of our subjectivity",[14] to give up "subjectivity as a bad job"[15] and to place ourselves:

> in a universe in which *we* are subject to the interplay of laws objectively established as independent of us, we create conditions for ourselves very similar to those of the table tennis ball—batted to and fro, often painfully perhaps, but at least without having to take the responsibility for it.[16]

My experiences of trying to get people to define *their* purposes is a small but not unimportant example of getting people to trust their intuitive sensitivity. Frequently when I ask people to state *their* purposes they will, as I have already indicated, repeat the purposes of their organization or church. This happened with a group of people holding national posts with whom I was working. After several failed attempts to get them to state *their* purposes one of them said, "Do you *really* mean that you want us to say what we feel in our gut that we are aiming for? I thought we were supposed to be objective. Is it right to work to our inner purposes?" Within minutes he was convinced of the importance. The relief and light on his face were moving. As profound definitions of *their* purposes poured out, the discussion, previously deadened by dull official statements of objectives, came to life. We have *our* purposes. They influence what we are and what we do, whether they are stated or not. Ignored, repressed and sublimated, they are more likely to have undesirable effects. Purposes are subjective realities that, as we saw earlier, are formed within us through complex subjective processes but point to things we wish to do beyond ourselves in the world "out there". Not working to our own subjective realities compromises our ability to work to the subjective realities of others and to get them to do the same.

This is but one of the many ways in which the processes described in this book are an antidote to this propensity in society and in the Church. They enable people to submit their intuitive sensitivity to critical examination and to

264

use it to get a purposeful purchase on things within and beyond them, on their experience of "subjectivity" and "objectivity", and to create an inner base for outgoing action. The orientation towards action prevents people from preoccupation with their inner selves by leading them to thoughtful or purposeful occupation in human and spiritual affairs. The subjective purchase is gained by putting the intuitive sensitivity to work for the common good. The processes we are discussing are relevant because they help people to do this and because they help all kinds and conditions of people to do this. The result is that people are changing the world by changing their worlds, their involvement in them. To quote Smail again:

> Until we change the way we act towards each other, and the social institutions we have constructed, we shall not get much relief from the symptoms of anxiety, depression and despair which beset all of us at some time in our lives, and some of us nearly all the time. The "experts" will not change the world—they will simply make a satisfactory living helping people to adjust to it; the world will only change when ordinary people realize what is making them unhappy, and do something about it.... Changing the world is of course, largely a political enterprise ... I wish to suggest not so much that people must change the world (though that would be nice!) as that they must change *their* worlds, and that to do that they must first develop their *own* grasp of what is happening in that limited personal world in which they pursue their existence[17].

III. CONTRIBUTIONS TO DE-PRIVATIZATION

Bishop Lesslie Newbigin's[18] socio-religious studies have helped me to see more clearly one of the contributions that the approaches described in this book make to the life and witness of the churches in contemporary Western culture. By comparing biblical, medieval and post-Enlightenment thinking, Newbigin shows that the biblical and medieval world views were integrated, corporate, and co-operative whereas those that followed the Enlightenment were fragmented, individualistic and privatized. The following quotations illustrate this.

> The Bible closes with a vision of the Holy City coming down from heaven to earth. It is the vision of a consummation which embraced both the public and private life of men and women. There is no dichotomy between these two.[19]
> The Medieval world-view, based on the Christian dogma, was one which embraced the whole life of society, public as well as private. It had as much to do with economics and social order as with prayer and the sacraments. Like the Bible, it assumed that human life is to be understood in its totality, that is to say as a life in which there is no dichotomy between the private and the public, between the believer and the citizen.[20]
> The story of the Church's attempt to respond to the challenge of the

Enlightenment is ... complex.... At the inevitable risk of over-simplification one may say that the Protestant churches gradually surrendered the public sphere ... and survived by retreating into the private sector. The typical form of living Christian faith in its Protestant forms from the eighteenth century onwards was pietism, a religion of the soul, of the inner life, of personal morals and of the home.... Christian faith became—for most people—a private and domestic matter strictly separated from the public worlds of politics and economics.[21]

Essentially the development processes described in this book direct and enable people to work for holistic and inter-related development in church and community through processes of adult education and the use of social and behavioural sciences for Christian ministry and church and community work. That brings together those church and community worlds separated through the privatization of religion[22] and causes people to work at the interfaces between biblical, church and secular worlds of experience. It also inter-relates the disciplines of ministry and mission, adult education and the behavioural sciences. Practised throughout the church, these processes will make significant contributions to the de-privatization of religion.

Just as we saw the need for frames of reference to guide and evaluate thoughtful action, Newbigin sees the need for new "fiduciary frameworks", i.e. frameworks held in trust:

I do plead, that the Church recognize with fresh clarity that it is the community entrusted with a "fiduciary framework" which offers a new starting point for understanding and coping with experience.... It must live in genuine and open dialogue with those who live by other "frameworks".[23]

No "fiduciary framework" or "pattern", in the sense that we are using these words, can exist except as it is held by a community. Science is the enterprise of a confraternity of scholars who share the same basic framework of thought; it would be impossible without this confraternity.... But the point is that no systematic science is possible except where there is some kind of community which sustains and protects the "fiduciary framework" within which research and discussion are conducted. And every such community has power.[24]

The processes of church and community development are designed to ensure that these conditions are met. They enable people to use the approaches and methods of the behavioural sciences and to understand the theory and theology on which they are based. They also help people to articulate and to "own" their frames of reference and to use them in their own work and in dialogue with others.

Thus, this approach to church and community development makes significant contributions towards de-privatization by enabling people to work privately, corporately and publicly at public and private aspects of their lives in co-operative ways. (See the discussion in Chapter 8 about "working privately and publicly".) It can do this without people being disorientated because it also enables them to get a subjective purchase on things within and beyond themselves, as we saw in the previous section.

IV. ENGENDERING EGALITARIAN WORKING RELATIONSHIPS

At all levels in churches and allied organizations there are growing theological commitments to and demands for shared ministry; for participative, collaborative and egalitarian rather than hierarchical working relationships; for non-directive, rather than directive approaches to working with people. These changes are easier to discern than to make. Generally speaking, they have to be made in churches and organizations with hierarchical structures of one kind or another (or the shadows of them) and with a variety of democratic practices and procedures. Attempts to make these changes are challenged and resisted by some people in churches and organizations in many different ways: some do so because they feel deeply that their vocation is to lead other people; others do so because they fear change or that things will get out of control.

People with authority and power working locally, regionally and nationally operate at the nexus of all this. Whatever their personal leadership style might be, they have primary responsibilities to see that churches and organizations are true to their vocation and to ensure that law, order and discipline are maintained amongst staff members and users. Generally speaking they have more models and experience of power and authority being used in autocratic, authoritarian and permissive than in egalitarian and non-directive ways. What they are looking for is help with human relations and the technical problems of translating their egalitarian theology into effective practice from their position of power and authority. Considerable numbers of people of all denominations have got such help from the processes, approaches and methods described in this book.

First, the analytical processes themselves give leaders tools to help them to work their way through authority and power problems and cases more systematically and systemically than they have done previously. Situational analyses have helped them to trace out with greater accuracy the power and authority structures (formal and informal, ascribed and acquired) and to find ways of improving them. Some church leaders have found the case-study method extraordinarily useful in dealing with clergy whose behaviour has been unacceptable.

Second, ability to use the processes equips leaders to give a strong lead to people over whom they have authority to think things through and to help them to do so with respect for their respective power and authority domains. That builds up trust and creative interaction between different domains of power and authority. What is involved in doing this is amply illustrated and modelled in this book and is discussed later in the section on consultancy.

Third, what does help people in authority is to see that non-directive and directive action are integral parts of the same creative process. This means, for instance, that the directive action they must take to maintain discipline and good order can work together with the non-directive action they can and must take to promote discussion about discipline and good order and all other matters related to human and spiritual well-being and development. The art, as we have seen, is to use them appropriately, not to choose between them *in toto*.

The following things have helped leaders to construct models of leadership consonant with their theological convictions about egalitarian action and apposite to them and their situations.

1. Stance and Strategy

A wide spectrum of approaches from dictatorial to *laissez-faire* is in operation in a church or organization at any one time. For the foreseeable future this situation is likely to remain. So, even if the spectrum is shortened and the distribution of approaches modified, this is the kind of situation in which leaders have to work for change. Changes of the kind required can be inaugurated but not achieved by edict. (Vatican II demonstrated that.) Even if they could, that would be a denial of the egalitarian approach; attempts to impose it deny its nature. The means of inducing it must embody the ends to be achieved; the substance of it must be in the process. Thus egalitarian participation emerges by slow and sometimes painful processes of interaction and dialogue between those who differ significantly in their approach. Church leaders highly committed to egalitarian ministry may feel disadvantaged in promoting it because their strong feelings about it might cause people to feel they have to accept it. They are disadvantaged only if they have not the means to promote it in an egalitarian manner. Both their stance and strategy must be egalitarian. Inevitably that involves being nondirective about the essential personal choices however directive one is in holding institutional boundaries and maintaining an organizational context in which the dialogue can mature.

2. Leadership Labels

Labels such as "democratic", "directive", or "non-directive" have a certain use when examining different forms of leadership. However, using them to decide the kind of lead to give in complex situations is unhelpful, possibly even dangerous. As we have already seen in Chapter 8, the kind of questions that help to determine appropriate forms of action in different situations are: "What must I do for these people? What must we do together? What must they do for themselves? When must I withdraw? How must I withdraw so that my waiting and returning promote processes of development?"[25] The questions are universally relevant; the answers, and therefore the leads to be given, vary enormously from one situation to another and as people and situations change.

When leaders decide to answer the questions themselves, or insist that others do, that aspect of their leadership is directive. Taking such action may well be a prelude to leaders doing things *with* people and therefore to collaborative, democratic or non-directive leadership. When leaders work out the answers to such questions *with* others, their leadership is variously consultative, collaborative, democratic, non-directive. (In this case the questions may be put in this way: "What do I need to do? What do you need from me? What can you yourselves do? What do you need to do for yourselves? Do you need any help to do these things? What arrangements do we need to make so that we are able to work together and separately to best effect and call on each other as needed? How long do you think I should be involved? What will be the best way to bring my involvement to an end?") When leaders leave others to find, formulate and answer the questions, their action (it can hardly be called leadership because there is no intervention) is first permissive or *laissez-faire* and then reactive. (The questions the people have to find and tackle are: "What do we want our leaders to do *for* us and *with* us? If we get our leaders involved, how do we ensure that they do not take over, that we remain in control of our projects and that they leave us to our own devices when we want to get on with things ourselves?")

Appropriate action, it follows, will generally be a combination of several kinds of leadership, apart, that is, from those that are autocratic, authoritarian, coercive or manipulative. Leaders are more likely to determine what is the appropriate form in given circumstances by tackling the questions (on their own and/or with others) in relation to key reference points (beliefs, purposes, needs, resources, key contextual factors), rather than by adhering to one style of leadership or another. *A composite form of leadership evolves from making situational choices in these ways. It is properly and effectively eclectic. In the development work in which I engage it is predominantly, but not exclusively non-directive.* It has no readily recognized title even though it models the way in which God relates to us in the Church and the world: God does things for us, does things with us and alongside us, equips us to do things for ourselves and with each other; God gives us a lead to do the same. All this shows just how misleading it can be to ask whether one should be directive or non-directive in relation to situations *in toto*.

3. "Leadership through Self-differentiation"[26]

The idea is that leaders need to define, occupy and maintain the unique position that is theirs in the system of which they are an integral part. This is not to be confused with independence; it is about "the ability of a leader to be a self while remaining part of the system".[27] The art of leadership is in fact to "define self and continue to stay in touch".[28] ("Any leader", says Friedman, "can maintain his or her position by cutting himself or herself off, but from that moment on, the leader is no longer a leader, only a head."[29]) To do this, Friedman says , leaders need to have the "capacity to deal with the sabotage", i.e. any attempt to put leaders "out of touch" or to place them in positions, possibly traditional positions, foreign to them. (I once worked with some provincials who were preparing to meet bishops to discuss for the first time their respective roles. A moment of disclosure occurred when they realized that inwardly they were relating to bishops as they knew and experienced them a generation previously. This would have made it difficult for the bishops to differentiate themselves.) Egalitarian working relationships depend upon differentiated selves working collaboratively: they do not develop when people feign to be what they are not.

4. Participation

To complete the picture it is necessary to say something about participation, even though it means going over some ground already covered in the previous chapter.

Those preoccupied with the disestablishment of hierarchy have used "participation" to represent thorough-going egalitarian sharing and partnerships. Such relationships are of great importance. However, treating them as the only mode of participation worthy of consideration is debilitating. It is tantamount to suggesting that a necessary pluriform system of participation in society should give way to a uniform one. As we saw in Chapter 11, the life of churches, organizations and communities depends upon an enormously wide range and varied pattern of participation. (Undoubtedly they all need to be improved. That is not in question.)

Some people, for instance, gladly and freely participate in what others organize and have no desire to be partners in its provision. Others wish to participate through discussions, consultations, negotiations, etc. Yet others wish to collaborate, to be in short- or long-term partnerships or to have responsibility delegated to them. *Each of these forms of participation can be based upon egalitarian relationships.* Establishing appropriate modes of participation is vital to human and spiritual well-being and development. Doctrinaire allegiance to one form prevents this. (Deep involvement, for example, can be damaging. We have all heard people say in anguish, "I wish I'd never got involved". Keeping people out of things in which they want to and should be involved has very bad effects.)

Appropriate modes of participation can be determined by considering the options in relation to workers and people, their capacities for responsible participation and their desires for it. One also has to take into account reference points and the realities of the working situation; for instance, initiating consultative procedures that cannot be completed before decisions are made have long- and short-term adverse effects upon getting people to take seriously invitations to participate. No one mode is necessarily correct. In living and developing working relationships the patterns are not fixed; they are flexible and changing as relationships grow organically.

270

Sufficient has been said, here and in Chapter 11, to illustrate the processes of demythologizing "participation" and examining its community and organizational anatomy as a prelude to discerning the purposeful uses of appropriate modes. Church leaders find this helps them to identify and put into effect the modes of participation related to the creative distribution of power, authority and responsibility—that which they must retain and that which they must share.

People with power and authority find that making distinctions and choices of the kind made in this section helps them to work with authority without being authoritarian; to establish their position and that of others; to analyse their situations, cases and problems and to design action programmes; to establish creative patterns of involvement and the power-sharing necessary to empower all participants; to determine rhythms of engagement and disengagement. All this helps them with two basic problems: managing a multiplicity of intersecting roles, and discerning the essential nature of their job. Church leaders of all kinds grappling with issues of authority, power and responsibility in collectives need this kind of apparatus.

V. CO-OPERATION AND DIALOGUE IN A COMPETITIVE AND PLURALISTIC SOCIETY

Co-operation is a hallmark of the ways of working set out in this book: the procedures require and engender it. The processes, approaches and methods constitute an in-depth approach to the promotion of co-operative effort in relation to the common good and to the dialogue necessary to sustain it. They enable people to think together at the depth that they can manage about their work and their personal orientation to it. Thought as well as action is characterized by co-operation: rhetoric and debate have no place in this kind of sensitive but penetrating exploration. As people work at things in this way they discover where their experiences, ideas, beliefs, etc., converge and diverge and just how much or how little they have in common. They will experience consensus and conflict and feel the associated resonances and dissonances. All this will enable them to decide realistically whether they have sufficient in common to enable them to undertake together shared tasks and to continue to explore their differences, i.e., to enter into a dialogue about work and faith as they work together.

Forging this kind of co-operation is demanding but rewarding. It has great internal strength. It is charged with power and energy. It has integrity. It is of a quality that does not evolve from superficial consensus. Combining thought with action gives a cutting edge to discussions which is simply not present when the conversation is open-ended. My experience is that these processes do build up relationships of trust and respect within which there are sharings about the deep things of life quite unrelated to the tasks, but which would not have taken place outside the context of working and struggling together. Soul friendships are formed. Consequently I place high value on both the processes and their product.

This book is based upon the belief that in order to promote the human and spiritual development of all people (poor and rich and those in between) and to ensure the well-being of those most vulnerable it is essential to extend and deepen the areas of qualitative co-operation throughout society and its religious and secular institutions. This is what church and community development is about and it is to this that I am committed. Co-operation is, of course, an integral part of the competitive society: groups, teams and organizations in church and community cooperate to survive, compete, win—or to beat or to destroy their rivals. Some people grow through it; others are marred and destroyed by it. The cooperation that is required for holistic development is that which brings together in collaborative and egalitarian endeavour, for the common good, people from secular and religious organizations and communities and from churches of different faiths. The intrinsic difficulties of extending such forms of co-operation and linking self-contained pools of narcissistic cooperation are exacerbated by the dedicated and militant way in which competition is being promoted in contemporary society. That kind of competition has now entered the fields of medical and social care.

Most of the work in which I have been engaged through church and community development has been promoting co-operation of this kind between people from different churches and denominations and people in local community and society at large with no religious affiliation. It has taken an enormous amount of effort to get co-operation for development across the Christian–secular socio-religious divides. These forms of co-operation are established and extending. They must not be neglected. Another challenge is opening before us, that of using these procedures to promote inter-faith co-operation through dialogue about work and faith. Hans Küng says that there is "no world peace without religious peace". These procedures are well-tested tools for interfaith work projects that will help to establish that peace.

VI. THE DEVELOPMENT OF A WORK CONSULTANCY INFRASTRUCTURE THAT SERVICES AND SUPPORTS WORKERS

Work consultancy is an enormous contemporary need. Chapter 5 describes a process which workers can use to think their way through their work on their own or with others. This is highly desirable. People and workers can become proficient in using the processes and helping each other to do so. When, for one reason or another, they are finding it difficult to work through the process on their own with sufficient objectivity, they can be helped to do so by others less involved, I call such helpers non-directive work consultants. Workers and consultants can use the same processes, approaches and methods: they are tools they have in common.[30]

Experiencing consultancy help is an admirable way to acquire understanding of and a facility to handle the processes. The workers in each of the four examples in Part One were helped by consultants to work on the problem, the case, the situation and the project. Temporarily the worker becomes the consultor. Consultants and consultors combine their resources in an alliance of minds to work on the consultors' work in relation to the consultors' reference points and what consultors feel they can do. Work consultancy operates through the complex interplay between consultors and consultants. Thoughts and beliefs and feelings about consultors' work and ways of approaching it are exchanged and mulled over. Consultors and consultants allow their respective perspectives and their perspectives on each other's perspectives to interact. The art and science of work consultancy is the fusion of these perspectives in processes that produce things within consultors which enable them themselves to do their work more effectively and efficiently and with more satisfaction than they would otherwise be able to do. The fusion must occur within the consultors themselves if the energy is to be released in them and subsequently in their work.

These processes facilitate this. It is of the essence of consultancy that consultors remain free to act in their own right in whatever way they and those with whom they work see to be right. Emphasizing this is necessary because the autonomy of workers can by default be easily and subtly compromised by being consultors: consultors can feel they must carry out just what was decided during consultancy sessions; consultants, on the other hand, can feel they want to ensure that what they see to be necessary is done. To circumvent this real danger, consultants must avoid any semblance of remote control. They cease to be consultants if they supervise or manage consultors and their work and they become co-workers if they undertake work that is properly that of the consultors. Of necessity, therefore, being and remaining a consultant and avoiding these and other dangers involves being non-directive in the ways defined by T. R. Batten.[31] It is the use of this approach that enables consultants and consultors to be vigorously proactive in ways that help consultors to be more creatively active. It facilitates the bonding of consultants and consultors that is necessary for productive consultancy sessions and gives consultors the freedom to be independent workers.

Generations of people engaged in the work of the Church and in social work have given outstanding service without consultancy help and many continue to do so. Why then is it now both a perceived and felt need far beyond the resources to meet it?[32] Briefly stated, I believe it is because of radical changes in the kind of work now undertaken by churches and in the ways of doing it. Those who were trained to say mass, conduct worship and to address audiences now work with groups openly to facilitate participatory worship and those trained to give pastoral advice have to counsel. Those who were trained to lead in an authoritarian manner are now expected to collaborate and lead. Those schooled to service, maintain and develop established programmes of church or educational work have now to design and manage diversified socio-religious programmes. Those who were trained to follow traditional ways of doing things have to think for themselves about how to do things and their motivation for doing them—and to get others to do the same. Those who once pursued their ministry with segregated like-minded people now have to relate to people of other denominations, religious cultures and ethnic backgrounds.

These changes make great practical, theoretical and theological demands upon workers. Accepting the practical aspects of these changes without examining the underlying theory and theology makes workers vulnerable because they cannot give adequate reasons for what they are doing. Yet examining the underlying theory is a complicated business. As we have seen, it involves foraging in many disciplines such as sociology, management and business studies, organizational theory and behaviour, social work and community development studies, and so on. An extraordinarily difficult thing to do. Rival claims and contradictory theories confuse laity and specialists alike. Also, no sooner have workers and people got hold of one idea than it is upstaged by another. Very few people can master even one discipline. Workers often find themselves on the practical and theoretical edges of all this—and they are workers and not academics. They have to decide and act now, not juggle with and speculate about ideas and theories indefinitely.

Meeting more of the needs for consultancy help involves increasing the number of people who can provide specialist consultancy services and building up the practice of workers giving to and receiving from each other consultancy help in their workplaces. It is imperative that these two modes of provision are developed concurrently as interdependent consultancy services. Certain consultancy needs can be met only by consultants who are autonomous and quite independent of any of the consultors, those with whom they work and their organizations—and are seen to be so. However, no matter how proficient and readily available such a service becomes, it could never meet all the consultancy needs that church and community development workers have. Some of those needs can only be met by people on the spot, by their colleagues or by others in their organization, including their bosses. And, in any case, a proficient and readily available specialist service could, through its very proficiency and availability, prevent other important needs being met.

One such need is the need to be as self-sufficient a worker as possible. Another need is for workers to build up their working and personal relationships by giving and receiving help from each other. One of the sad things about the evolution of social work is that it has in some circumstances stripped neighbours of the confidence to counsel and care for each other because they feel that they are not qualified to do so because they are not "experts",[33] whereas in fact they are the local experts. Should this happen through the provision of consultancy services for clergy, religious and laity it would be a travesty of the purpose of the whole enterprise because it would diminish rather than enhance workers and local resources; it would not be an exercise in church and community development. Building up co-consultancy infrastructures reduces this danger and also minimizes other dangers inherent in specialist consultancy relationships. There are the dangers, for instance, of workers becoming unhealthily dependent upon consultants, insecure in their own judgements, hesitant or unable to act without having consulted. These things impair workers and relationships with any who resent the procrastination that ensues and what must appear to be the powerful say of an absentee consultant.

Consultants must take action to avoid these and other problems, but so must consultors. They need to be aware of these dangers and how to avoid them. They will be best able to do so through being helped and trained to be as self-sufficient as possible in thinking through their own work. They need to be able to use the analytical and design tools used in consultancies in a dialogue with themselves, to become self-consultants. Having got as far as they can on their own they then need to be able to turn for help to those working alongside them with confidence that they will get consultancy help rather than advice. In these ways workers act as first-aid consultants to each other and build up their own DIY consultancy services.

So we are forced back again to the need for both specialist and local consultancy provision. Combined, they strengthen the workforce of any church or organization and enhance its power through creating highly desirable work consultancy infrastructures. Skills apart, the provision of these services must meet two critical conditions: people must opt to use them freely because they want to, they should not be mandatory; they must be strictly confidential.

The ability to use these processes will enhance the effectiveness of work reviews, which are becoming established and sometimes mandatory procedures for people at all levels in churches and allied organizations. These reviews are variously described as "appraisal", "assessment", "audit" and "evaluation". As Michael Jacobs[34] shows, the terminology is not used in a consistent way. There is some overlap between these activities and work consultancy. Work consultancy does involve helping people to evaluate their work. Evaluative schemes and audits are of themselves discussions about work. Whether or not the parties proceed from assessment to work consultancy will depend upon whether or not they are able to analyse situations and design action programmes along the lines described earlier.

Both institutionalized evaluative schemes and work consultancy aim for better and more satisfying work and for better workers. However the activities must not be confused. They have different immediate foci: the one focuses on evaluation and the other on work development. Workers are often required to participate in the first, whereas they participate freely in the other. Clearly one of the advantages of assessments is that they provide opportunities to discuss work with people who would not do so if it were not required of them by their organization. Work consultancy approaches and methods help people to

275

conduct appraisals. Work consultancy also provides a quite independent service by helping people to work out the implications of their evaluations.

The processes are also useful to those who train people as they do the job through various forms of supervision, apprenticeship schemes and "mentoring" (non-directive help offered by an experienced expert to a novice working in the same field of work but independently). These relationships are established so that some people can help others to learn their job. Supervision and apprenticeships imply that those who instruct and teach have some control over their student workers, they observe them at work and intervene quite freely and directly. These are significantly different working relationships from those established between consultors and consultants. Work consultancy is an activity associated with the reflective and proactive side of a worker's working life aimed to help people to learn how to do their job better.

The process described in Chapter 5 provides a structure for consultations and courses. It is widely used in this way, as can be seen from Part One. From time to time people who have attended Avec courses set up local co-consultancy groups, some of which have proved to be very helpful.

I am highly committed to developing these consultancy processes because they have such profound and far-reaching effects. I am planning to write a book on the subject as a companion volume to this one.

A lot of effort and considerable resources are needed to make the kind of comprehensive provision which I claim to be needed (and needed urgently). It will include the following:

- multiplying endlessly and continuously the evaluated experiences of work consultancy and supervised opportunities to practise it for people in all spheres of church and community work—lay, religious and ordained;

- getting both those who offer consultancy help and those who receive it to study the theory, theology and practice of it;

- training all church workers (lay, religious and ordained) at an early stage in their pre-service training to be effective consultors and subsequently retraining them throughout their working life through in-service work consultancy programmes;

- getting people to think of work consultancy as a healthy and not a pathological activity;

- educating people and workers about the nature of, and the need for, comprehensive consultancy provision and thus creating an environment of thought conducive to its practice and funding;

- building up a cadre of specialist regional/national consultants who are committed to building up the kind of provision described in this book rather than an elitist consultancy service;

276

- establishing as an element of good practice the budgeting of fees for consultancy services and support for workers (lay and ordained) and for projects;

- developing ecumenical, inter-church and inter-organizational collaboration in making overall provision and particularly in providing consultancy services for one another[35] (people in one denomination or diocese, for example, can provide consultancy help for some people in another which they could not provide for people in their own);

- researching the experience of providing and receiving consultancy help;

- providing more literature on the subject.

Pursuing such a tenfold course of action would, by putting the processes described in this book to work in different modes, build up communities of workers suffused by a culture of work consultancy even though the process is an off-stage, back-room activity.

VII. THE PROVISION OF INVALUABLE DATA ABOUT CHURCH AND COMMUNITY DEVELOPMENT

A vast amount of broad-based experience of the use and research of these processes at all levels is accumulating. (Some of the research has been written up in reports and for further degrees.[36]) Insights and information wrapped up in this experience are invaluable to all those concerned in any way whatsoever with church and community development. These data are one of the products of people searching for ways and means of doing their work more effectively and with greater job satisfaction. They are the result of trial and error; success and failure; studying, analysing, designing, evaluating and researching. Their genesis makes them hard-gained reliable information about the actualities of the aspirations and frustrations of workers, the actualities of working situations and what workers feel about them, what works and what does not work and what it is actually like to work in them.

Using these kinds of processes, Avec staff have studied in depth with almost four thousand people, individually and in small and large groups, the work in which they are engaged, with the express purpose of enhancing their effectiveness and abilities. Most of the work in which the participants were engaged was in Great Britain, but some of it was in twenty other countries. These work studies cover eight denominations and are equally representative of Anglican, Methodist and Roman Catholic church and community work in its many forms at local, regional and national levels. They were undertaken in the strictest confidence and give unique subjective perspectives on what it is like to work in these situations. Some of this work has been written up.[37] Marc Europe has conducted an independent postal survey of most of this work.[38] Each stage of the work has been evaluated by all those engaged in it. New insights have been used by those concerned to refine the processes and the ways in which they are used. The study of these work situations undertaken entirely for the sake of the work under consideration has much to teach us about:

— critical contemporary features of church and community working situations in the UK and overseas;

— the changes taking place in church and community work;

— the difficulties actually experienced in adopting the non-directive mode of working with people in church and community (the efficacy of this mode of working has already been thoroughly researched[39]);

— the theological implications of church and community development work;

— the kind of workers required and the aptitudes and skills they need;

— recruiting, selecting, training and deploying full and part-time workers for church and community development work;

— equipping the clergy and laity for church and community development work;

— analysing, designing and carrying out programmes aimed at promoting inter-related development;

— critical contextual problems;

— the implications of all this for the church, religious orders, Christian voluntary organizations and all those with whom they collaborate.

By describing the processes of church and community development this book makes a small contribution to providing information on some of these subjects and shows that research can be done without breaching the confidentiality of the work studies. However, there is a mine of information and insights that will be made generally available only when the resources to do the necessary research are made available.

VIII. THE PROMOTION OF A SPIRITUALITY OF CHURCH AND COMMUNITY DEVELOPMENT

The approaches, methods and processes we are considering, adopted and internalized, contribute a distinctive work culture that influences our being and

278

doing. They are not simply a collection of techniques or technical tools. In fact, they characterize the nature of our involvement in human affairs, become a way of life and generate a spirituality all of their own, the spirituality of church and community development.

Spirituality, a concept much in use now by people in religious and secular organizations, is defined by Dr Gordon Wakefield as "a word which has come much into vogue to describe those attitudes, beliefs and practices which animate people's lives and help them to reach out towards super-sensible realities".[40] This definition helps me to distinguish inter-related aspects of spirituality: the things that generate it (beliefs, attitudes and practices); its affective content within individuals and groups (the "core spirituality"); the feelings, ethos, atmosphere that it engenders; (the "projected spirituality"); and those things that it facilitates within, between and through people. The first and fourth of these are comparatively easily described; the second and third are directly communicated to the senses but elusive to description. Thus understood, "spirituality" points to the essential substance of human being and doing, not to something vague, amorphous and "religious". Figure 12:1 helps me to conceptualize this.

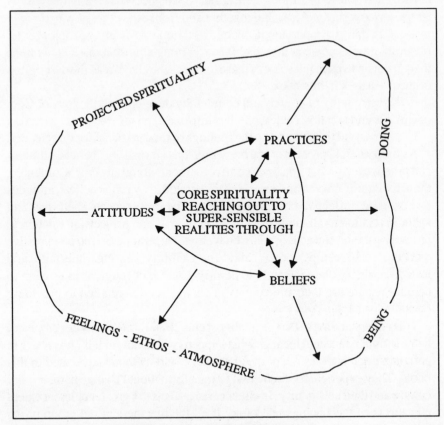

FIGURE 12:1. ATTRIBUTES OF SPIRITUALITY

At the heart of the spirituality that characterizes church and community development are the beliefs, practices and attitudes that enable people in all kinds of situations and circumstances to initiate and sustain imaginative critical thought and action relevant to the complexities of contemporary society. These processes of thought and action engender an ethos and an atmosphere in which people feel they matter and know instinctively that they and their interests are being taken seriously. It is an atmosphere in which they feel equal and enjoy equality of opportunity and participation and in which they know with deep personal assurance that they are significant. It is an environment within which people know that they are accepted for what they are, non-judgmentally and without patronage or condescension. The freedom to think, to think aloud and to think again is in the air.

The ethos encourages all forms of exploration and the facing up to differences; it discourages argumentation, rhetoric and debate; it is therefore unitive rather than divisive. It is characterized by receptivity, affective as well as intellectual responses, waiting or attentiveness and the acceptance of pain as intrinsic to the bringing forth of life.[41] It constrains people to stop and think, stimulates them to go and act and deters them from being quietists or activists. It is a spirituality of being and doing. The atmosphere is that which goes with creative activity—people discovering and learning together and from each other how to do or to make something of importance to them. It is the ethos of healthy people at work rather than sick people at therapy. It is a learning atmosphere. It is my hope that readers will have felt some of these things as they have read the description of the processes in this book.

In the spirituality of church and community development the love of God, neighbour and creation coalesce.[42] It is informed and infused by the vocation of Christians and the church and the findings of modern behavioural sciences.

A compounding process is at work within this spirituality: beliefs, attitudes and practices engender a distinctive affective content and an ethos. Combined, these facilitate things in human affairs; integrated, they refine beliefs, attitudes and practices, affective content and ethos. The cycle repeats itself over and again in relation to all kinds of work programmes and projects; in relation to promoting thoughtful action, holistic development, egalitarian and co-operative working relationships, power and responsibility sharing, interfaith and interdisciplinary dialogue and the de-privatization of religion; in relation to helping people use their subjectivity creatively; and in relation to providing consultancy support services.

This understanding of the spirituality of church and community development helps to understand and manage what happens when individuals and groups in complex organizations adopt the approaches and methods advocated in this book. They experience incremental or transformational change in their work culture and their spirituality. In either case it affects to a greater or lesser extent all aspects of their being and doing. If all the members of the group or the organization adopt the approaches, they manage the processes of loss and change together and work out what they want to conserve. However, the most likely situation is that only some of the members of an organization or group will be attracted to these approaches. When this happens, an alternative spirituality—it might be a sub-spirituality or a counter-spirituality—is generated.[43] The interaction between normative and alternative spiritualities determines the pattern of development that ensues. It is more likely to be for the common good if the beliefs, practices and attitudes of the alternative spirituality are brought to bear on the dynamics of the interaction, whatever they might be.

All my experience convinces me that church and community development is a movement of the second half of the twentieth century that has much to contribute through its methodology and spirituality to Christian mission and ministry in the twenty-first century, through equipping practitioners, churches and communities for creative reflective action.

NOTES AND REFERENCES

1. Stamp, Gillian, *Well-Being and Stress at Work* (Brunel Institute of Organizational & Social Studies, BIOSS, Sep. 1988).

2. *Op. cit.*, pp. 3 & 6.

3. *Op. cit.*, p. 7.

4. See note 15 to Chapter 5.

5. Church Publishing House, 1985.

6. David Smail has set out the results of his research in *Illusion and Reality: The Meaning of Anxiety* (London: Dent, 1984).

7. *Op. cit.*, p. 36.

8. *Op. cit.*, p. 37.

9. *Op. cit.*, p. 34.

10. *Op. cit.*, p. 88.

11. *Op. cit.*, p. 92 ff.

12. *Op. cit.*, p. 90.

13. *Op. cit.*, p. 83 cf. p.42.

14. *Op. cit.*, p. 30.

15. *Op. cit.*, p. 50.

16. *Op. cit.*, p. 51.

17. *Op. cit.*, p. 2 cf. p. 137.

18. Newbigin, Lesslie, *The Other Side of 1984—Questions for the Churches* (Geneva: World Council of Churches, 1983): cf. sequels to this by Newbigin: *Foolishness to the Greeks—The Gospel and Western Culture* (Geneva: World Council of Churches, 1986); and *The Gospel in a Pluralistic Society* (London: SPCK, 1989).

19. *The Other Side of 1984,* p. 35.

20. *Op. cit.*, p. 21.

21. *Op. cit.*, p. 22.

22. *Op. cit.*, p. 35.

23. *Op. cit.*, p. 31.

24. *Op. cit.*, p. 29 f.

25. Cf. Lovell, George, *Human and Religious Factors in Church and Community Work* (Grail Publications, 1982), p. 27 ff. Lovell, *Diagrammatic Modelling* (Avec Publication, 1191, 2nd ed. 1992), p. 28 ff. Lovell, "Leadership and Decision Making—Some Thoughts on a Given Theme", *Community* No. 26 (Spring 1980).

26. Friedman, Edwin H., *Generation to Generation: Family Process in Church and Synagogue* (New York & London: The Guilford Press, 1985), pp. 228–249.

27. *Ibid.*, p. 229.

28. *Ibid.*, p. 229.

29. *Ibid.*, p. 230.

30. The same processes can be used by facilitators. The overlap of these roles obscures differences of considerable practical importance between the technical and process expertise.

Consultants, unlike "facilitators" of processes, do need other tools and knowledge of the subject matter. I act as a facilitator when I help a group of Benedictines to examine critically their monastic life and the theology and praxis on which it is based. My experience is in the process, not in the subject-matter. I act as a consultant if I help the same group to design a church and community development project, because that is my field. This distinction helped a recent consultation of facilitators and consultants to see that sometimes with the same group they find themselves changing from one role to the other and that it is essential to be clear about this and to negotiate role changes. Cf. *Consultants and Facilitators for Religious: A Brief Report on a Consultation Organized Jointly by The CMRS and Avec on the 26th & 27th November 1991* (An Avec Report).

31. Batten, T. R. and M., *The Non-Directive Approach* (Avec Publication, 1988).

32. Lippitt, Gordon and Ronald Lippitt, *The Consulting Process In Action* (University Associates, Inc., 1986), give four reasons for "the growth and development of consultation resources": technological development and its impact on life styles; crisis in human resources and "the under utilization, underdevelopment and misuse of such resources as racial and ethnic minority groups"; undeveloped consulting skills of workers; discretionary time to spend beyond wage-earning activities (p. 2 f).

33. Cf. for example Seabrook, Jeremy, *What Went Wrong? Working People and the Ideals of the Labour Movement* (London: Gollancz, 1978). Writing of working people in Bradford, Seabrook says, "Human skills (no less than work skills) absorbed unselfconsciously by the family have been taken away from them without effort and laboriously invested in professional social workers, who have to be taught them: an act of human plunder" (p. 116: cf. pp. 100, 211, 214).

34. Jacobs, Michael, *Holding In Trust: The Appraisal of Ministry* (London: SPCK, 1989). Cf. pp. 19 ff.

35. Cf. Lippitt & Lippitt *op. cit.,* p. 203 f.

36. The research completed is: Lovell, George, *An Action Research Project To Test The Applicability of the Non-Directive Concept in a Church, Youth and Community Setting:* Thesis submitted for the Degree of Doctor of Philosophy in the Institute of Education, Faculty of Arts, University of London, 1973; Lovell & Catherine Widdicombe *Churches and Communities: An Approach to Development in the Local Church* (Tunbridge Wells: Search Press, 1978); Widdicombe, Catherine, *The Roman Catholic Church and Vatican II: Action Research Into Means Of Implementation:* Thesis submitted for the Degree of Master of Philosophy in the Institute of Education, Faculty of Education, University of London, 1984; New, Charles, *Development in Church and Community: Promoting Personal Growth Through Community Development and Curriculum Development Methods:* Thesis submitted for the Degree of Master of Philosophy in the University of Liverpool, 1987; Mellor, G. Howard, *A Theological Examination of the Non-Directive Approach to Church and Community Development with a Special Reference to the Nature of Evangelism:* Thesis submitted for the Degree of Master of Arts in Theology in the Theology Department, Faculty of Arts, University of Durham, 1990.

37. Members of the two-year part-time diploma courses run by Avec and validated by Roehampton Institute write an action-research dissertation. So far there are thirty-four completed dissertations.

38. Europe, Marc, *Viva l'avec* (November 1990).

39. See the research listed under reference 36.

40. Wakefield, Gordon S. (ed.), *A Dictionary of Spirituality* (London: SCM Press, 3d impression, 1986), Article on "Spirituality", p. 361.

41. I am drawing here on an article in *A Dictionary of Spirituality* (see note 40 above) by Professor Nancy C. Ring entitled "Feminine Spirituality". She says, "... one can say that

feminine spirituality as appropriated by both male and female is characterized by receptivity, affective response, waiting or attentiveness and the acceptance of pain as intrinsic to the bringing forth of life" (p. 149).

42. Cf. Wakefield, *op. cit.*, p. 362; cf. the article in the same dictionary by Professor Dominic Maruca, SJ, on "Roman Catholic Spirituality".

43. I was helped to see the significance of this by Charles Elliott *Comfortable Compassion: Poverty, Power and the Church* (London: Hodder & Stoughton, 1987) and particularly what he had to say about "alternative consciousness and spiritual growth" (p. 119 *et al*), and the change process outlined on pp. 176 ff.

Bibliography

In this book I have expounded a particular approach to analysis and design, I have not attempted to describe and compare similar and dissimilar approaches. So, in this bibliography, I have limited myself to books about this approach. To help people to decide what further reading could be of use to them I have annotated it. For those who wish to study and research the methods in greater depth I have included notes of theses even though these are not generally available.

The books and theses variously describe: the non-directive approach and processes of analysis and design in action in church and community development work; aids to working with people analytically and creatively, individually and in groups, churches and communities; basic underlying theoretical and theological concepts; action-research methods in operation. Classifying the books is not very helpful because most of them touch on several of the aspects I have just mentioned. So I have listed them under the authors. A list of dissertations based on the methods of analysis and design described in this book, written by those who completed the Avec/Roehampton Institute Diploma in Church and Community Development, is available from "Resources", address below.

Copies of all the books and theses referred to below are in the Avec reference library. This is to be rehoused because Avec and its work are currently being re-organized radically. Avec papers and all the books listed below that are in print can be obtained from "RESOURCES", The Grail, 125 Waxwell Lane, Pinner, Middlesex, HA5 3ER along with information about Avec. "Resources" has been set up by The Revd John V. Budd, Ms Catherine Widdcombe and The Revd Dr George Lovell in association with the Grail to continue to make available books and papers about working with people in church and community.

Batten, T. R. (1962), *Training for Community Development: A Critical Study of Method* (Oxford University Press), 192pp.
This book, out of print, describes how Batten got people to analyse and design community development work. It is particularly helpful on promoting group discussions. It describes the analysis of some problems and cases.

Batten, T. R. with the collaboration of Madge Batten (1965), *The Human Factor in Community Work* (Oxford University Press), 184pp.

Batten, T. R. with the collaboration of Madge Batten (1970), *The Human Factor in Youth Work* (Oxford University Press), 170pp.

These two books, out of print, are based upon systematic discussions about real-life situations; the first with community and the second with youth workers, trainers and administrators. These real-life situations are called cases and they were contributed and worked on by members of training courses. They further illustrate the method described in Chapter 1. *The Human Factor in Community Work* presents thirty-seven cases grouped under the chapter headings: Meeting Requests for Help, Suggesting Community Projects, Introducing Improvement, Establishing Groups, Working with Groups, Working with Leaders, Dealing with Faction and Asking for Help. Most of these cases come from working situations overseas but have much to say to all working contexts. *The Human Factor in Youth Work* contains nineteen analysed problems and many that are not analysed. These cases are from the British scene. They are grouped under the following chapter headings: Problems with Members, Working with Management Committees, Working with Helpers and Working in the Community.

Batten T. R. in collaboration with Madge Batten (1967), *The Non-Directive Approach in Group and Community Work* (Oxford University Press), 148pp.

This book is a critical study of the nature, scope and limitations of the non-directive approach—the approach underlying the approach I have described in this present book. It is in four parts: in the first part the directive and non-directive approaches are defined and contrasted and their relative uses discussed; in the second part the functions performed by a non-directive worker are described; and the third and fourth parts are about training people to practise the non-directive approach. It is as relevant to consultants as to workers. Sadly it is out of print, but the first two parts have been reprinted: Batten T. R. & M. Batten (1988), *The Non-Directive Approach* (Avec Publications), 53pp.

Grundy, Malcolm (ed.) (1994), *The Parchmore Story: George Lovell, Garth Rogers and Peter Sharrocks* (Chester House Publications, 1994).

This is probably a unique story. The Parchmore Road Methodist Church in Croydon, South London, has had four consecutive ministers who have, since 1966, attempted to develop the life of this local congregation by using church and community development methods and policies. This book—the stories of the first three covering twenty-five years with a contribution from the fourth who is the present minister of Parchmore—encourages us to see how much more can be achieved when the methods described in this book are employed consistently. A measure of the effectiveness of the Parchmore ministry through these three men is one way in which relationships with the police and the local community were maintained through more than twenty years of tension and change. This is a revealing Christian story. Many lessons about analysis and design can be learned from it that are of importance for all those who are involved in church and community ministry through the work of a local church.

Lovell, George (1992 originally published in 1972 as a Grail & Chester House Publication), *The Church and Community Development: An Introduction* (Avec Publications), 80pp.

A concise and readable introduction, in non-technical language, to church and community development work. It describes how local churches can work *with* rather than *for* people. It gives illustrations of projects and schemes. It discusses the biblical theology underlying this approach. First published in 1972, there have now been three editions of this book because it has proved to be so useful in the induction of people into this approach to thinking things through with people.

Lovell, George (1973), *An Action Research Project to Test the Applicability of the Non-Directive Concept in a Church, Youth and Community Centre Setting* (thesis submitted for the Degree of Doctor of Philosophy in the Institute of Education, Faculty of Arts, University of London), 677pp.

This thesis is a factual study of a community development action-research project. It tests the applicability of the non-directive approach to working with people (as defined by T. R. Batten) in a church, youth and community centre setting in Thornton Heath, Surrey. It describes the origins of the project; the training in community development of the Methodist minister who acted as "worker"; the help he received from a consultant; and the theoretical background to the non-directive approach. It reports in detail the developments that took place over three years in youth, community and church work and in programmes of Christian education and worship and the ways in which workers and people analysed their situation, designed their programmes, put them into action and evaluated developments.

It considers the relevance of action-research and the worker's role as an "active participant observer" in the sequential analysis of community development processes. It describes a way of documenting projects and the use of "indicators" for evaluating "change for the better" in people. It analyses various critical responses to the worker's use of the non-directive approach, the ways in which he responded and subsequent changes in people's attitudes.

It concludes that the use of the non-directive approach helps people to "change for the better" and is applicable to work undertaken in church, youth and community centre settings. It is demonstrated that consultants who understand and practise the non-directive approach can greatly help workers —and through them others—to achieve their purposes. It recommends that church and community workers be trained in the non-directive approach and states the need for more consultancy help.

Lovell, George & Catherine Widdicombe (1978), *Churches and Communities: An Approach to Development in the Local Church* (Search Press), 218pp.

This book describes how clergy and laity of sixteen churches of seven denominations in Ronsey (a pseudonym), helped by an ecumenical team, learnt about the non-directive approach to working with people and tried it out on a wide range of church and community work. It shows how they found the experience of analysing, designing and doing their work in this way deeply satisfying and highly productive. It contains an extremely practical collection of case-studies of analytical development work with individuals, groups, ecumenical organizations and churches. It describes the evaluation by the people of what had happened and how they felt strongly that what they had learnt should be widely known for the sake of the church as well as the community. It also describes how key people in all major denominations were involved in discussions about the project from beginning to end, and what they thought about it.

Lovell, George (1982), *Human and Religious Factors in Church and Community Work.* Based on the Beckly Social Service Lecture 1981. (Grail Publications), 64pp.

This book gives the background to the development of church and community development, discusses the critical features of church and community development, gives a good example of analysis through participant observation and describes what is involved in working with churches as institutions.

Lovell, George (1991), *Diagrammatic Modelling: An aid to theological reflection in church and community development work* (Avec Publications, originally published as Occasional Paper No. 4, 1980, by the William Temple Foundation), 62pp.

A Report of some work done over a three-year period by the community Development Group of the Methodist Church in co-operation with the "Core Group" of the William Temple Foundation. It has Preface by Bishop David Jenkins. The title is an accurate description of the contents of this booklet which shows the use of models in analysis and design. Drawing heavily upon the work of Bishop Ian Ramsey, models are described and diagrammatic modelling is illustrated. Three creative experiences of disclosure models are described and the reflective and analytical processes that led to them are outlined in some detail.

Lovell, George (1994), *Reflective Practitioners in Church and Community Work, Avec's 1992 Annual Meeting Lecture* (Resources Publication), 27pp. Originally published as: *Analysis and Design; Ways of Realising the Learning Potential in Church and Community Work* (1992).

This lecture demonstrates how the approaches and methods used by Avec help clergy, religious and lay people and church organizations and communities to become more effective agents of reflective action. It shows that the non-directive approach is a medium for learning as well as for working with people and explores ways in which analysing and designing church and community work creates reflective practitioners. The lecture concludes by indicating the application of this approach to the work of the church in the contemporary setting.

Mellor, G. Howard (1990), *A Theological Examination of the Non-Directive Approach to Church and Community Development with a Special Reference to the Nature of Evangelism* (thesis submitted for the degree of Master of Arts in Theology in the Theology Department, Faculty of Arts, University of Durham), 235pp.

This thesis is an examination by Howard Mellor, now Principal of Cliff College, of the nature and value of the non-directive approach to studying and doing church and community work in the context of evangelical ministry. It originates out of Howard Mellor's seven-year evangelical ministry in Addiscombe, Croydon, and describes the process of adopting a non-directive approach to that ministry, first of all intuitively and then systematically. It considers the origins, nature and application of church and community development and the directive and non-directive approaches.

Evangelistic ministry is analysed by noting the characteristics common to all evangelicals and then constructing in some detail a typology of evangelicals against which to test the applicability of the non-directive approach. It then critically reviews the theology of church and community development. It tests out the non-directive concept against the biblical narrative, considering Jesus' use of parable; the exercise of authority, and use of charismatic gifts within the church. It examines three areas which seem predisposed to show dissonance between evangelistic ministry and the non-directive approach: decision-making, theology of evangelical conversion, and proclamation of the evangel. The conclusion is that the biblical teaching supports the non-directive approach, whilst also recognizing certain aspects as non-negotiable. It concludes that the non-directive approach is not only consonant with evangelistic ministry but could be a vital partner to such a ministry and increase its effectiveness.

New, Charles (1987), *Development in Church and Community: Promoting personal growth through community development and curriculum development methods* (thesis submitted for the degree of Master of Philosophy in the University of Liverpool), 368pp.

This thesis is about a Methodist Circuit Minister (the Revd Charles New) and a church of which he was minister for ten years (Moreton Methodist Church, Wirral). It describes in detail a three-year period during which important changes occurred in the church and in his role and function as the minister. His assessment of the significance of these changes and of the part he played in promoting them is tested by researching the opinions and attitudes of some of the church members who were there at the time, community groups who used the church premises, and neighbourhood agencies whose work brought them into contact with the church.

It also describes and evaluates principles and concepts from community development to which he worked in his ministry. It shows how curriculum-development models used in formal education and the principles and concepts from which they are constructed can assist ministers and other local church workers to promote human and spiritual growth amongst the people.

Insights from both community and curriculum development practices are incorporated into a tentative model by which local church workers could analyse and design and evaluate their work.

Widdicombe, Catherine (1984), *The Roman Catholic Church and Vatican II: Action-research into means of implementation* (thesis submitted for the Degree of Master of Philosophy in the Institute of Education, Faculty of Education, University of London), 425pp.

This thesis studies work done between 1970 and 1981 with Roman Catholics in positions of authority, particularly at local level, through two ecumenical community-development action-research programmes undertaken in the United Kingdom: Project 70–75 and Avec, a Service Agency for Church and Community Work. It is about the introduction of new ideas and practices required by the Second Vatican Council (1962–5) into the Roman Catholic Church through initiating clergy, religious and full-time church workers into the appropriate and skilled use of directive and non-directive approaches. It describes the approaches and methods as used in training, projects and work consultancy to help people analyse, design and evaluate their work.

It discusses the nature of the changes at the heart of Vatican II and outlines the way the Roman Catholic Church has attempted to implement it and with what result. It describes work done with a large number of clergy, religious and church workers; the problems they were currently facing in introducing Vatican II and the ways found of overcoming or ameliorating them. It shows that through this work many Roman Catholics in positions of authority have undergone a change of attitude and approach to their work with people.

It concludes that Roman Catholics in positions of authority at every level in the Church would be helped to implement the innovatory ideas and practices of Vatican II if they were able to use the non-directive approach and to do that they need training and support.

Widdicombe, Catherine (1994), *Group Meetings That Work: a practical guide for working with different kinds of groups* (St Pauls), 205pp.

This is a practical book about working together in groups. It is essentially a "how to" book, and is arranged so that you can easily find what you need for a particular group or situation. It is therefore, a book to be used as a helpmate rather than to be read through from start to finish. It could be used as a manual by study groups. It is written for anyone who wants to help others to think and discuss together and to tackle their common task in a collaborative way. This means pooling ideas, insights and expertise in the conviction that individuals, groups and communities flourish best when people have a say in decisions that affect them.

Report by the Community Development Group, William Temple Foundation in collaboration with the Community Work Advisory Group, British Council of Churches (1980), *Involvement in Community: A Christian Contribution* (The William Temple Foundation), 107pp.

This is a theological critique of church and community development work by a group of people which met over a period of some three years under the aegis of the William Temple Foundation. They were Revd Tony Addy, Revd Dr John Atherton, Revd Alan Gawith, Revd Dr George Lovell, Revd Prof. David Jenkins (later the Bishop of Durham), Revd Harry Salmon, Fr Austin Smith, Mr Richard Tetlow, Revd Dr Gerry Wheale and Revd Clifford Wright. From a Christian perspective it critically explores the nature and necessity of critical, analytical involvement in community and its limitations. It discusses the commitments required. It argues the necessity for a theory of involvement in community and discusses what is involved in formulating one. It concludes that this way of working is in fact a way of life.

Index of Subjects

Index of Names

APPENDIX

Notes on Work Papers: A Proposed Outline

Introduction

Participants are required to write a paper by way of preparation. These papers are shared amongst those taking part in the course who have undertaken, in writing, to treat them confidentially. They provide an opportunity for you to reflect on different aspects of your work and ministry, and your thoughts about them. Of itself this can be useful. They also facilitate the exchange of information and the development of mutual understanding. They will provide the background to the session on each participant's work situation and help us together to give shape to the course.

Detailed guidelines to the parts of the paper are given below to aid and prompt your reflection. Your own reflections are most important. Follow the suggestions where they are helpful. Supplement these to add things that are important to you and which you would like to include in your writing. Use the opportunity to write as fully and freely as you wish but 2000 words is a useful guide. No more than a quarter of the paper should be given to Part 1. This is not a questionnaire.

Part 1 - My working life, journey and story

This first part invites you to reflect and write about your vocational story up to now and to assess your present position. The following headings may help you to do so:

> The major landmarks in my vocational journey to the present.
>
> People and ideas that have influenced me and my ministry.
>
> Ways in which my present work fits into the story or my journey.
>
> The aspects of my ministry that I find enjoyable and fulfilling; difficult and frustrating; and those that occupy most of my time and thought.
>
> Dimensions of my ministry that I would like to develop.

No more than a quarter of the paper should be given to Part 1.

Part 2 - My beliefs, purposes and approaches

This part is for you to indicate the beliefs, principles, concepts, assumptions, ideas and purposes that are and have been fundamental to your life and work. Also indicate what you have learnt about working with and ministering to people that now informs the ways in which you work and minister.

Part 3 - The section of the Church (Parish, Circuit, Diocese, District, etc.) for which I am responsible

My present job or appointment

Describe the principal aspects of your present job, the overall context in which you have to do it and how they relate.

Features

Describe the features of the Church or Organization in which you work and the geographical area within which it operates, the activities in which it is engaged and the people for whom you work.

Describe the way you see the different church, organizational and community entities with which you work and the relationships between them.

Tasks and Purposes

Describe and rank in order of importance as you perceive them the main tasks and purposes of the part of the church or organization in which you work and the way it is organized to carry out its tasks.

Who is responsible for what areas of work?

Who makes decisions and carries them out?

The process by which decisions are made.

Ways in which people are accountable for the effectiveness and well-being of your church or organization.

Relationships in theory and practice between national, regional and local levels.

Your views of these aspects.

My place in my church and organization

The way you see the place and role that you occupy in your Church or Organization.

The primary responsibilities and tasks that you undertake within your Church or Organization.

The ways in which you are supported from above and below.

Aspects of the Church's or Organization's life and structure which you find helpful and those which hinder.

How would you describe the primary working and personal relationships you have? For example: with colleagues, with other Churches and religious orders or organizations, with others working professionally with you.

The Context

Can you state the positive and negative factors for you in the contemporary Christian, ecclesiastical and social contexts.

Change and Development

Describe any significant patterns you discern in the way in which things are proceeding and developing in your work. Note the things you consider to be sound, to be evolving satisfactorily, to need considering, to be ripe for change or assessment, to be problematic. Can you do a similar exercise on the way in which you are developing in your vocation/profession?

Do you discern any implications in all this for you?

Part 4 - What I would like to get out of the course. Note just what you yourself want to get out of the course.

Books of general Christian interest as well as books on theology, scripture, spirituality and mysticism are published by Burns & Oates Limited.

A free catalogue will be sent on request:

Burns and Oates Dept A,
Wellwood, North Farm Road, Tunbridge Wells,
Kent TN2 3DR, England
Tel (01892) 510850, Fax (01892) 515903